COMMUNICATIVE JUSTICE IN THE PLURIVERSE

This volume examines communicative justice from the perspective of the pluriverse and explores how it is employed to work towards key pluriverse goals of environmental, cognitive, sociocultural, sociopolitical, and political economy justice.

The book identifies and explains the unequal power relations in place that limit the possibilities of communication justice, the challenges and difficulties faced by activists and communities, the ways in which communities and movements have confronted power structures through discourse and material action, and their successes and limitations in creating new structures that promote the right to, and facilitate a future for, communicative justice. The volume features contributions based on experiences of resistance and transformation in the Global South—Bolivia, Ecuador, India, Malawi, and collaborations between the continents of Latin America and Africa—as well as notable studies from the Global North—Japan, Spain, and the United Kingdom—that defy hegemonic models.

This book is essential for students and scholars interested in media and communication activism, media practice for development and social change, and communication for development and social change, as well as those actively engaged with activism and social justice.

Joan Pedro-Carañana is Assistant Professor of Journalism and New Media at the Universidad Complutense de Madrid, Spain. He is interested in the role of media, education, and culture in the reproduction and transformation of societies. He is a coeditor of *El Modelo de Propaganda y el Control de los Medios*, *The Propaganda Model Today: Filtering Perception and Awareness*, and *Talking Back to Globalization: Texts and Practices*.

Eliana Herrera-Huérfano is Dean of the Communication School at Uniminuto, Corporación Universitaria Minuto de Dios, Colombia. Her research is based on participatory methodologies that involve interaction with Indigenous communities and other social or community leaders. Her publications include *Emergencia del territorio y comunicación local* and *Communicology of the South The Bases of a New Critical Theory of Communication*.

Juana Ochoa Almanza is Research Professor in Communication, Development, and Social Change at the Corporación Universitaria Minuto de Dios, Colombia. She is interested in the studies of gender, feminisms, and communication in Latin American context. Her latest articles have been published in *Revista* Conrado, University of Cienfuegos, Cuba, and *Revista* Improntas de la Historia y la Comunicación, Universidad Nacional de la Plata, Argentina.

Media and Communication Activism: The Empowerment Practices of Social Movements

Series editors: Claudia Magallanes Blanco, Alice Mattoni, and Charlotte Ryan

This Routledge series edited by Claudia Magallanes Blanco, Alice Mattoni, and Charlotte Ryan grapples with recurring issues facing practitioners, teachers, students, and scholars of communication activism; it addresses challenges to communication activism as well as emancipatory practices that build culturally resonant, richly networked, multi-faceted, movement communication systems. Core series themes include:

- The power structures of media and communication activism;
- Rights in the framework of media and communication activism;
- Outcomes, learning and sustainable futures in media and communication activism.

This is a global series published in English, and the editors welcome submissions from authors who work primarily in other languages.

Indigenous Media Activism in Argentina
Francesca Belotti

Communicative Justice in the Pluriverse
An International Dialogue
Edited by Joan Pedro-Carañana, Eliana Herrera-Huérfano, and Juana Ochoa Almanza

For more information about the series, please visit: www.routledge.com/ Media-and-Communication-Activism/book-series/MCA

COMMUNICATIVE JUSTICE IN THE PLURIVERSE

An International Dialogue

Edited by Joan Pedro-Carañana,
Eliana Herrera-Huérfano, and
Juana Ochoa Almanza

Routledge
Taylor & Francis Group

NEW YORK AND LONDON

Cover image: Arina Kumysheva/Getty Images

First published 2023
by Routledge
605 Third Avenue, New York, NY 10158

and by Routledge
4 Park Square, Milton Park, Abingdon, Oxon, OX14 4RN

Routledge is an imprint of the Taylor & Francis Group, an informa business

© 2023 selection and editorial matter, Joan Pedro-Carañana, Eliana Herrera-Huérfano, and Juana Ochoa Almanza; individual chapters, the contributors

The right of Joan Pedro-Carañana, Eliana Herrera-Huérfano, and Juana Ochoa Almanza to be identified as the authors of the editorial material, and of the authors for their individual chapters, has been asserted in accordance with sections 77 and 78 of the Copyright, Designs and Patents Act 1988.

ISBN: 978-1-032-32689-4 (hbk)
ISBN: 978-1-032-32618-4 (pbk)
ISBN: 978-1-003-31622-0 (ebk)

DOI: 10.4324/9781003316220

Typeset in Bembo
by Apex CoVantage, LLC

CONTENTS

CONTRIBUTORS

Editors/Authors

Joan Pedro-Carañana is in the Department of Journalism and New Media, Universidad Complutense de Madrid, Spain. He is co-editor of *El Modelo de Propaganda y el Control de los Medios*, *The Propaganda Model Today: Filtering Perception and Awareness*, and *Talking Back to Globalization: Texts and Practices*.

Eliana Herrera-Huérfano is Dean of the Communication School at Uniminuto, Corporación Universitaria Minuto, Colombia. Her publications include *Emergencia del territorio y comunicación local* and *Communicology of the South The Bases of a New Critical Theory of Communication*.

Juana Ochoa Almanza is Research Professor at the Master's programme in Communication, Development, and Social Change at the Corporación Universitaria Minuto de Dios, Colombia. Her work has been published in *Revista Conrado*, University of Cienfuegos, Cuba, and *Revista Improntas de la Historia y la Comunicación*, Universidad Nacional de la Plata, Argentina.

Authors

Alberto Acosta is Ecuadorian Economist, Grandfather, Companion of the struggles of social movements, University Professor, Minister of Energy and Mines, and President of the Constitutional Assembly (2007–2008). He is coeditor of *A Post-Development Dictionary* (2018) and Author of *El Buen Vivir. Sumak Kawsay, una oportunidad para imaginar otros mundos* (2013).

Karen Andrade Mendoza is Professor at the Faculty of Social Communication of the Central University of Ecuador, Ecuador. She worked in spaces of social, political, and environmental conflict as an independent consultant. Her research topics include preservation of cultural heritage, management of protected areas, agroforestry and conservation projects, environmental impact, and political advocacy and communication in a variety of forms.

Gabriel Baglo is Journalist, Expert, and Consultant in Communication and Media Development. Senegal. He is Advocate for Press Freedom, Freedom of Expression, and Access to Information. He worked in public broadcast and the independent print media and was Secretary-General of Togo Union of Journalists.

Sara-Nathalie Brombart is Head of the Office of the Friedrich-Ebert-Stiftung in Lima, Peru. She is Editor of Obregón, R. & Vega, J. (2019) Voices with Purpose—A Manual on Communication Strategies for Development and Social Change. Participant's Module. Windhoek: Friedrich Ebert Stiftung Fesmedia Africa.

Daniel Broudy is Professor of Rhetoric and Applied Linguistics in the Graduate School of Intercultural Communication at Okinawa Christian University, United States. His recent publications include "Who Wants to be a Slave? The Technocratic Convergence of Humans and Data" and The Propaganda Model Today: Filtering Perception and Awareness.

Elvira Espejo Ayca is Artist, Weaver, Narrator of oral tradition, Documentarist, and Poet in Bolivia. She has participated in the project "Sonares Comunes" of El Parafonista and has received several awards including the Prize of Indigenous Literatures of Casa de las Américas in Cuba.

Des Freedman is Professor of Media and Communication Studies at the University of London and Co-Director of the Goldsmiths Leverhulme Media Research Centre, United Kingdom. His latest books include Misunderstanding the Internet and The Contradictions of Media Power.

Begoña Gutiérrez-Martínez teaches communication at Universidad Internacional de La Rioja, Spain. She has published chapters in the volumes Entender el Artivismo (Peter Lang, 2019) and European Cinema in the Twenty-First Century (Palgrave Macmillan, 2020).

Ariko Ikehara is Director of Koza X MiXtopia Research Center in Okinawa and Lecturer in Communication at Okinawa Christian University, Japan. Her recent publications include the Champurū Text: Postwar Okinawan Writing and Third Space as Decolonial Con/Text: Okinawa's American Champurū.

Ashish Kothari is one of the founders of Kalpavriksh, an Indian environmental NGO, India. He is the author or editor of over 30 books, including Churning the Earth: Making of Global India; Alternative Futures: India Unshackled; and Pluriverse: A Post-Development Dictionary.

Vedabhyas Kundu is Programme Officer of Gandhi Smriti and Darshan Samiti, the national memorial of Mahatma Gandhi. India. His expertise is in nonviolent communication and media and information literacy. He has been training and conducting workshops in these areas for more than two decades.

Aura Isabel Mora is Research Professor at the Master's programme in Communication Education in Culture at the Corporación Universitaria Minuto de Dios, Colombia. She has also investigated the decolonial perspective and the proposals of "good living" and "good life".

Rafael Obregón Gálvez is Country Representative at UNICEF Paraguay, Colombia. He was Former Chief of Communication for Development, UNICEF NY. He was Professor in the School of Media Arts and Studies and Director of the Communication and Development Studies Program at Ohio University.

Josep Pedro is Assistant Professor at Universidad Carlos III de Madrid. Spain. He has published articles in journals such as Atlantic Studies, Signa, Jazz Research Journal, and EU-topías and has written chapters in the volumes Talking Back to Globalization: Texts and Practices, Jazz and Totalitarianism, and The Cambridge Companion to the Singer-Songwriter.

Galo Plaza Vanegas is Teacher of Sociological Theory at the Universidad of Guayaquil, Ecuador. He has worked in a variety of field projects, including Rural Advisor and Director of Planning for the 29 municipalities in the Province of Guayas, Administration Director of the Wilson Galarza Foundation, and Coordinator of Logistics at Comandato-Ecuacolor.

Carlos A. Segovia is Associate Professor of religious studies at Saint Louis University, Madrid, Spain. His recent publications include "Re-theorising the Social and Its Models after Lévi-Strauss's and Pierre Clastres's Study of Stateless Social Assemblages" and "Metaphoric Recursiveness and Ternary Ontology: Another Look at the Language and Worldview of the Yaminahua".

Jair Vega-Casanova is Professor in the Department of Social Communication, Researcher for PBX, Communication, Culture and Social Change Research Group, and Coordinator of Master in Communication at Universidad del Norte, Colombia. His research and consulting topics include Communication for Social and Behavioural Change, Health Communication, and Popular and Community Communication.

Translators

Sheila Agenjo Alcaide received his Bachelor's degree in English Philology at Universidad Complutense de Madrid. She currently works as an English teacher in a secondary state school, IES Altaír. She collaborates with the European Project *Women's Legacy: Our Cultural Heritage for Equity*.

Catalina Campuzano Rodríguez is Research Professor at Corporación Universitaria Minuto de Dios, Colombia. Her research focus is on communication, education, and art concerning the sacred conceptions in indigenous cultures. She has worked in several universities and as a consultant in community processes. She holds an M.A. degree in Education from La Salle University and a Ph.D. degree in Communication.

BY WAY OF PROLOGUE

From development to the pluriverse, an emancipatory step

Gustavo Esteva (1936–2022) said that "the world is falling to pieces around us. The ideas that shaped the Modern mentality in the last two hundred years are falling down". The situation is such that the current and multiple planetary crises confront us with the true possibility of Humanity becoming extinct on the planet. In the best scenario, the great majority of human beings are going through a growing and increasingly accelerated decline in the already deplorable situation. Let's face it frankly, never before have so many crucial aspects of life failed simultaneously. And in this setting, while the promises of Modernity fade away, inequities and violence expand. In short, if the present is overwhelming, expectations for the future are increasingly uncertain and disturbing.[1]

These multiple dimensions of the crisis respond not only to the process of dehumanisation of humanity but also to the denaturalisation of nature. No matter how powerful the *denialists* may be, let us admit it, environmental problems cannot be concealed. Besides, we cannot hide either the enormous socio-economic inequalities that are growing at the same time as *progress*—or its stepchild, *development*—spreads around the world like a mutant virus. This crisis can be seen and felt in every sphere: economic, social, environmental, political, ethical, cultural, spiritual, and so on.

Ironically, these crises are even fed by the support of many of the system's very victims, trapped by false but attractive images. Demolishing those images is not easy. Their seductive logic is widely internalised. The dominance of the corporate media, as highlighted in this powerful and motivating book, conceals systemic injustices through instruments designed to ideologically discipline populations. Therefore, the fear and tension, caused and sustained—again and again—by the various instances of power, allow the introduction of *solutions*, otherwise undeniable, even magical, wrapped in the unfulfillable promise of development and progress. As a result of this convulsive scenario, loaded with media manipulations, consumerism and productivism, violence and corruption, and authoritarianism and repression, the fragile democratic institutions are wrapped and weakened.

The South emulates the North, captivated by its stunning lifestyles on an apparently unstoppable course that causes more and more social and environmental problems. Seven decades after the concept of *development* officially appeared, the whole world is immersed in *maldevelopment*. Even countries that consider themselves to be developed find themselves in an increasingly complex position, not only because their lifestyles are unrepeatable on a global scale but also because inequalities, frustrations, violence, and pollution are expanding more and more. All of this occurs in a situation in which wars are the order of the day, shaping spaces of confrontation not only of jingoistic imperialisms but, mainly, of corporate imperialism.

Without accepting pessimistic readings or visions of wishful optimism, we cannot sink into despair, even when we understand that reality itself is terrible. Reading the cases discussed in this book, we get the idea that humanity does not give up. They are only a few examples, however, they are powerful, not only in their content but also in their message. The experiences, which deal with different areas of human action, speak to us of options that go beyond the visions normally offered by communication and monocultural research. This is so in enriched countries (*societies of externalisation*, that is, enriched at the expense of other societies): Japan, the United Kingdom, and Spain, as well as in impoverished countries: Malawi, Ecuador, Bolivia, and India, and, in continental terms, in Africa and Latin America. From the beginning, in this text, horizontal dialogue and understanding between cultures are suggested, seeking common grounds while always valuing differences.

Postdevelopment as an initial step

Surprising as it may seem at first glance, the discourse of *development* consolidates the global crisis. This crisis is not circumstantial. In fact, it is structural and historical. It is therefore urgent to think and act beyond development, seeking a deep reorganisation of relations within and between societies, as well as relations between Humanity and Nature, which we are part of.

Without denying the need to have an impact on every level of action—from the local to the global, without forgetting the national and the regional—we must understand that the construction of alternatives of civilising scale is being promoted from diverse community spaces around the world. This implies, as proposed in the cases analysed in these pages, a Copernican turn of the civilising screw: moving from visions and actions, marked by the verticality of power, to horizontal ones, which are the basis for understanding the world through other perspectives and, of course, for building those other possible and desirable worlds for humans and nonhumans.

When we open the door to postdevelopment, we bring up the need to go beyond development as an organising principle of life. We even question the fetish of progress. What is interesting today is that the bulk of the criticism of development is emerging in a powerful way through alternative proposals and actions from neighbourhoods and rural communities, but mainly, from Indigenous people and from feminist and environmental movements, that is, from many traditionally marginalised groups in society. All of them are victims of development. This criticism is increasing in academic spaces, some of which have understood the importance of being in tune with those processes of popular origin, as it is the case of the analyses in this book.

Without playing down all these efforts and without assuming in a simplistic way that all those actions bring about civilising changes, it should be acknowledged that the prefix *post* simply points out what is not wanted. This is essential. Niccolo Machiavelli recommended, in his classic book, published more than 500 years ago: *one must know the ways of hell in order to avoid them!* However, while this recognition is important, it is not enough. We need to transition towards a pluriversal world with historical meaning—the utopian—and certainly with practical content—the concrete.

In this endeavour, there is a resurgence of existing Indigenous cosmogonies. Besides, there is also the emergence of new visions and practices that present systemic alternatives to ensure the integral well-being of all human and nonhuman beings. This increasingly vigorous process is forcing the decolonisation of knowledge and communication systems, breaking down many of the dualisms that patriarchal and colonial paradigms have conceived, such as the awkward attempt to separate Humanity from Nature. This is reflected in a traditional but no less evil dichotomy: the cultural and the natural.

Postdevelopment is also deeply related to overcoming economicism, which finds one of its strongholds in the religion of economic growth or in the theory of the rational choice of individuals, that is, the supposedly natural tendency to selfishly maximise profits. Postdevelopment questions the system of capital domination, based on greed and endless accumulation. However, it is not enough to criticise and avoid what we do not want. We need to complete what comes after the *post*.

In short, it is not a question of looking for alternatives within development, incorporating new names to it, such as, for example, sustainable development or development on a human scale. In a deeper sense, we require alternatives to this development, with the aim of breaking with the cultural and ideological bases of progress, stuffing this process of change—a profound *metamorphosis* of civilising scope—with other imaginaries, objectives, and practices.

If we accept what has been previously stated, we must avoid false solutions proposed by those in power, in an attempt to give an ecological image to development or an almost magical character to technological solutions. Above all, the path of the permanent and continuous commodification of life must be avoided. Let's face it, the economy is in an extremely complex dilemma. The problems besetting it, and the challenges it has to face, are becoming bigger and more difficult to cope with. It is unbearable to see how the economy—as a machine designed and built to maximise results with a greater or lesser involvement of the state and/or the market—has transformed itself into a sort of great *totem* to which permanent and submissive honour is paid. Actions are deployed to protect it, presenting them as alternatives to try to solve the very problems caused by this economy. This way *sustainable, circular,* or *coloured* economies emerge, be they *green, blue, orange, violet,* or whatever one wants to call them or *colour* them. However, without disregarding some good intentions, these economies end up not questioning the perverse essence of economicism and even less of capitalism.

We, therefore, argue that the time has come to deepen and broaden an agenda that allows us to learn about, and debate a variety of worldviews and practices related to the collective search for an ecologically and socially sustainable world, which should be framed in a process of permanent radicalisation of democracy. A world that demands a dialogue of knowledges and wisdoms in line with the category of cognitive justice made from the perspective of the pluriverse. That means valuing multiple ways of thinking and feeling, inhabiting the world, and knowing beyond the limits of the Western literate matrix of the Modern/colonial world system. As this book, clearly and vigorously, concludes, this is an urgent task to overcome the technocratic, corporate, and oppressive monoculture of communication that responds to the established logic of Modernity. From this reading, emerge transformative alternatives to the dominant processes of current globalised development, including the deep structural roots of Modernity, in essence, capitalism, which is sustained by the predominance of the commodification of life, as well as patriarchy and coloniality.

Criticising Modernity does not place us in the area of reactionary conservatives. It does not imply a rejection of all technological advances. Nor does it synthesise an unconditional acceptance of all that is *traditional,* which, more often than not sustains unequal and unjust societies. The critique of Modernity concentrates on its hegemonic, unidirectional, and universalist aspects.

The postdevelopment agenda must investigate the what, the how, the who, and the why of everything that is transformative and also what is not. Likewise, those who promote postdevelopment must overcome a number of weaknesses in their argumentation, they must accept that the idea of development is still present, and focus on the structural changes needed to face deep social fractures and the ecological collapse. All these efforts must never make us lose sight of the essential construction of alternatives to the problems of everyday life or of utopian horizons.

Some postdevelopmentalist horizons

The exploration of alternatives to development has already found a specific expression in a large number of new concepts and practices, such as degrowth or conviviality, or the ones that made a comeback, such as *Buen Vivir, swaraj, Ubuntu,* or *kyosei.* At the same time, the demand for common goods and proposals such as food and energy sovereignty is emerging. An important place is occupied by all efforts to prioritise the principle of care. All these struggles and alternatives are becoming not only more visible but also increasingly possible. However, they remain marginal in comparison to the narrative and practice of the dominant development, especially, because of the weight of media injustice. It is therefore a good time to promote general awareness of these alternatives, as well as to build bridges between them, while respecting their geopolitical and epistemic specificities. It is also essential to establish a bond between these alternatives and popular groups and movements that resist the dominant economic and political systems.

The list of issues that this effort demands is enormous. By way of example, we can highlight some of them. The absence of an analysis of the historical and structural roots of poverty, hunger, criminality, and inequalities would include the essence of the centralisation of state power and capitalist monopolies: scant importance given to direct democracy, indispensable in decision-making in order to ensure control over our own lives; the failure to recognise the biophysical limits of economic growth and the sociocultural damage it causes; the continued submission to private capital; the inability or unwillingness to democratise the economy or to transform it completely from its roots; the exaltation of modern science and technology as a supposed panacea, ignoring their limitations and marginalising other forms of knowledge and in particular those knowledges coming from outside Modernity itself; the marginalisation of culture, ethics, and spirituality; unstoppable consumerism as one of the greatest aberrations of extreme individualism, transformed into a real social disease; and the absence of global relations built on the foundations of justice, transparency, and equity, which deepens the growing loss of sovereignty of peoples. Both, injustice and media inequity, close this circle of domination.

Despite these barriers, a variety of different and complementary notions or visions of the world have emerged in various regions of the world, which seek to imagine and achieve a real transformation that is impossible to achieve through traditional approaches, no matter how much they are concealed under the guise of the green economy or sustainable development. Some of these are a revival of the worldviews of Indigenous peoples. Some have emerged from recent social and environmental movements related to old traditions and philosophies. Some emerge from specific actions in different areas of people's lives. Coming from different cultural and social contexts, they sometimes differ in their prescriptions, but they share much of the same diagnosis; they are worldviews related to each other by the urgent need to promote a harmonious life in the world among human beings and between human beings and Nature—a life that places at the centre the self-sufficiency and self-management of human beings living in community, strengthening the bonds of interdependence. This effort of multiple transformations must be focused on concrete contents, rather than forms, institutions, or regulations.

Unlike development, which is a concept based on a false consensus, these alternative visions cannot be reduced to a single vision and, therefore, cannot aspire to be adopted as a common goal by large international organisations. These ideas were born as radical proposals for change from the local to the global. They express disagreement with current representations of the world and propose systemic alternatives. In this way, they are a critique of the current hegemony of development, which means a critique of the homogenisation of cultures that adopt patterns and lifestyles loaded with models of consumption and production coming from the Global North.

Accepting the complexity of the task, the deconstruction of development opens the door to a wide range of ideas (new and old) within a complex and rich matrix of alternatives. These include *Buen Vivir* (*Vivir Bien*, *sumak kawsay*, *suma qamaña*, *ñandareko/teko pora*, *küme mogen*, etc.) a culture of life with different denominations and varieties in different regions of South America; *Ubuntu*, with its emphasis on human reciprocity in Africa; *Swaraj*, with its emphasis on self-reliance and self-governance, in India, and many others.

What is important here is the fact that, although many are old, these options are reemerging both in their original forms and with modifications, in the heart of various narratives within movements that struggle against development in all its versions. The postulates from feminists and ecofeminists, as well as ecosocialism, represent aspects that could fit within this postdevelopmentalist rainbow. And to the aforementioned must be added the whole decolonial contribution.

These worldviews are not new in the 21st century but rather part of a long search for alternative ways of living, forged in the crucible of humanity's struggle for emancipation *within* (rather than outside) the womb of nature. What makes such alternative proposals remarkable, however, is the fact that they often emerge from traditionally marginalised groups, the ones forgotten by history and by the mainstream press. Many of these worldviews differ from those of the dominant West by emerging from noncapitalist communities. They are, therefore, independent from the anthropocentric and androcentric logic of capitalism, the dominant civilisation, and the different models of state socialism (in practice, state capitalism) that have existed up to now. But there are other approaches and practices emerging from the *belly of the beast*, which can also break the dominant logic, as it is the case of degrowth or postextractivism, for example, to mention a couple of visions that are expanding firmly, building bridges between the Global North and the Global South.

What should be done? Development, as a worldwide adopted/imposed mental construct, needs to be overcome, regardless of its various names. But this task is not easy. Due to the politics of the media powers in society, it is difficult to unmask this reality. It is often more important what remains unsaid than what is said. Manipulating the facts in order to inoculate the audience with a certain framework to understand reality is another of its perversities. Imposing the topics of discussion is another of its baseness. Thus, using this broad and powerful instrument of domination, they systematically hide existing alternatives and even distort horizons with civilising content, such as Buen Vivir.

The matter covers a crudely perverse aspect when we see that this type of vision of civilising change has been sucked dry in its essence. The United Nations tried to use *Buen Vivir* as a tool within the green economy. And the *progressive* governments of Ecuador and Bolivia, which encouraged its adoption in touted constitutional texts, transformed *Buen Vivir/Vivir Bien* into mere power devices and into vulgar propaganda tools for merely trying to modernise capitalism, something truly aberrant.

The results of the aspirations to change, without questioning the matrix of Modernisation, are easy to see. Material accumulation—mechanistic and endless accumulation of goods—assumed as progress, has no future. Neither does development, which comes from such progress. The limits of lifestyles based on anthropocentric prosperity—unequal and inequitable, in fact—are becoming increasingly noticeable and worrying. In short, the traditional concept of development must be overturned. However, it is not just a matter of criticising and destroying it. Different constructive points of view, rich in content as well as complexity, are needed to make sense of what comes after development.

That is why these alternative approaches are necessary to challenge the ideas of the dominant economy in all its aspects. It is also the case of technologies as unquestioned panaceas. Let us dare to think of other worlds based on diversity, relationality, reciprocity, solidarity, commonality, empathy, resonance, interconnectivity, simplicity, inclusiveness, equity and nonhierarchicality, sufficiency, and not just efficiency. In short, pluriversality. It also assumes the challenge of acknowledging that we are Nature and that she, Mother Earth, is the one who really gives us the right to our existence.

Walking in the pluriverse

At a time when wild neoliberalism and extractivism brutalise the daily lives of societies around the world, particularly those in the Global South, it is essential that protesting voices and people's movements engage in a concentrated effort of research, participation, dialogue, and action in the key of the pluriverse. Acts of resistance give hope here and now. Resistance is crucial, but it is not enough. And these resistances, which are often parallel acts of reexistence, must be translated into renewed narratives and proposals in a pluriversal key.

We have a long road ahead of us. There is much to discuss and construct in order to enter the pluriverse. Actually, if we are honest and thorough in our analyses, we must accept that the pluriverse has always been present, although hidden and marginalised by the standardising visions and proposals of the universe.

We only need to look at the cases presented in this book. A chapter rich in concrete experiences analyses how in Bolivia Indigenous textile practices are promoted, characterised by the harmonious and sustainable production of raw materials, natural dyes, and fabrics that support local communities and the extended community (the *ayllu*). Another chapter reflects on the understanding and practice of communicative justice in line with decolonial practices. On Puná Island, in the Gulf of Guayaquil, a forgotten region of Ecuadorian society, communication is present in the multiple conflicts its inhabitants deal with in their daily activities in the face of natural resources exploitation; an issue that conflicts with the possibility of building harmonious relationships between ecosystems and cultures, giving way to complex capitalist outlets for survival, lacking the potential for civilisational change. The decolonial practices implemented in several Malawian communities in Africa serve to challenge colonial developmentalist strategies, which are essentially inept, even proposing solutions to nonexistent problems. The message of this case is extremely powerful to revalue the epistemological idiosyncrasy of each culture, that is, different knowledges situated in a concrete reality, in concrete territories, and specific to each situation. A paradigmatic example can be found in India, where nonviolent communication expands teachings of Mahatma Gandhi to become an alternative to the dominant violent communicative ecosystem. It proposes to build emotional and cognitive bridges within and between communities through a variety of techniques and strategies. The theory and practice of nonviolence aims to counteract and eventually eradicate violent communication. But there are also other nonviolent noncommunicative structures and practices that may be found, as the chapter shows, in legal systems, law enforcement, or even in some youth cultures.

It is surprising what a leap one can make wandering around in this pluriverse when arriving in Japan. Okinawa's history is almost unknown. Preserving and reinforcing the remains of its unique identity, culture, history, and language is motivating. Since the Japanese colonisation of the Ryukyu Kingdom in the late 19th century, the smallest archipelago of Ryukyu, renamed Okinawa, has been relegated to an exotic, feminine, and inferior cultural haven. It assumes the role of Japan's inner periphery geographically, politically, and socioeconomically. The chapter analysing this case study questions the dependent development of this region in terms of *postdevelopment*. A task that is also explored through the perspective of sociocultural, environmental, political economy, and communicative justice.

In another highly motivating twist, this book moves forward in the analysis of what the worldwide spreading of popular music means, taking as examples two emerging female bands in relation to their performances on International Women's Day. This chapter, based on a Spanish experience, presents examples of cooperation, solidarity, diversity, female inspiration, and empowerment through the ways in which popular music and *glocal*—local/global—music scenes stimulate intercultural and intergenerational dialogue. A real challenge since as is widely accepted, music appears as another mechanism for imposing labour models, consumption patterns, and uniformed ways of life. Recovering art from the claws of capital demands multiplying different voices that integrate the dimension of justices—yes, justices in the plural—in the diverse worlds that make up the pluriverse.

The aforementioned case is in line with an experience in the United Kingdom, which highlights the importance of cultural rituals to break with visions and actions imposed "from above" regarding communication public policies. It is essential, this case of analysis tells us, a reverse political transfer, which overcomes the dominant axes from North to South, from West to East. This exercise of reflection, which starts from a Northern country, undoubtedly finds a multiplicity of experiences in many other parts of the planet. The search for participatory communication, the activism of social movements, and radical democracy must overcome the values and practices imposed by the influence of the "imperial way of life".

These latter contributions based on the geographic north present experiences of communicative justice in which people from both the south and the north cooperate as allies of the Global South. The last chapter worthwhile mentioning in this prologue is significant for its coverage of a collaborative South–South project between Latin America and Africa. The chapter presents the lessons learnt, through exchanges, alliances, and mutual support, to apply communication strategies in favour of a social and behavioural change from a pluriversal point of view.

In summary, we urgently need to recover the rich variety of worldviews and practices related to the collective search for a world where other worlds fit, in a Zapatista key, ensuring a dignified life for human and nonhuman beings. We have to move forward in the definition of which are the transformative alternatives, show how they differ from false solutions, and also explore how they can be articulated.

To conclude, these practices and worldviews—alternatives to development—seek to repoliticise the debate in processes of socioecological transitions, ratifying dissidence with respect to current representations of the world (such as the much-promoted sustainable development), as well as seeking other paths. Overcoming the modern ontology of a single world expands the multiplicity of possible worlds. It strengthens the relationality of all forms of human and nonhuman life, in line with a multiple world, the pluriverse.

This implies having in mind a civilisational change. Modernity is falling apart and postmodernity must be overcome as an era of disenchantment. The devastating "development", whose major paradigms—inherited from Modernity—are progress, extreme individualism, domination of Nature, and unsustainable economic growth cannot continue to dominate. It will be necessary, then, to overcome the idea of progress, understood especially as the permanent accumulation of material goods. And, therefore, to reverse the evil processes of dehumanisation of humanity and denaturalisation of nature.

In this endeavour, communicative justice occupies a fundamental position. As noted in the book, this implies a permanent awareness and questioning of how societies represent differences and diversity, as well as how they represent themselves and each other. This is intimately related to intersectionality inasmuch as communicative justice, based on this awareness, leads not only to revealing and denouncing stereotypes but also to overcoming them in discourse and action.

We know that there are no recipes or models to propose and build different societies. Nor are there any set paths or defined alternatives. They need to be built. And not having a predetermined path is not a problem. Quite the contrary. It frees us from dogmatic visions, although it requires us to be clearer about the destination we want to reach, assuming transitions as concrete options in a plural and radical journey towards pluriversal horizons. It is not only the destination that counts but also the ways to achieve human life in dignity guaranteeing all beings—human and nonhuman—a present and a future on the planet.

Alberto Acosta
Translated by Sheila Agenjo Alcaide

Note

1. *This text is based on the reflections made by the author and previously published in various texts*, but especially those made jointly with Ashish Kothari, Ariel Salleh, Arturo Escobar and Federico Demaria, with whom he edited the book *Pluriverse—A Post-Development Dictionary* (2019, Tulika Books, India) (editions already exist in Ecuador, Spain, Peru/Bolivia, Colombia, Brazil, Italy). For reasons of space and, to facilitate the reading of this prologue, the bibliographical quotes have been sacrificed, but it should be noted that, in addition to the four people mentioned, this text draws on contributions from many others, such as Aníbal Quijano, Bruno Latour, Boaventura de Sousa Santos, Eduardo Gudynas, Gustavo Esteva, Enrique Dussel, Enrique Leff, Iván Illich, Joan Martínez Alier, José María Tortosa, Miriam Lang, Maristella Svampa, Markus Wissen, Nina Pacari, Rita Segato, Stephan Lesenich, Ulrich Brand, Walter Mignolo, and so on.

ACKNOWLEDGEMENTS

The editors of this volume would like to express our gratitude first to each of the authors for believing in this project, sharing their research, and patiently weaving links until the end result was achieved. Together we have learned from each other.

We have also learned from several communities and social movements that have allowed us to recognise that the pluriverse is not only a concept, an approach, and a perspective but also realities. Without interaction with them, it would be more difficult to question our own frameworks of knowledge, sense, and feeling. They are our inspiration.

This journey has been possible thanks to the editors of the series, Claudia Magallanes Blanco, Charlotte Ryan, and Alice Mattoni. They have been a loving, dedicated, knowledgeable, and respectful accompaniment, guide, and support. Thank you for encouraging us not to lose ourselves in this process.

Indeed, we have learned a lot from dialogues with fellow scholars who are engaged in critical and emancipatory research.

We are also grateful to our universities—Uniminuto and Complutense de Madrid—for allowing us to focus on this work and incorporate these important debates into their daily academic life.

Finally, and more importantly, we extend our gratitude to our close and extended family for their love and support.

INTRODUCTION

*Eliana Herrera-Huérfano, Joan Pedro-Carañana,
and Juana Ochoa Almanza*

This volume brings together a plurality of academic and practical experiences of communicative justice from the perspective of the pluriverse. Following Arturo Escobar (2012a, p. xxviii), the pluriverse is understood as "a world where many worlds fit", without the oppression of anyone and ensuring the dignity of all. In the face of the dominant conception of the world as a universe with a unique, Euro and US-centric regime of truth and existence, the pluriverse acknowledges the existence of multiple, interconnected "worlds and knowledges otherwise" (Escobar, 2012a, p. xxviii). Thus, this book analyses how a variety of communicative justice experiences are involved in the struggles for expanding "worlds and knowledges constructed on the basis of different ontological commitments, epistemic configurations, and practices of being, knowing, and doing" (2012a, p. xxviii). Specifically, the book explores how communicative justice is related to the key dimensions of the pluriverse, namely, cognitive justice, environmental justice, sociocultural and spiritual justice, sociopolitical justice, and political economy justice, which are defined in Chapter 1.

The focus on communicative justice allows us to further the knowledge of both hegemonic structures and counterhegemonic ecologies and practices that might contribute to overcoming them. The contributions in this book delve into experiences of communicative justice, allowing us to rethink communication from a decolonial perspective in relation to other dimensions of justice and to an ecology of communication in the face of a Modern, capitalist, patriarchal, and racist communication monoculture.

The volume features contributions based on experiences of and from the Global South. We understand this term as including not merely the countries that have lower income than those in the Global North but also the experiences

DOI: 10.4324/9781003316220-1

of resistance and transformation which are taking place within countries of the geographical north in so far as they are part of the epistemologies of the South (Santos, 2015). Thus, the volume includes experiences and authors from the epistemological South in both the geographical south and north, although it gives more space to the geographical south as a matter of cognitive justice. Within the limited space of a volume, we have made the selection of chapters with the aim of addressing as much geographical diversity as possible. That is why the volume features contributions from experiences in Latin America, Europe, Asia, and Africa. Specifically, the book includes studies on processes of communicative justice in Japan, the United Kingdom, and Spain that defy hegemonic models of the Global North, as well as practices in Malawi, Ecuador, Bolivia, India, and broader South–South collaborations between Latin America and Africa that intend to extend the pluriverse and facilitate social change.

All the contributions to this volume are by invitation of the editors of the volume after learning about the research and reflective experiences of the authors in academic meetings, congresses, social activism, and publications. In addition to the focus on the global south, the selection aimed to include academic and activist work on communicative justice as an experience of struggle, that is, as a way to promote other forms of justice within the framework of the recognition of the pluriverse of ontologies and epistemologies that cross human experiences on the planet, generating models different from those expanded through the monocultures of the Western, modern, literate, patriarchal, Anglo-centred matrix.

All the chapters included in this volume engage with experiences that are representative of communicative justice as part of the pluriverse. They identify and explain the challenges and difficulties faced by activists and communities, the strategies developed to overcome such problems, and the achievements made from a communicative perspective. They identify the unequal power relations that limit the possibilities of communication justice, the ways in which movements have confronted power structures through discourse and material action, and their successes and limitations in the creation of new structures that promote the right to communication and facilitate a sustainable future for communicative justice. This volume, therefore, builds a dialogue with experiences that show how the pluriverse emerges in different parts of the world and among diverse populations as a possibility to resist, transform, and stop the violence of monocultures.

The contributors to the book continue with this dialogue by focusing on concrete experiences through theoretical reflections and case studies. The cases and reflections emphasise the development and preservation of local knowledges and how to place them in dialogue with other traditions of thought and struggle. Although not homogeneous in structure, the chapters bring to light alternative ways of learning and thinking produced by oppressed populations, reflect upon them in the context of the pluriverse and the ecologies of the epistemologies of the South, connect them with communicative justice, and show their heuristic value for better understanding societies. The dialogue is rounded off in the Conclusion chapter of the book by way of articulating the various forms of knowledge explored throughout the volume.

As editors, we have structured the volume according to the general relations between communicative justice and other dimensions of the pluriverse. In Chapter 1, we develop a dialogue of knowledges and set out the key common features of the experiences discussed in the book, namely, the theoretical framework of the pluriverse, the focus on communicative justice, and its interrelations with other dimensions of justice of the pluriverse. Moreover, we present participant-engaged methodologies as a general framework to host different methodological approaches based on fieldwork with communities in diverse contexts as the most appropriate for conducting pluriversal studies.

The dialogue between communicative justice and sociocultural and spiritual justice is explored in Chapters 2–4. Elvira Espejo Ayca and Aura Isabel Mora present in Chapter 2 a collective of Bolivian women weavers who, through Women's Science, reclaim, communicate and make visible ancestral techniques and traditions, confronting the process of discrimination and eradication of their traditional knowledge. In Chapter 3, Vedabhyas Kundu challenges the current violent communicative ecosystem and its role in the dissemination of hate speech, radicalisation, xenophobia, and political polarisation of society. In response to this situation, the author takes up the commitments of the Gandhian peace movement to propose an ecosystem that fosters soul-to-soul communication and the building of emotional bridges through nonviolent communication. Finally, Chapter 4, written by Jair Vega-Casanova, Rafael Obregón Galvez, Sara-Nathalie Brombart, and Gabriel Baglo, explores the South–South collaborative dialogue between Latin America and Africa through the consolidation and adjustment of a manual called "Voices with Purpose—A Manual on Communication Strategies for Development and Social Change", which allowed for the exploration of central sociocultural elements of each region for the strengthening of the communication skills and capacities of social organisations.

Chapters 5–7 take up the dialogue between sociopolitical justice, political economy justice, and communicative justice, exploring experiences of active and critical citizenship. In Chapter 5, Karen Andrade Mendoza and Galo Plaza Vanegas present the communicative and political tensions between different actors in the Gulf of Guayaquil and Puna Island, Ecuador, around the processes of exploitation of natural resources in the area. Environmental groups and Indigenous communities make visible the damage by capitalist economic productivity by emphasising environmental justice in articulation with the other dimensions of justice that are discussed. In Chapter 6, Des Freedman discusses pluriversal media policy based on anticolonial and anticapitalist struggles, as well as on cognitive, sociopolitical, cultural, and political economy justice to transform the hegemonic media system as a way of fostering the pluriverse. The author assesses the communication justice activism of the Media Reform Coalition in the United Kingdom in this light. Finally, Josep Pedro and Begoña Gutierrez-Martínez explore in

Chapter 7 the planetarisation of popular music by examining two emerging female bands in relation to their performances on International Women's Day (8 March 2019, Madrid—Spain). These cases explore the ways in which women from different countries and cultural traditions organise themselves through music and foster communicative justice to confront different forms of exclusion and discrimination.

The dimension of cognitive justice and its dialogue with communicative justice are explored in Chapters 8 and 9. In Chapter 8, Daniel Broudy and Ariko Ikehara delve into antidemocratic development to analyse *artivism* in Okinawa's (Japan) pluriverse, revealing the need to value worldviews and relational ontologies based on the traditional cultural and historical uniqueness of the area, as a response to US military colonisation and neoliberal capitalist projects. Finally, Carlos A. Segovia in Chapter 9 focuses on Malawi and short-sighted colonial developmentalist experiences that propose solutions to nonexistent problems. The author expresses the urgency of cognitive justice not only at the epistemological level but also with regard to the ontologies of communities to move towards a pluriverse that allows for the recovery of Malawi's precolonial agricultural practices, its economic self-sufficiency, and its resilience in the face of climate change.

Based on the reflections, debates, findings, and conclusions developed in each of the chapters, the Conclusion of the book develops a further dialogue of knowledges around the central category of communicative justice in opposition to the monoculture of communication. It explains the need for communicative justice, its characteristics and protagonists, the media that it employs, and how it relates to other dimensions of pluriversal justice. With this volume, the editors and authors endeavour to provide clues for new readings of communication and media experiences, structures, processes, practices, and contexts that contribute to making visible and expanding the pluriverse and, thus, allow for the affirmation of life itself in all its human and environmental richness and diversity.

References

Escobar, A. (2012a). *Encountering development: The making and unmaking of the third world.* Princeton University Press.

Santos, B. D. S. (2015). *Epistemologies of the South: Justice against epistemicide.* Routledge.

1
DIALOGUE OF KNOWLEDGES IN THE PLURIVERSE[1]

Eliana Herrera-Huérfano, Joan Pedro-Carañana, and Juana Ochoa Almanza

The theoretical and methodological discussion presented in this chapter reviews three academic strands from different disciplinary origins: (1) the foundations of the concept and perspective of the pluriverse developed by Arturo Escobar (anthropology); (2) the decolonial approach, especially anchored in Latin American authors such as Anibal Quijano, Walter Mignolo, Santiago Castro-Gómez, Enrique Dussel, Nelson Maldonado-Torres, and Edgardo Lander, among others (philosophy, cultural studies, and sociology); and (3) the understanding of monocultures and ecologies of southern epistemologies proposed by Boaventura de Sousa Santos (sociology of emergencies). On the basis of the journey through these strands of thought, we wish to establish a dialogue between the different social and human sciences that converge here with the field of communication studies in the analysis of communicative justice.

Pluriverse: concept, perspective, and reality

The aim of this chapter is to introduce readers to the academic and practical importance of *communicative justice* in the perspective of the pluriverse within the sociohistorical and intellectual context in which this perspective is emerging. Given that the role of communication in the pluriverse has been less explored by scholarship than other dimensions, we focus on the concept of communicative justice, which, not incidentally, also contributes to other forms of justice. The perspective of the pluriverse challenges dominant structures of oppression and facilitates horizontal dialogue and understanding among cultures by finding commonalities while valuing differences.

In the following pages, we trace the academic contributions of a variety of perspectives which, faithful to the spirit of pluriversality, we propose to combine

DOI: 10.4324/9781003316220-2

and articulate in order to provide a nonreductionist, comprehensive, and flexible model of analysis for the study of the pluriverse and its concomitant critique of the Modern world system.

The pluriverse is a concept that "questions the concept of universality, one of the pillars of Western Modernity" (Escobar, 2018, p. 43). The concept of the pluriverse is instead inspired by Foucault's understanding of utopias and hetero-topias as different spaces that generate their own autonomies outside the regular order of the homogeneous and universal system that creates exclusions:

> I found it interesting to try to understand our society and our civilisation through its systems of exclusion, its forms of rejection and denial, through what is not wanted, its limits, and the feeling of obligation that prompts to suppress a certain number of things, of people, of processes and, there-fore, through what is left hidden under the cloak of oblivion; in short, I'm interested in analysing the repression–elimination systems typical of society.
>
> *(Foucault, 1999, p. 28)*

Based on Foucault's critical perspective, Arturo Escobar considers that the pluriverse has become a concept, an approach, a perspective, and also a reality, to the extent that the world—reality—is made up of many worlds, of many realities (Personal Communication, 2020). The perspective of the pluriverse maps the multiple transitions and existing alternatives on the planet as spaces of opposition to the Modern/colonial world system (Escobar, 2014). The pluriverse seeks to recognise and interpret all the realities that present alternatives to what is called development, economic growth, and neoliberalism, that is, to show the map of transitions or transformative experiences in the face of the global capitalist system.

The perspective of the pluriverse is the culmination of a series of academic works that take a critical look at capitalist development. Since the publication of *Discourse and Power in Development* (1984), Escobar has analysed how the dis-course of development is a social, cultural, and neoliberal force of submission and domination, which makes other cultural and social forms invisible. Start-ing from the conception of postdevelopment as a social concept and practice, Escobar joined the debates of critical development studies and opened the way to understanding alternatives to development enacted by social movements and grassroots activism. The pluriversal perspective consists in understanding that there is a diversity of viable realities outside the established script of the univer-sality of capitalism and that they foster postdevelopment practices or alternatives to development.

In recent years, the discussion has focused on understanding the discourses and practices of the transitions towards another civilisational model that moves away from the universality of global capitalism to the pluriverse. In Escobar's (2014) view, pluriversal studies:

> Are oriented, on the one hand, to present viable alternatives to the discourse and practices of the one world for those Modern uni-worldists already tired of their empty universalist narratives; and, on the other, to understand the multiple projects based on other ontological commitments and ways of planetarising life, and the many ways in which these struggles weaken the project of the one-world and at the same time contribute to expanding its spaces of re-existence.
>
> *(p. 21)*

The evolving perspective of the pluriverse is grounded in decolonial scholarship and comes from the practices that communities and social movements around the world are implementing to question the Modern hegemonic paradigm and improve the degrees of justice. Kothari et al. (2018, p. xxviii) define the pluriverse following the Zapatista conceptualisation as "a world where many worlds fit". In the face of the dominant conception of the world as a universe with a unique regime of thought, the term pluriverse acknowledges the existence of multiple, interconnected "worlds and knowledges otherwise" (Escobar, 2012a, p. xxviii). Recognition of this diversity requires the decolonisation of knowledge, cognitive justice, and complex intercultural and interepistemic processes that make visible a multiplicity of ontologies and the need for decolonisation.

The perspective of the pluriverse understands that dominant ideologies and scholarship culturally legitimate injustice(s) in the world. Since the Modern hegemonic paradigm has been produced by and spread from Western countries, it is only natural that the perspective of the pluriverse critically questions Western, mainstream scholarship. The perspective of the pluriverse is actually born from a need to provide alternative knowledge and as a critique of the hegemonic paradigm that has marginalised alternative ways of thinking. Visvanathan (2006, p. 167) refers to cognitive justice not as "an esoteric plea but a practical idea, an appeal by marginal and traditional societies who felt that they had something to add to Western science, to its ideas of complexity, time and sustainability". This demand for cognitive justice made from the perspective of the pluriverse values multiple ways of thinking, inhabiting the world, and knowing beyond the limits of the Western literate matrix of the Modern/colonial world system.

Accordingly, the perspective of the pluriverse criticises the globalisation paradigm for privileging both homogenisation under Western commercial standards and fragmentation based on market niches and excluding identities. Pluriversal scholarship draws on the struggles for social change that oppose the globalisation of capitalism with the planetarisation of diverse, noncommodified social relations. In the face of a massive concentration of wealth and power, the pluriverse fosters its distribution and dispersion. Instead of uncritically accepting the globalisation of capitalist markets, patriarchy, and racism, the pluriverse observes and critiques multiple inequalities and inequities. Based on this diagnosis, the pluriverse brings to the fore alternatives for the planetarisation of forms of imagining, discovering, creating, and sharing in which humans as well as other living beings can interrelate to enrich each other, expand epistemic and ontological plurality, improve social equality, and engage in harmonious forms of relating with nature (Escobar, 2012a).

The perspective of the pluriverse also questions the notion of the Habermasian public sphere and its attached liberal pluralism for obscuring the multiple conflicts and dominations that are constitutive of communication spaces mediated by capital, coloniality, and state. As Enrique Dussel (2015, p. 18) has noted, a project of systemic justice should aim to develop a culture "with a rich pluriversality resulting from an authentic intercultural dialogue, which ought to take clearly into account existing asymmetries". The pluriverse is attentive to unequal power relations that often lead to a false consensus that hinders opposition, diversity, and innovation. The pluriverse aims to foster dialogue and understanding in fair conditions by prioritising grassroots voices. These voices, capable of both expanding understanding and generating conflict, are precisely those that liberal pluralism has marginalised. Even more so, the dominant conception of the Habermasian public sphere does not even conceive the existence of the voice of the subalterns[2] and other marginalised populations. The liberal approach detaches the analysis of communication from the capitalist conditions of production and, by doing so, hides both the structural limitations they establish and the voices that challenge them.

If the liberal framework provides an understanding of the public sphere as a rational conversation between white educated gentlemen, the pluriverse attempts to facilitate the free exercise of reason by looking at the conditions of enunciation and response and, at the same time, by combining rationality with the ontologies of emotions, affects, intimacy, and spirituality. In accordance with critical theory, it also attempts to unveil the instrumental rationality of domination, that is, the means-ends of classist, racial, and gender exploitation and subjugation. It does not only allow space for educated men but also gives priority to a variety of exploited, oppressed, and intersectional actors. In the face of liberal ethnocentrism, the pluriverse attempts to foster equal ontological and epistemological dialogue oriented towards social change among the diverse populations of the planet and, thereby, facilitate the reduction of ethnocentrism in all cultures. The need for the voices of the pluriverse to be heard is indicative of the failure of the so-called *marketplace of ideas*. The existence itself of excluded voices demands an alternative framework that allows for real inclusion and diversity based on equality on a planetary level. Both academically and socially, the perspective and practices of the pluriverse endeavour to expand the spaces for systemic justice. It does not aim to make the existing exclusionary system a bit more inclusive but to generate new spaces, structures, and, eventually, systems grounded on the strength of both difference and equality.

Decolonial scholars have given the first steps to elaborate the academic approach of the pluriverse by observing and listening to the existing pluriversal practices carried out by social movements and grassroots organisations around the world. We further argue for a never-ending construction of this theoretical perspective grounded on the decolonial project of the epistemologies of the South (Santos, 2016), which oppose dualism and positivism with relational frameworks and apply participatory methodologies that defy mainstream sociological and ethnographic approaches.

Moreover, we contend that the encompassing, interdimensional focus of the pluriverse requires this perspective to draw from complementary approaches, including decolonial and postcolonial scholarship, intersectionality, and the study of communication and social justice. Accordingly, in this first chapter, we start to develop a dialogue of knowledges that allows building a comprehensive analytical framework for the study of the pluriverse in the context of the Modern world system. This dialogue is construed as a decolonial reading of the pluriverse: the key criteria used for the selection of the perspectives and authors which are discussed are that they share a central preoccupation with the oppressed, especially the subaltern, and a critique of the dominant paradigm.

In the next section, we provide an overview of the postcolonial and decolonial critiques of the Modern world system and their proposals of justice which inform the pluriversal perspective (Section 2). This overview allows us to identify the foundations of pluriversal theory and its place within scholarship and history.

After this, we propose theoretical and empirical articulations of the dimensions of the pluriverse with what Boaventura de Sousa Santos (2007, 2016) has called ecologies in the framework of the epistemologies of the South. We crystallise these articulations in a model of analysis of the pluriverse based on a series of key interrelated dimensions that conform to systemic justice–injustice: cognitive, environmental, sociocultural and spiritual, political economy, sociopolitical, and communicative dimensions of justice (Section 3).

Section 4 discusses communicative justice based on scholarship on the decoloniality of communication, and, lastly, Section 5 presents some closing remarks.

Postcolonialism and decoloniality

The term pluriverse has been developed within decolonial scholarship, which, in turn, is closely related to postcolonial studies. As developed by Cruz Tornay-Márquez (2017), both perspectives emerge from within cultural studies and share the key criterion of seeing the phenomenon of colonialism and its ongoing consequences *from below*, i.e., from the locus of the oppressed popula- tions, especially the subalterns. This way of seeing inevitably leads to the critique of the hegemonic paradigm as well as to the recovery of the voices of the colo- nised after centuries of being systematically silenced and ignored.

Based on the work conducted by Bhambra (2014), Grosfoguel (2011), Lim (2019), and Mignolo (2000, 2011), we can observe some differences, but espe- cially important similarities, between postcolonial and decolonial scholarship. In general terms, each perspective has focused on distinct spatial and tempo- ral frameworks, used a different language, and resorted to alternative intellectual references. However, it is more relevant that they share a preoccupation with coloniality—understood as racialisation—and Modernity, the subaltern, and intersectionality as the key tenets of theoretical and empirical analysis. These are key concepts for the study and practical expansion of the pluriverse as we develop next.

The subalterns

Postcolonial scholar pioneer Gayatri Spivak (1988) introduced the idea of focus- ing on the subalterns, understood as heterogeneous populations who can surely express themselves but are not heard by the dominant West. In Spivak's work, the subalterns are colonised people in the East who do not have the power to present themselves to colonising countries but are mainly represented exogenously by the West. The term subaltern has had a variety of uses since Antonio Gramsci first coined it and today usually refers to people who are ranked as inferior based on race, class, gender, and other forms of oppression. The key to this framework is the change of focus towards the excluded and marginalised. The similarities with the epistemic question posed by decolonial author Ramón Grosfoguel (2011) can be readily observed:

> How would the world-system look like if we moved the locus of enuncia- tion from the European man to Indigenous women in the Americas, to, say, Rigoberta Menchú in Guatemala or Domitila Barrios de Chungara in Bolivia? I do not pretend to speak for or represent the perspective of these Indigenous women. What I attempt to do is to shift the location from which these paradigms are thinking.
>
> *(p. 7)*

This attempt to think from below is also the key focus of the epistemologies of the South. Grounded in postcolonial and decolonial frameworks, the work of Boaventura de Sousa Santos (2007, 2016) reclaims the just valuation of the invisi- bilised knowledges of marginalised communities and advocates for an intercultural dialogue through what he calls an ecology of knowledges (see Section 3).

Coloniality

Anibal Quijano (1993, 2000, 2003) coined the term coloniality to refer to the process that allowed the development of Modernity and of Europe, that is, the hierarchical construction, differentiation, and domination of other cultures based on the invention of "races". Conversely, the identity of the colonised has also been strongly influenced by this process of racist classification.

Since coloniality expresses itself through a variety of means, decolonial studies have further distinguished three dimensions of coloniality: coloniality of power, coloniality of knowledge, and coloniality of being. The first dimension refers to racism, the second to epistemic Eurocentrism, and the third to Westernisation.

According to Quijano (Ibid.), the coloniality of power refers to the socio-historical construction of race which began with the conquest of America. In this view, the main feature in the creation and development of the world system is the production of a mode of hierarchical classification of the members of the human species based on their phenotypes which allowed European whites to project themselves as racially superior. As Grosfoguel (2011, p. 11) notes, "what is new in the 'coloniality of power' perspective is how the idea of race and racism becomes the organising principle that structures all of the multiple hierarchies of the world-system". Quijano (2003) notes that "races" consist of a mental construction that expresses the basic form of colonial domination by producing new social identities (blacks, Indians, indigenous, mestizos, whites). Even though there is no biological basis to support the existence of "races", their existence in the mind of racists means that there are real, empirical consequences for both the dominant and the dominated populations. Thus, the existence of "races" as a sociocultural construction was and still is used to legitimise white, Western domination and diverse forms of violence based on an imagined higher rank. The objective of racial profiling is to provide a self-justification based on the alleged superiority of the endogroup as well as to foster obedience and subordination on the side of the exogroup.

Second, the coloniality of knowledge refers to the Eurocentric hierarchy of epistemologies that privileges Euro-centric knowledge and cosmology over non-Western (Grosfoguel, 2011; Mignolo, 1995, 2000; Quijano, 1993). Thus, it is understood that the alleged validity of knowledge rests on the criteria of Modern rationality and not on its value to society. This coloniality of knowledge has been institutionalised in the university systems around the world, contributing to the invisibilisation of alternative ways of knowing and imagining.

Finally, the coloniality of being is a concept developed by Mignolo and Wynter (2003) and Maldonado-Torres (2007) to refer to the lived experience of colonialism. In this view, the outcome of the colonialities of power and knowledge is a subalterisation of the colonised as nonbeings. The colonised can only exist as an imitation of Western culture, but not as themselves. This form of coloniality refers to the ontological dimension of autorepresentation.

Following this line of thought, the pluriverse is understood as an approach for the oppressed to critique dominant epistemologies and narratives and to construct decolonial ways of relating, knowing, and being. In the pluriverse, power relations are made more symmetrical as knowledge is exchanged and cooperation extends within a framework of equality and mutual aid.

Intersectionality

Grosfoguel (2011) advocates for extending the scope of decolonial scholarship by investigating the intersections of race with other sources of domination. This author contends that, since the world system presents many interconnected sources of oppression, social struggles cannot focus solely on one dimension (say antiracism, anticapitalism, or feminism) but instead should aim at an antisystemic liberation. Accordingly, Grosfoguel advocates for a nonreductionist, intersectional approach that addresses the interrelations between the sexual, gendered, spiritual, epistemic, economic, political, linguistic, aesthetic, pedagogical, racial, ecologic, and communicative hierarchies. This author borrows the concept of intersectionality from U.S. Third World Feminism and black feminism (see Crenshaw Williams, 1989; Collins, 2000; Sandoval, 1991; Davis, 2011) and understands it as an entanglement of multiple and heterogeneous global hierarchies or "heterarchies" (Kontopoulos, 1993). This interest in intersectionality is of manifest importance for the pluriverse and ought to be further pursued.

Decolonial and postcolonial feminism (Espinosa, 2009; Espinosa et al., 2014; Mohanty, 2008) are at the forefront of this articulation of the different forms of oppression and of liberation. An essential contribution of this approach is the critique of white, heterosexual, middle-class, and liberal feminism, whose Eurocentrism has led to the characterisation of women as a homogeneous group devoid of stories and contexts, as well as to supporting the hegemonic, unilinear conception of progress. Moreover, decolonial feminism has moved beyond the critique of the cultural construction of oppression to also study feminist solidarity and the role of racialised people in the anticapitalist struggle.

The relevance of postcolonial and decolonial studies for the pluriverse resides in that they provide theoretical tools for the critical analysis of Western dominant ideologies based on hierarchical otherising and bring to the fore the experiences and voices of colonised populations. By looking at power relations among actors, pluriversal analysis allows understanding of the symbolic construction of the Other in a context of inequality.

It can be observed that decolonial and postcolonial studies have focused mostly—although not exclusively—on the study of race, epistemology, and gender in the formation and expansion of the world system. That is to say that most of this scholarship has remained focused on the cultural sphere. However, this book addresses equally the material sphere (environmental, political economy, and sociopolitical dimensions of society) and communication (in its cultural and material dimensions) and emphasises their intersections with culture following the articulations initiated by decolonial feminism, intersectionality, and a class and political economy reading of coloniality (Trigo, 2014; Wallerstein & Balibar, 1991).

The pluriversal perspective ought to pursue the investigation of diverse geographical and sociohistorical sites and actors by drawing on epistemological and linguistic pluralism. As previously noted, the shared preoccupation for the voice of the oppressed—especially the subaltern—and the questioning of dominant narratives and structures are key for the pluriverse. Moreover, the intersections between different cultural and material dimensions are essential for a comprehensive understanding of the pluriverse, as developed in the overarching theoretical model presented in Section 3.

Monocultures, ecologies, and the pluriverse[3]

The insights provided by the perspectives that have been presented allow identifying important dimensions of the pluriverse. In this section, we discuss further contributions of the epistemologies of the South and the ecologies by Santos in dialogue with the reflections on the pluriverse provided by Escobar and other decolonial scholars. This dialogue of knowledges is crystallised in the model of analysis presented at the end of the section in Table 1.1. It includes the monocultures that conform to the Modern paradigm, the ecologies that challenge them, and their relation with the different forms of justice that the pluriverse requires for its existence and extension.

The proposal of the epistemologies of the South led by Boaventura de Sousa Santos and the collaborators of the ALICE[4] project at the School of Coimbra is based on several discussions that started to take place at the beginning of the millennium: (1) The loss of epistemic confidence in science in the 20th century, given the impossibility of finding explanations and solutions to current challenges; (2) the implications of knowledge, positioned epistemologies and the social production of knowledge (Haraway, Harding, Longino cited by Santos, 2010) under specific conditions by actors with a locus of enunciation from which evaluation and validation criteria can be established according to local contexts; (3) the questioning to classical dualisms (nature/culture; subject/object; individual/society); (4) the understanding of the production of knowledge from the perspective of the ontological practices of the production of knowledge (Latour cited by Santos, 2010); (5) the philosophical debate against the sovereignty of Western knowledge initiated by the pragmatic approach to knowledge and science (Berstein, Jaimes, Pierce, and Dewey cited by Santos, 2010); and (6) encounters with the South in research and knowledge productions socially committed to their realities and with the need to reinvent social emancipation against injustices and inequalities (Santos, 2004).

These debates allow the understanding of the demarcation of an abyssal line of thought that creates absences or nonexistence(s), visible and invisible distinctions, in a sociology of absences. A diversity of social and cultural practices, ways of being, knowledge, and cognitive frameworks are actively treated as nonexistent or as hardly feasible alternatives. Faced with this sociology of absences, Santos proposes a sociology of emergences which configures a postabyssal thought that seeks the visibility of said absences (Santos, 2010).

Decolonisation requires turning absences, nonexistence, or historical invisibilities into presences. Such nonexistents are produced, according to Santos, from logics that embody five monocultures that represent different forms of coloniality: the *monoculture of knowledge* centred in Modern science as an excluding and allegedly exact form of knowledge production and high culture as an aesthetic canon; the *monoculture of globality* and universality as the dominant scale; a *monoculture of the naturalisation of the differences* in social classifications and hierarchies based on race, colour, origin, or sex, which implement an invisible logic of inferiority and superiority; the *monoculture of linear time* as an understanding of historicities, of the dynamics of progress and, therefore, as a parameter to measure what is considered backward and obsolete, a past that really continues to be present; and the *monoculture of capitalist productivity* centred on economic aspects, the private property of the means of production, consumption, and fast production (Santos, 2010, pp. 110–112). To these five monocultures defined by Santos, we have incorporated the *monoculture of liberal democracy*, proposed by Aguiló Bonet (2017) as a hegemonic conception that denies other forms of democracy. Moreover, as the discussion on decolonial communication scholarship suggests, there is a *monoculture of Modern communication*, which pluriversal and decolonial scholarships have not investigated sufficiently yet and is a central constriction to communicative justice (see Section 5).

Social and peasant movements, Indigenous Peoples, Afro-descendants, women, LGBTIQ+ communities, and environmentalists are some of the references for Santos and Escobar in their proposal to identify, in the face of Western monocultures, five ecologies (Santos, 2010). These ecologies are understood as paths for the recognition of the existence of multiple worlds and knowledge interconnected in various ways that contribute to expanding the pluriverse (Escobar, 2012). In this sense, Santos (2010) proposes the concept of ecology "because it is based on the recognition of the plurality of heterogeneous knowledge . . . and on the continuous and dynamic interconnections between them without compromising their autonomy. The ecology of knowledge is based on the idea that knowledge is inter-knowledge" (Santos, 2010, p. 182). Knowledge is always generated in collective processes.

The central axis of the project of the epistemologies of the South is the recognition of an epistemic diversity, which is made evident by the plurality of thoughts and principles that cross daily practices and the lifeworld. The canon of universal Modernity is only one of these cognitive frameworks. The ecology of knowledges implies recognition not only of the otherness of thoughts but also of other ecologies that would make up the pluriverse.

The model of analysis collects the relationships we have found between the ecologies proposed by de Sousa Santos and the different dimensions of the pluriverse proposal based on Escobar's work and other decolonial and postcolonial authors. This model has been developed as a tool to design the cultural and ecological transitions required to face today's civilisational crisis.

The epistemologies of the South, with their ecologies, propose an epistemic pragmatism in which the diverse forms of thought are characterised by their incompleteness and incommensurability, that is, their impossibility of understanding or explaining and of measuring or evaluating all kinds of possible interventions in the world (Santos, 2010). This standpoint understands that there are both elements in common and profound differences among cultures and that intercultural dialogue is the basis for the planetarisation of the pluriverse on the grounds of defending both difference and unity.

Faced with the monoculture of Modern knowledge, an *ecology of knowledges* aims to make visible the value of popular, peasant, traditional, Indigenous, and practical knowledges, which provide other criteria of rigour that give contextual credibility to knowledge. This ecology is consistent with forms of *cognitive justice* that recognise other epistemologies and ontologies (Descola & Pons, 2012), that is, achieve the transition from a dualistic ontology to a relational ontology (Escobar, 2012b, 2018).

The incommensurability and incompleteness of cultures open the possibility of recognising other epistemologies—ways of knowing and learning—which differ from Modern culture by revealing ontologies that are not dual (e.g., subject-object) but instead have their basis in relationality or interconnection between everything. This is what the transition to the pluriverse is about.

> This transition implies moving from the Modern understanding of the world as a universe to viewing the world as a pluriverse (without universal pre-existents) or . . . moving from a paradigm of "globalisation" to one of "planetarisation". If the former privileges economic and cultural integration and homogenisation under a series of universal (Eurocentric) principles, the latter advocates communicability between a multiplicity of cultural worlds on the basis of a shared ecological and political understanding (Santos, 2007, cited in original). To put it succinctly, the transition to the pluriverse requires a broader concept of translation that includes the ontological and epistemic dimensions.
>
> *(Escobar, 2012b, p. 39)*

We understand that there is a coherent relationship between ontologies, epistemologies, and research methodologies. Therefore, pluriversal studies require a commitment to participatory methodologies, which allow the researcher to engage with communities based on their own epistemic and ontological perspectives in the reconstruction of knowledge based on diversity (see Section 6).

To cross the abyssal line of the monoculture of globality and universality as the dominant scale, an *ecology of transscales* advocates for a simultaneous recovery of the tensions and articulations between the local and the global, in accordance with a *sociocultural and spiritual justice* that revitalises the commons and plurinationality as a located space from where (communitarian, communalists, communal, peaceful, intercultural, etc.) interactions are built and from where relationships ranging from the local to the global—and not only from the global to the local—are woven.

Such *sociocultural and spiritual justice* is also correlated with the proposal of an *ecology of recognition*, understood as processes of collective, emancipatory action for the inclusion of social and cultural diversity, and as struggles for cultural, spiritual, and social organisation autonomy (Escobar, 2018). This dimension of pluriversal justice involves self-management, evident in social movements, as a way of transforming the absences created by hierarchical classifications into self-determination of the peoples with historical memory, cultural self-appreciation, cooperation, solidarity, and horizontal (democratic) relations that allow building unity within diversity. In the face of the monoculture of linear time, Santos proposes an *ecology of temporalities*, which recognises the coexistence of different durations and rhythms, such as the sense of cycles and circular time, as well as the coexistence of slow and fast forms that take place in different social organisations and production processes, which should not be mistaken with being advanced or backward. For this reason, this *ecology of temporalities* is directly complemented by an *ecology of productivities*, which, in the face of the monoculture of capitalist production, make visible alternative production systems based on the protection of land and territory, which are generated in popular economic organisations through collective ownership, self-management, cooperative organisation, and solidarity. These two ecologies have their correlation with the idea of *environmental justice* in a pluriverse of alternatives to capitalist development in which alternative human/nonhuman relations (Descola & Pons, 2012), the rights of nature, biocentrism, and meta-citizenship are made visible by "philosophies of well-being that finally equip humans to live in mutual improvement with each other and with the land" (Escobar, 2018, p. xi). They also have an intricate relation with *political economy justice* in economies created with cultural and political autonomy, degrowth, a slowdown in consumption (Elizalde, 2008), and demarketisation, within the framework of an ontological pluralisation of politics as a transformation of the concept of "politics as power disputes within a singular world, to another that includes the possibility of adverse relations between worlds: a pluriversal politics" (De la Cadena, 2010, p. 360). This liberatory entanglement of economics and politics can lead to an economy of the Commons in which the public sector also contributes to postextractivist and post-development self-sustainable models based on cooperative self-management, solidarity, and equality.

The monoculture of liberal democracy currently requires an *ecology of demodiversity*, understood as emancipatory praxis of alternative ethical–political interventions that recognise the plurality of powers and legal orders (Santos, 2010, pp. 287–288) and the "peaceful or conflictive coexistence of different democratic models and practices beyond the liberal political imaginary" (Santos and Avritzer cited by Aguiló Bonet, 2017, p. 27). This requires struggles in relation to *sociopolitical justice*, that is, the meaning of democracy, the incorporation of new political subjects, more participatory spaces for democratic construction and democratic practices entrenched in popular experiences of direct democracy such as assemblies, protest, and plebiscites, as well as other forms of alternative sociality beyond individualism and consumerism, such as communality.

Finally, we reflect on how to promote *communicative justice* as an *ecology of communication* that allows decentralising the understanding of communication away from the logic of the monoculture of Modern communication based on mass media resources, media monopolies, and dominant technologies controlled by corporations.

The monoculture of Modern communication began with elite control of the printing press and continues today with the power over communication and information technologies. This control grants a dominant position, which allows the definition of what is published and what is not, thus determining the discourses and ideas that are put into circulation. This monoculture has generated a digital divide in the processes of appropriation of technologies, which in the framework of unequal consumption societies are more of a luxury than a right. In addition, the monoculture of Modern communication is based on corporate and conglomerate ownership of communication technologies that have generated a structure of cultural industries in which "the consolidation and concentration of large groups or dominant players conspire against informational pluralism (affects the cultural ecosystem) against the diversity of voices within a society" (Mastrini & Becerra, 2006, p. 66). Therefore, this monoculture limits the visibility of the pluriverse, since it produces and reproduces hegemonic discourses and makes invisible the pluriverse of transition experiences as a function of other justices—cognitive, sociocultural, spiritual, environmental, and so on.

The monoculture of Modern communication centred on the discourse of domination runs through all kinds of communication practices, representations, and production of meanings imposing exclusions. It represents the options of the pluriverse as romantic, utopian, or as a mere illusion. As social movements are all too aware, monocultural communication presents as dreamy and unviable overcoming or even moderating wild capitalism, its attached consumerism, and the forms of relationships that it produces based on the logics of hierarchies, exclusions, or the denial of existence.

In the face of this monoculture, we propose the ecology of communication and the search for communicative justice (see Table 1.1). This implies the recognition of the right to communication in a broader and more comprehensive way than the conception of the right to information, as we explain in greater detail in the next section.

TABLE 1.1 Model of analysis: relations among monocultures, ecologies, and dimensions of the pluriverse.

Monocultures	Ecologies	Dimensions of the pluriverse
Monoculture of Modern knowledge	**Ecology of knowledges:** Value of other knowledges and criteria of rigour that give contextual credibility to knowledges	**Cognitive justice:** Relational epistemologies/ontologies Recognition of knowledges (popular, peasant, traditional, indigenous, practical knowledges)
Monoculture of the naturalisation of differences	**Ecology of recognitions:** Recognitions of social movements, social and cultural diversity, autonomy, emancipation, and collective action	**Sociocultural and spiritual justice:** Communitarisms, communalisms, cooperation and solidarity, plurinational communities and states, peace, horizontal (democratic) relations, self-management, unity within diversity, historical memory, cultural self-appreciation, interculturality, and relations from the local to the global
Monoculture of globality/ universality	**Ecology of trans-scales:** Simultaneous recovery of tensions and articulations between the local and the global, as the community	**Environmental justice:** Rethink the relationships of the human being with nature, human and nonhuman relationships, rights of nature, biocentrism, alternatives to development, and ecological metacitizenship
Monoculture of linear time	**Ecology of temporalities:** Recover the sense of cycles, circular and radial time that are typical of biological processes and nature	**Political economy justice:** Self-sustainable economies, postextractivism, solidarity economy, cooperatives, self-management, equality, the commons, the public, degrowth, postdevelopment, demarketisation, slowdown of consumption, and autonomy

Monoculture of capitalist productivity	**Ecology of productivities:** Recover and value alternative production systems that are carried out in popular economic organisations through self-management, cooperative organisation, solidarity, and protection of the land and territory	**Sociopolitical justice:** New political subjects, legalities and powers, participatory spaces, popular experiences, assemblies, protest, plebiscites, communality, and direct democracy
Monoculture of liberal democracy	**Ecology of demodiversity:** Different models and practices of democracy, plurality of powers, and legalities	
Monoculture of Modern communication	**Ecology of communication** Decentralising understanding of communication to ensure the right to communication and diverse and egalitarian communication	**COMMUNICATIVE JUSTICE** Recovery of different ways of thinking communication and communication studies, critique of colonial communication and mainstream media, subaltern communication, access, public policies, right to communication, democratisation of mediations, representations, practices, technologies, and media systems

Communicative justice

From the perspective of the pluriverse, communicative justice aims to make visible the existence of forms of communication that go beyond the monoculture of Modern communication of media conglomerates and digital social networks. It facilitates crossing the abyssal line to recognise the plurality of communication practices and forms outside of the mainstream practices and representations that render alternatives invisible.

Communicative justice involves a series of social processes, practices, representations, ways of narrating, and mediations that are at the heart of the autonomy of peoples and communities and that move away from the structures and impositions of the hegemonic vision both of communication (generally reduced to information) and of the discourses that sustain the world system. It constitutes a communicative praxis that informs and communicates the existence of alternative viable, constructible realities.

Communicative justice comprises different lines of research and transformation, some of which are addressed in this chapter. It includes debates on public policies, which not only focus on access to ICTs but also recognise alternative ways of understanding communication and place limits on media concentration and exclusionary representations by fostering the democratisation of ownership and discourse. It also includes the recognition of the centrality of daily and interpersonal communicative practices beyond industrialised technologies, such as fabrics, embroidery, artisanal handicrafts, and other expressions emanating from the multiple ways of narrating first, ancestral and Indigenous communities, Afro-descendants, popular neighbourhoods, peasants, activists, the youth, and LGBTIQ+ people, among others.

A first characteristic of *communicative justice* is the development of communication and information legislation that favours the appropriation of media and the redistribution of use and access to information and communication technologies to communities, social organisations, and cultural groups, whose access to technologies had been limited or denied. This involves the enactment of public policies for the visibility of organisations, circulation of discourses, and openness to a communicability of diverse cultural, social, economic, and political agents, as fostered by media activism struggles. It also includes autonomy of communities and social movements in the development of technologies of their own, as achieved by Indigenous people in Oaxaca (Mexico) (Baca-Feldman, 2016; Baca-Feldman & Huerta Velázquez, 2018) and other groupings around the world.

In addition to favourable legislation for the appropriation of media, communicative justice focuses on legitimate practices in which communication is recognised as a central right that enables the fight for other rights. The basic right is to be able to communicate (including to be heard and responded to) as a key articulator of struggles, in order to protest, resist, and achieve other rights. Therefore, beyond legality (of legislation or policies), communicative justice requires the recognition of the legitimacy of communicative practices, which enable the advancement of social struggles based on the autonomy and self-determination of peoples, communities, or cultures. This includes the recognition of other ways of understanding communication beyond the human being, such as communication with other beings that inhabit Mother Earth, an approach typical of Indigenous, Afro-descendant, and peasant communities in different latitudes of the planet.

Communicative justice gives legitimacy to the various communicative practices that make visible all those invisible processes in mediated and nonmediated discourses. It gives legitimacy to what exists on the other side of that abyssal line, that is, to the realities that are part of the pluriverse. For this reason, *communicative justice* is the precondition that makes other justices possible (cognitive, sociocultural and spiritual, environmental, political economy, and sociopolitical). It consists of an ecology of communication that makes possible the opening to other ecologies (demodiversity, productivities, temporalities, transscales, and recognition of knowledge).

It is thus understood that communicative justice includes epistemological and ontological visions of communication that emerge from ways of knowing different from western mainstream knowledge. Communicative justice requires the development of "worlds and knowledges otherwise—that is, worlds and knowledge constructed on the basis of different ontological commitments, epistemic configurations and practices of being, knowing and doing" (Escobar, 2012b, p. 49). In this regard, it intersects with *cognitive justice* and, therefore, with the proposal of an ecology of knowledge.

Communicative justice implies a permanent awareness and questioning of how societies represent differences and diversity, as well as how they represent themselves and others. This is closely related to intersectionality inasmuch as communicative justice based on this awareness leads not only to revealing and denouncing stereotypes but also to overcoming them in speech and action.

The idea of *communicative justice* draws on the decolonial perspective of communication in Latin America as an inspiring line of thought to think communication beyond the media and focus on historical, political, cultural, and social mediations (Martín-Barbero, 1998), as well as, more recently, in epistemic and ontological mediations.

From the perspective of the pluriverse, we explore how communication can not only function to reproduce systemic injustice but also work to foster justice. In this regard, we understand that communicative justice is expanded when the critical analysis of mainstream media systems is combined with communication practices of and for autonomy, creativity, and transformation.

The advancement of *communicative justice* also benefits from the recognition and recapitulation of the Latin American debates on communication/development/social change, which show that there is a special *locus* of enunciation that challenges the positivist, dualist, and liberal tradition of studies of the Global North. Therefore, this decolonial perspective captures the potential of communicative justice for the transitions of the pluriverse.

Erick Torrico-Villanueva (2018) proposes to think about the decoloniality of communication by recovering Latin American scholarship as the production of a critical episteme. This perspective views Latin America as a particular locus of enunciation against the mainstream tradition of social studies proposed in Europe and North America. The liberation pedagogy of Paulo Freire, the liberation communicology of Luis Ramiro Beltrán, and the questioning of the dominant positivist–functionalist–behaviourist paradigm by Antonio Pasquali are precedents of a fundamental critical episteme and the inspiring pillars of the decolonisation of communication, "which involves a new utopian journey in the fight against epistemic segregation and whose purpose is to re-establish the communication that humanises" (Torrico-Villanueva, 2018, p. 80); and it humanises when it brings out the altruistic values of human beings.

The contributions to the decoloniality of communication have addressed four key topics: (1) the archaeology of Latin American doings and knowings of communication within the critical thought of the Latin American School and its decolonising potential (Valencia Rincón, 2012; Torrico-Villanueva, 2016, 2017, 2018; Herrera et al., 2016); (2) rethinking the disciplinary and epistemological perspective, as well as the academic logics (including those of cognitive capitalism) from which communication theory is made in Latin America, exploring paths towards a so-called epistemic disobedience (Castro-Lara, 2016; Flores-Prieto et al., 2018); (3) the understanding of colonial communication practices (Padilla, 2018); and (4) the understanding of subaltern communicative practices of Indigenous groups, Afro-descendants, and other popular cultures that allow us to see the forms of resistance and reexistence, as well as the epistemes and ontologies that underlie such practices (Cebrelli & Arancibia, 2018; Larrea & Saladrigas, 2018).

The analysis provided in this section allows pluriversal studies to include the role of communication in coloniality as well as the practices for the decoloniality of media systems. In the context of the permanent technological revolution that is taking place, one of the key strengths of the framework of analysis of communicative justice is that it can be applied to different types of media. This is so precisely because its focus is not the media itself but the practices, relations, and mediations of communication. In contrast to technocentric perspectives, communicative justice in the perspective of the pluriverse allows us to look beyond specific technologies by providing a general, flexible framework to understand both the monoculture of communication and the pluriculture of communicative justice in different types of mediated and nonmediated communications. Therefore, it can not only be applied to different technologies, including the new digitalisation, datafication, and platformisation of media, but it may also be applied in the future when new technologies appear. From a pluriversal perspective, what really matters are the concrete practices of communicative justice vis-à-vis hegemonic structures. It understands the different technological possibilities as instruments that can be designed and used in different directions, to expand or restrict justice. From this point of view, the characteristics of the technology are subordinated to the structural, hegemonic–counterhegemonic power relations that affect them and which communicative justice aims to alter in favour of the pluriverse. In synthesis, pluriversal communicative justice provides analytical tools to decentre media studies and analyse both mainstream and alternative communication in different channels used in the present or that may be used in the future.

Participant-engaged methodologies[5]

Different methodologies can be applied to the study and improvement of the pluriverse. We emphasise the value of participant and engaged methodologies as a general framework to host different methodological approaches based on fieldwork with communities in diverse contexts (methods are always contingent on the situation and research).

Participatory and engaged methodologies are framed within the interpretative-hermeneutical approach, in accordance with Mardones's reflections on the philosophy of science. This philosophical approach resonates with the need to subvert or, at least, question the monocultural model of the scientific construction of Western knowledge based on objectivity, generalisation, and the theoretical inflection of positivism. This questioning involves transitioning from the monovision of the universe or the universality of science to the vision of the pluriverse.

> The efforts of hermeneutics, phenomenologists, and linguists does not mean ignoring "scientific rationality" as understood by the empiricist tradition; they only contradict its reductionism. . . . The result shows that the human sciences are an especially suitable place to show the partiality of the causal explanation. Scientific objectivism falls to pieces when discovering the strategies of silence that it weaves around the subject and his/her contributions. Scientific knowledge is framed within the fabric of life. It cannot be separated from the process of daily life, communicative interaction and common language.
>
> *(Mardones & Ursua, 1999, p. 148)*

Thinking about participatory methodologies implies the understanding of reflective philosophy as a possibility of permanent understanding of oneself as a subject that investigates seeking to achieve a hermeneutical displacement, "which from now on puts the accent on being-in-the-world and in the participative belonging that precedes any relation of a subject with the object before him" (Ricoeur, 2000, p. 206). These methodologies propose a logical reflection and a dialectic of subject-subject, based on "subverting the idea of the knowable object, in the realm of the material object, by the idea of another subject in the construction of knowledge", which provides "a first sense of reciprocity and horizontality in the interaction" (Herrera et al., 2016, p. 93). The awareness of a subject-subject relationship is framed within the awareness of the incompleteness of the cultures, which paves the way for Boaventura de Sousa Santos's proposal of a diatopic hermeneutics (Santos, 2010, p. 93) that makes effective the dialogue between scholars and other social subjects to produce consistent knowledge about what we call social realities.

The pluriverse is interested in all the participant-engaged methodologies that are characterised by building a permanent dialectical relationship with subjects of the community and with themselves as researchers, in order to search for knowledge of social meanings to reconstruct the logics and coherence inherent in the culture of the community. This approach takes into account the differences and conflicts that may arise within the community and aims to understand the different degrees of cohesion, adherence, separation, or belonging of the subjects to their cultural social identity (Giménez, 1997). This implies,

> the incorporation of the subjective aspects of the researcher as genuine and legitimate tools of knowledge; field work as experience for the organisation of knowledge; the importance of techniques linked to participation; recovery for anthropological and social knowledge from the point of view of the informant.
>
> *(Guber, 2004, pp. 25–26)*

Following the work of Orlando Fals Borda and other scholars who have used participatory methodologies, the pluriversal perspective is interested in interactions in which "investigating is not returning to the peasants the data collected by external researchers, but the process of recalling the past and analysing it together" (Rappapor, 2018, p. 140). In other words, research is conducted with and from the members of communities who seek to exercise their right to communication, that is, foster communicative justice against mainstream monoculture and control.

These participatory methodologies also have as their starting point two very particular political, methodological, and conceptual tools that have been developed in Latin America: Participatory Action Research (PAR) and Popular Education (PE).

PAR was first developed in Colombia, especially by Orlando Fals Borda (1999). Its point of departure consists in approaching the people who participate in the research process as active agents in every step who will allow the collective construction and transformation of knowledge (Villegas, 2000). As a collective research-learning method, its main purpose is the action for transformation based on a contextual and historical critical analysis.

> Its principles involved decolonization of the method to bring it closer not only to the understanding but also to the transformation of realities; developing interdisciplinary approaches that enable a broader and more complex understanding of contexts; reframing the "neutral" and "non-evaluative" character of positive science through a transformation of the researcher toward an intellectual committed to processes of change; and rethinking

the relationship between researcher and researched in order to build a more horizontal and dialogic relationship between individuals and produce trans-formative knowledge.

(Vega-Casanova, 2021, pp. 120–121)

PE has as one of its main exponents the Brazilian pedagogue Paulo Freire. This proposal bases each person's learning process on their practice, experience, ration-alising exercises, and social context. In this way, learning is given by the environ-ment and society in which the subject develops. Freire understands education as a critical tool that allows human liberation through the critical knowledge of reality and a commitment to the utopia of social transformation (Freire, 1973).

Consistent with this political stance and with hermeneutic philosophy, we privilege experiences based on methods for interaction with and from the com-munities with the purpose of favouring joint constructive action in the long path of the dialogue of knowledges. This proposal is inspired by theoretical perspec-tives that relate communication to interaction and intersubjectivity, as Mexican researcher Marta Rizo (2009) notes:

The reflection focuses on intersubjective relationships, under the angle of interaction, and a relevant role is given to the elements of negotiation and communication in the social construction of the referents of meaning that enable dialogue, negotiation and/or conflict in any encounter or situation of human interaction.

(p. 29)

From this basis, participatory methodologies emerge as a questioning of the posi-tivist and Western colonisation of knowledge, making visible the inability of the social sciences and traditional education to generate real processes of transforma-tion of social structures. Likewise, participatory methodologies are grounded on the practical transformations of societies emerging from local and community processes while taking into account the national and transnational scales.

In this line, the Maori indigenous researcher Linda Smith proposes research that is relentless in its search for social justice in order to account for the vindication, reformulation, and reconstruction of indigenous cultures -an aspect that should be extended to other traditionally subalternised communities (Smith, 2006). This implies that their methodologies must start from the recognition of local commu-nities and processes; something which goes beyond a practical approach:

Within an indigenous framework, methodological debates are those con-cerned with the broader politics and strategic goals of indigenous research. It is at this level that researchers have to clarify and justify their intentions. Methods become the means and procedures through which the central problems of the research are addressed.

(Smith, 2006, p. 143)

For Tomás R. Villasante, it is necessary to ask two basic epistemological questions that should accompany any participatory or implicative methodological proposal: what for? And for whom? This enters into dialogue with Smith's proposal. Answering these questions implies recognising the interests, influences, and prejudices that come with the research exercise, as well as eliminating the idea that any methodology can be "applied" to any population by assuming that populations are objects of research, denying the historical subject that constitutes them (2019). Thus, methodologies start by recognising the different social actors who are immersed in the research and the interests of each one, "It is not only a question of ethics or ideology, it is a basic methodological question that we raise" (Villasante, 2019, p. 216). Thus, participatory or implicative methodologies propose that the researcher has some questions to ask, but that there are also other questions that arise from the experiences of people or communities, and most importantly, " 'we have to build' the answers with the people affected, involved, and from 'their truths', not from ours. . . . In the process of construction of action and knowledge we can all intervene, from different positions, but the role of the professional must be above all to have rigour in the methodology" (Villasante, 2019, p. 217). Thus, and under the logic of finding all the questions, the implicative or participatory methodologies start the work with participation to be able to understand the whole context from where the questions arise. After that, it can focus on all the necessary techniques to carry out the research.

Thus, the emphasis proposed by these methodologies does not lie on the specific method or technique, but on the questions behind them and on the relationship that has been previously built with the people and the communities. Under this logic, the relevance and use of interviews (of any type), discussion groups, mapping, participant observation, or any other method or technique will depend on the questions that have been built together with participation, dialogue, and recognition of the historical subjects and communities involved in the research process.

> In all community approaches process—that is, methodology and method—is highly important. In many projects the process is far more important than the outcome. Processes are expected to be respectful, to enable people, to heal and to educate. They are expected to lead one small step further towards self-determination.
>
> *(Smith, 2006, pp. 127–128)*

Closing remarks

The pluriverse opposes systemic justice to systemic injustice. The starting point of our understanding of justice is that it consists of a natural impulse towards making ethical decisions that favour the diversity and equality that are needed for the exercise of real freedom. This involves the removal of authoritarian and unjust social structures that constrain human creativity, as well as the establishment of harmonious relations with the natural environment. Applied to media and communication, it involves destructuring the corporate monoculture of communication through the expansion of an ecology based on communicative justice.

As has been developed in this chapter, justice and injustice are interdimensional; they appear across different sites of conflict and manifest in cognitive, sociocultural and spiritual, environmental, political economy and sociopolitical dimensions of life. The same happens with communication; communicative justice and injustice appear across different dimensions of life. A new line of research in pluriversal studies is to critically analyse the phenomenology of such forms of communication and how they interrelate with other dimensions of life. It can do so by looking at the corporate hegemonic media system and the experiences of communicative justice organised at a grassroots level. By doing so, pluriversal studies can contribute further dialogue and critique for the visibilisation, strengthening, and planetarisation of the pluriverse.

Pluriversal scholarship makes use of general models of analysis and available data combining them with decolonial participatory methods. Methodologically, pluriversal studies have the differential advantage of being capable of obtaining extremely rich data based on the practices and voices of communities and movements that are unobtainable through other methods. Macro models and quantitative data are only made relevant when related to concrete experiences, data, and models based on micro and meso levels. Even more so, pluriversal studies based on participatory methods provide an important contribution with, from, and to the community, which not only participates in the investigation but also is the centre of it, provides interpretations, and makes decisions for action.

Notes

1. The theoretical and methodological debate presented here emerges as part of the research projects *Communication/education practices and maintenance of symbolic capitals of indigenous peoples* financed by the Corporación Universitaria Minuto De Dios-UNIMINUTO- (2018–2022); *La contemporaneidad clásica y su dislocación: de Weber a Foucault* (PID2020–113413RB-C31); and *Problemas públicos y controversias: diversidad y participación en la esfera mediática* (CSO2017–82109-R).
2. As we will develop further on in this chapter, the academic demand for recognition of such voices started to take place in postcolonial and decolonial studies.
3. An important part of the discussion presented here is included in the theoretical framework of the Ph.D. thesis: Herrera-Huérfano, E. (2022). *Prácticas de comunicación y pueblos indígenas: Mediaciones de la cultura y el desarrollo local en la amazonia colombiana* [PhD thesis, Universidad de Sevilla] (mimeo).
4. ALICE-Strage Mirrors is a research project that aims to rethink and renew social scientific knowledge by developing new theoretical and political paradigms of social transformation based on different perspectives that have been marginalised, forgotten, or considered strange. It is a response to the feeling of political and intellectual exhaustion in the 21st century. The details of this project can be reviewed here: https://alice.ces.uc.pt/
5. With the term *engaged methodologies*, we take up the theoretical and practical development carried out from the *metodologías implicativas* proposed by Latin America authors.

References

Aguiló Bonet, A. (2017). Descolonizar la democracia: Apuntes sobre demodiversidad y nuevo constitucionalismo en Bolivia. *Astrolabio: Revista internacional de filosofía, 19,* 26–36.

Baca-Feldman, C. (2016). Experiencias resonantes de comunicación en pueblos indígenas de Oaxaca, México. *Universitas Humanística, 81*(81).

Baca-Feldman, C., y Huerta Velázquez, E. (2018, May). Tejiendo autonomía tecnológica en los pueblos indígenas: Telefonía celular comunitaria en Oaxaca, México. En L. Belli y O. Cavalli (Eds.), *Gobernanza y regulaciones de Internet en América Latina: Análisis sobre infraestructura, privacidad, bioseguridad y evoluciones en honor de los diez años de la South school on internet governance.* FGV Direito Rio.

Bhambra, G. K. (2014). Postcolonial and decolonial dialogues. *Postcolonial Studies, 17*(2), 115–121.

Castro-Lara, E. (2016). Reflexiones para decolonizar la cultura académica latinoamericana en Comunicación. *Chasqui: Revista Latinoamericana de Comunicación, 131,* 107–122.

Cebrelli, A., y Arancibia, V (2018). *Hacia una teoría de la comunicación decolonial. Representaciones nodales y discurso político* (pp. 30–39). XIV Congreso de la Asociación Latinoamericana de Comunicación -ALAIC- GI (4) Comunicación Decolonialidad.

Collins, P. H. (2000). *Black feminist thought: Knowledge, consciousness and the politics of empowerment.* Routledge.

Crenshaw Williams, K. (1989). *Demarginalizing the intersection of race and sex: A Black feminist critique of antidis- crimination doctrine, feminist theory and antiracist politics* (p. 139). University of Chicago Legal Forum.

Davis, A. Y. (2011). *Women, race, & class.* Vintage.

De la Cadena, M. (2010). Indigenous cosmopolitics in the Andes: Conceptual reflections beyond politics. *Cultural Anthropology, 25*(2), 334–370. http://dx.doi.org/10.1111/j.1548-1360.2010.01061.x

Descola, P., & Pons, H. (2012). *Más allá de la naturaleza y cultura.* Amorrortu.

Dussel, E. (2015, January 23). *Transmodernidad e Interculturalidad (Interpretación desde la Filosofía de la Liberación).* http://enriquedussel.com/txt/TRANSMODERNIDAD%20e%20interculturalidad.pdf

Elizalde, A. (2008). Las adicciones civilizatorias: Consumo y energía.¿ Caminos hacia la felicidad. *Papeles de relaciones ecosociales y cambio global, 102,* 47–76.

Escobar, A. (1984). Discourse and power in development: Michel Foucault and the relevance of his work to the third world. *Alternatives, 10*(3), 377–400.

Escobar, A. (2012a). *Encountering development: The making and unmaking of the third world.* Princeton University Press.

Escobar, A. (2012b). Más allá del desarrollo: Postdesarrollo y transiciones hacia el pluriverso. *Revista de Antropología Social, 21,* 23–62.

Escobar, A. (2014). *Sentipensar con la tierra: Nuevas lecturas sobre desarrollo, territorio y diferencia.* Universidad Autónoma Latinoamericana UNAULA.

Escobar, A. (2018). *Otro posible es posible: Caminando hacia las transiciones desde Abya Yala/Afro/Latino-América.* Ediciones desde abajo.

Espinosa, Y. (2009). Etnocentrismo y colonialidad en los feminismos latinoamericanos: Complicidades y consolidación de las hegemonías feministas en el espacio transnacional. *Revista Venezolana de Estudios de la Mujer, 14*(33).

Espinosa, Y., Gómez, D., & Ochoa, K. (2014). *Tejiendo de otro modo: Feminismo, epistemología y apuestas descoloniales en Abya Yala.* Editorial Universidad del Cauca.

Fals Borda, O. (1999, Septiembre–Diciembre). Orígenes universales y retos actuales de la IAP (Investigación Acción Participativa). *Análisis Político, 3.*

Flores-Prieto, P., Pozo, K., & Crawford, L. (2018). La comunicación en América Latina: Un debate pendiente más allá de las resistencias. *Signo y Pensamiento, 37*(72), 95–105. https://dx.doi.org/10.11144/javeriana.syp37-72.camd

Foucault, M. (1999). *El cuerpo utópico: Heterotopías.* Nueva Visión.

Freire, P. (1973). *Pedagogía del oprimido.* Siglo XXI.

Giménez, G. (1997, Julio–Diciembre). Materiales para una teoría de las identidades sociales. *Frontera Norte,* 9(18). https://fronteranorte.colef.mx/index.php/fronteranorte/article/viewFile/1441/891

Grosfoguel, R. (2011). Decolonizing postcolonial studies and paradigms of political-economy: Transmodernity, decolonial thinking, and global coloniality. *Transmodernity: Journal of Peripheral Cultural Production of the Luso-Hispanic World,* 1(1).

Guber, R. (2004). *El salvaje metropolitano, reconstrucción del conocimiento social en el trabajo de campo.* Paidós Estudios de Comunicación.

Herrera-Huérfano, E. (2022). *Prácticas de comunicación y pueblos indígenas: Mediaciones de la cultura y el desarrollo local en la amazonia colombiana* [PhD thesis, Universidad de Sevilla] (mimeo).

Herrera, E., Sierra, F., & Del Valle, C. (2016). Hacia una Epistemología del Sur. Decolonialidad del saber-poder informativo y nueva Comunicología Latinoamericana. Una lectura crítica de la mediación desde las culturas indígenas. *Chasqui: Revista latinoamericana de comunicación, 131,* 77–105.

Kontopoulos, K. (1993). *The logics of social structure.* Routledge.

Kothari, A., Salleh, A., Escobar, A., Demaria, F., & Acosta, A. (2018). *Pluriverse: A post-development dictionary.* Authors Up Front.

Larrea, C. A. L., y Saladrigas, H. (2018). *Epistemología del Sur en el contexto del Movimiento indígena de Chimborazo, un acercamiento comunicacional* (pp. 40–43). XIV Congreso de la Asociación Latinoamericana de Comunicación -ALAIC Comunicación-Decolonialidad.

Lim, C. M. S. (2019). Appendix 1: Postcolonial and decolonial: 'Same same but different'. In *Contextual biblical hermeneutics as multicentric dialogue* (pp. 193–194). Brill.

Maldonado-Torres, N. (2007). Sobre la colonialidad del ser: Contribuciones al desarrollo de un concepto. In S. Castro-Gómez y R. Grosfoguel (Eds.), *El giro decolonial: Reflexiones para una diversidad epistémica más allá del capitalismo global* (pp. 127–167). Iesco-Pensar-Siglo del Hombre.

Mardones, J. M., y Ursua, N. (1999). *Filosofía de las ciencias humanas y sociales.* Ediciones Coyuacán.

Martín-Barbero, J. (1998). *De los medios a las mediaciones: Comunicación, cultura y hegemonía.* Convenio Andrés Bello.

Mastrini, G., & Becerra, M. (2006). *Periodistas y magnates: Estructura y concentración de las industrias culturales en América Latina.* Prometeo.

Mignolo, W. (1995). *The darker side of the renaissance: Literacy, territoriality and colonization.* The University of Michigan Press.

Mignolo, W. (2000). *Local histories/global designs: Essays on the coloniality of power, subaltern knowledges and border thinking.* Princeton University Press.

Mignolo, W. (2011). *The darker side of western modernity: Global futures, decolonial options.* Duke University Press.

Mignolo, W., & Wynter, S. (2003). Unsettling the coloniality of being/ power/truth/freedom: Towards the human, after man, its overrepresentation-an argumente. *The New Centennial Review, 3,* 257–337.

Mohanty, C. (2008). De vuelta a 'Bajo los ojos de Occidente': La solidaridad feminista a través de las luchas anticapitalistas. In L. Suárez Navas y R. Aída Hernández (Eds.), *Descolonizando el feminismo: Teorías y prácticas desde los márgenes* (pp. 407–463). Cátedra.

Padilla, R. (2018). *Los inicios de la fotografía en México: Exotismo e imaginarios de colonialidad* (pp. 97–102). XIV Congreso de la Asociación Latinoamericana de Comunicación - ALAIC- GI (4) Comunicación Decolonialidad.

Quijano, A. (1993). 'Raza', 'Etnia' y 'Nación' en Mariátegui: Cuestiones abiertas. In R. Forgues (Ed.), *José Carlos Mariategui y Europa: El Otro Aspecto del Descubrimiento* (pp. 167–187). Empresa Editora Amauta.

Quijano, A. (2000). Coloniality of power, ethnocentrism, and Latin America. *Nepantla, 1*(3), 533–580.

Quijano, A. (2003). Colonialidad del poder, eurocentrismo y América Latina. In E. Lander (Comp.). *La colonialidad del saber: Eurocentrismo y ciencias sociales. Perspectivas latinoamericanas* (pp. 201–246). CLACSO/UNESCO.

Rappaport, J. (2018). Visualidad y escritura como acción: Investigación Acción Participativa en la Costa Caribe colombiana. *Revista Colombiana de Sociología, 41*(I), 133–156. https://doi/10.15446/resv41n1.66272

Ricoeur, P. (2000). Narratividad, fenomenología y hermenéutica. *Anàlisi: Quaderns de comunicació i cultura, 25*, 189–207.

Rizo, M. (2009). Sociología fenomenológica y comunicología: Sociología Fenomenológica y sus aportes a la comunicación interpersonal y mediática. *Fronteiras-estudos midiáticos, 11*(1), 25–32.

Sandoval, C. (1991). US third world feminism: The theory and method of oppositional consciousness in the postmodern world. *Genders, 10*, 1–24.

Santos, B. D. S. (2004). *Reinventar la democracia: Reinventar el Estado*. Editorial Abya Yala.

Santos, B. D. S. (2007). Beyond abyssal thinking: From global lines to ecologies of knowledges. *Review (Fernand Braudel Center)*, 45–89.

Santos, B. D. S. (2010). *Para descolonizar occidente: Más allá del pensamiento abismal*. CLACSO.

Santos, B. D. S. (2016). Epistemologies of the South and the future. *From the European South: A Transdisciplinary Journal of Postcolonial Humanities, 1*, 17–29.

Smith, L. (2006). *Decolonizing methodologies: Research and indigenous peoples*. Zed Books, University of Otago Press.

Spivak, G. C. (1988). *Can the subaltern speak? Reflections on the history of an idea*. Columbia University Press.

Tornay-Márquez, M. C. (2017). *Comunicación, subalternidad y género: Experiencias comunicativas comunitarias de mujeres afrodescendientes e indígenas en América Latina* [PhD Thesis, Universidad de Sevilla].

Torrico-Villanueva, E. (2016). La comunicación en clave latinoamericana. *Chasqui: Revista Latinoamericana de Comunicación*, 72–81. https://doi.org/10.16921/chasqui.v0i132.2888

Torrico-Villanueva, E. (2017). La rehumanización, sentido último de la decolonización comunicacional. *Rev aportes de la comunicación, 23*, 31–38. ISSN:2306-8671

Torrico-Villanueva, E. (2018). La comunicación decolonial—Revista latinoamericana de Ciencias de la Comunicación. *Alaic, 15*(28) 72–81. www.Alaic.Org/revista/index.Php/alaic/article/view/1150

Trigo, A. (2014, June 25). *Una lectura materialista de la colonialidad*. Ohio State University. https://kb.osu.edu/bitstream/handle/1811/64795/1/CLAS_AN_AU14_Trigo_UnaLectura.pdf

Valencia Rincón, J. (2012). Mediaciones, comunicación y colonialidad: Encuentros y des-encuentros de los estudios culturales y la comunicación en Latinoamérica. *Signo Y Pensamiento*, *30*(60), 156–165.

Vega-Casanova, J. (2021). Disenchantment as a path toward autonomy: Orlando Fals Borda, participatory action research, communication and social change. In *The evolution of popular communication in Latin America* (pp. 109–128). Palgrave Macmillan.

Villasante, T. (2019). Metodologías ¿Para qué? ¿Para quién?. En Y. Mellado (Ed.), *La dinámica del contacto: Movilidad, encuentro y conflicto en las relaciones interculturales*. CIDOB Edicións.

Villegas, R. (2000). *Investigación Participativa en Pérez, G. Modelos de Investigación Cualitativa en la Educación Social y Animación Sociocultural. Aplicaciones Práticas*. Ed Nancea.

Visvanathan, S. (2006). Alternative science. *Theory, Culture & Society*, *23*(2–3), 164–169.

Wallerstein, I. M., & Balibar, É. (1991). *Race, nation, class: Ambiguous identities*. Verso.

2

WEAVING LIFE

The women of the Andes in their decolonial work

Elvira Espejo Ayca and Aura Isabel Mora

Introduction

The women of the ancient Andean world were responsible for the ceremonies dedicated to the feminine divinities consecrated to fertility; therefore, they were in charge of the plots and weavings. Today, they continue to be so, updating their realities to the dynamics of culture. In this chapter, we show how the knowledge and wisdom of Andean women expressed in Andean textiles are embedded in the perspective of *other possible worlds*. We reveal how Andean textile processes and production chains are rescued, valued, and recognised as fundamental to think about the strategic issues of today's social life.

Approaching the role and knowledge of women in textile production from a decolonial perspective generates new forms of recognition of the other. From this perspective, dualities such as superior/inferior knowledge, developed/underdeveloped societies, and literate/illiterate people, among many others, are not valid. This approach avoids the possibility of thinking about these women and their knowledge as inferior, premodern, underdeveloped, illiterate, and so on.

We begin by discussing ceremonies (Sánchez Riaño & Mora, 2019) and other practices of mutual nurturing through which humans and other beings develop harmonious relations as part of the same unity. We then present the main features of Women's Science, including its cosmological relationship with nature and the resistance and subversion nurtured by women weavers through the production chain of textiles. Next, we address the role of communication in the production of textiles; we explain how these are based on the senses especially knowledge conveyed via visual communication that involves a form of writing and reading of the community. This discussion leads us to understand textiles as living beings since women weavers have developed the epistemology and ontology that textiles actually become persons.

DOI: 10.4324/9781003316220-3

The practices of mutual nurturing

One of the ancestral inheritances of Andean women and women weavers is the epistemological inheritance of the concept of *uywaña*, which means mutual nurturing or upbringing. This mutual nurturing develops in life cycles matching the life of animals and plants accompanied by humans. These life cycles demand the complementary help of the human species with the other species and vice versa. In life cycles, weavers are aware that the raw material for their textiles is offered for human care by camelids. In this sense and as a sign of reciprocity, they follow the animals in the process of offering wool and meat, through ceremonies that accompany the process of life together.

Mutual nurturing or *uywaña* is far removed from the colonial idea of the world that separates man from nature. According to Mora, there is

> an anthropocentric idea of the world in which man is separated and placed outside of nature, thus creating a dichotomy between the human world and the natural world. This vision holds the imaginary of nature as a resource, which is infinite, usable for development and to be exploited in a sustained way for the benefit of humans.
>
> *(2016, p. 33)*

In this understanding of the world, reciprocal relationships between species are not possible. Animal species are excluded from life to become a commodity.

The anthropocentric vision places women within nature, as well as animals and plants that need to be dominated in their trajectory. This anthropocentric and macho vision of the West arises from the conception that the human being is the king of creation and that everything that exists is for his benefit. This is based on the fact that their god is male, their only son is also male, and in creation, the first human being is male (Huanacuni Mamani, 2015). It points to development systems based on economic growth, where individual action guarantees the success of the subject with the use of resources, that is, of the sources of life and exploitation of the other species.

In applying the concept of mutual nurturing, women weavers in Bolivia celebrate different ceremonies over the course of the year to produce the circle of life that define specific moments for textile production. The first ceremony is the crossing of the camelids and takes place in January. This ceremony is related to the carnival dates. In it, a specialised use of light is made with aguayos and ponchos to cover males and females according to certain colours of nature. The women of the community explain that if the animals are exposed to light the colour of the coat of the young will be light, if it receives little light the coat will be dark. Thus, females and males are covered with light aguayos when they want pups with light fur, and with dark aguayos when they want pups with dark fur.

The second ceremony is related to the selection of the animals from which the wool for textiles is to be obtained. This selection is called *marcado*—marking. At this time, the llamas are adorned with earrings and necklaces. These earrings are made according to the colour of the lineage of the family that owns the animals, the village, or the region to which they belong. There is always a predominant colour, even though a colour is added each time a member of the family is born. The earrings with which the animals are adorned provide information about the village, community, and family to which the group of camelids belongs. It is like a database that identifies the herd. After placing the earrings, the stable where they rest is arranged. Sacred flowers, sacred foods, and sacred poems that are specific to this ceremony are placed.

The third ceremony is to accompany the camelids. This is the time when the yearlings are weaned. This moment is called *llamado*—calling. In this selection, the females stay with their mothers. The males are taken to the *purta*, an exclusive territory for the stallions.

The three ceremonies are very important for the fibre obtained from the wool of the animals to be of high quality and to give the desired colour. When the ceremonies are not performed, the animals do not roam the territory, they are not at festivities, and they are not happy. This can introduce changes in the quality of their wool.

In April, animal sanitation begins. Camelids are given vitamins and dewormed. The Aymara select ashes from local bushes and pour them into the camelids' wallowing place called *qarwa sink'uña*. The herd is turned there, and the dust from the ash, which passes through the wool, removes pests or ticks. In May, they mark the breeding animals. They are no longer marked with earrings, but with wool on the neck as a collar or tufts of red wool attached to the back. This indicates that the camelid male must be cared for so that next year he can be a stallion. Animal health and breeding marks are very important because crossbreeding between animals affects the fibres.

In June, there are two very important ceremonies. The young of the litter that had passed to the *purta*, a territory for the male llamas, are selected for their first trip to the valleys. The shepherds watch the behaviour of these young males, to see which are the most suitable for the reproduction process. In the community, sacks and ropes are collected per family to travel to the valleys with the animals. The community also decides who will travel with the animals and how many camelids will go.

A day before the journey, a ceremony is held so that there is no lack of water or food and so that animals and people are always together on the road as friends and colleagues. So that they can cross the roads to reach the valleys, where they collect food and exchange corn and wool with other *Ayllus* or families who live in the valleys.

In July, there is another ceremony for the return from the valleys. It is that of the good arrival. It begins with the preparation of incense and copal incense. In the drink, called chicha, coca leaves are put to give thanks for the walk and the work. Families continue to hold ceremonies throughout the remaining months of the year to mark other production milestones.

The rituals that accompany the textile process demonstrate the detailed articulation and connection of the life cycles of animals, human populations, and the environment. They show the intimate connection of a cosmology with the daily life of a population, which promotes other forms of relationships that question anthropocentrism as the only form of organisation.

Women's Science

Andean textile women have subverted, resisted, and reexisted[1] the colonial categories of the world through the rescue of their textiles as a living art. That is why we call them textiles of resistance and subversion. The resistance of the women of textiles has consisted in questioning the ways in which textiles have been conceptualised from the European world and in developing their own textile theory. This form of subversion of knowledge can be found in the work of Elvira Espejo and the weavers involved in the Science of Women.

The Science of Women, developed by the weavers, is the production of knowledge around the entire operative chain of textile production. In it are the "original knowledges that are not normally appreciated and do not enjoy the status of science, but are very important for thinking about the organisation of social life" (Mora, 2018, p. 210). They result from the techniques and technologies developed by women weavers operating in their native culture (see Figure 2.1).

Through their textiles, the weavers express their cosmological relationships with nature, for example, with songs to the rain, to planting, and to the earth. They express their political positions, showing how the production of knowledge is linked to the senses and experience. In textiles, the production of knowledge through a tactile formation, that is, systematised practice, resists the Western idea that the knowledge of native peoples is an obstacle to social life and progress. Often, reading a text is more difficult because it is necessary to read and imagine. In the visual and tactile education of the communities, one absorbs how the tool works through sight, being next to the person. You observe how the person uses the tool and, by using it, you see how the person and tool complement each other in a field of action.

Contrary to colonial heritage, in which the original peoples of the Americas are credited with no production of knowledge, the weavers of the Andes have forged their own history of knowledge, know-how, technology, and science, which contributes to development. Women's Science is generated from a deep understanding of the knowledge that exists in the daily practices of the community. This knowledge produces the textiles and is accompanied by art, dance, and songs that give life to the textile. The knowledge produced through textile practice was systematised and is published in five texts: La Ciencia de las Mujeres (2019a),

FIGURE 2.1   A woman's hands spinning wool. Photograph by Elvira Espejo.

Ciencia de Tejer en los Andes (2019b), El Textil Tridimensional (2013), and Los Términos Textiles Aymaras Actuales de la Región de Asanaque e Hilos Sueltos (2008). These books introduce a science indispensable for thinking about current problems, especially in the relationship between species.

Communication: the Andean textile as subject, resistance, and subversion

In the Andean world, textiles are traditionally a concrete way of expressing being a woman. Through them, the political power of women is evidenced. They are a form of visual communication that has its own form of writing and reading (see Figure 2.2). Textiles are evidence that there was writing in the Americas prior to their conquest and subsequent colonialisation. Textiles as a form of communication challenge the flawed and unfounded arrogance of Western colonisers who, believing themselfes superior, ignored and/or denied forms of writing and reading through the textiles of other civilisations, such as the Incas. Denise Arnold, Juan de Dios Yapita, and Elvira Espejo (2008) argue that a subversive function of textiles was to serve as territorial maps, demonstrating a direct relationship between textiles in Bolivia and the territory. In addition to being one

FIGURE 2.2   Weaving in process. Photograph by Elvira Espejo.

of the most important technologies in the Andes, textiles could carry political messages.

However, during the colonial period, more specifically during the Tupac Amaru I Rebellion, textile figuration was prohibited for fear that the indigenous people would send religious and ideological messages hidden in this iconography (Arnold & Espejo, 2019a). The colonisers feared that in the future (as indeed happened), the atrocities carried out against the peoples of *Abya Yala* (The Great America) would be evidenced through textiles (Arnold & Espejo, 2019a). This was the form of resistance of the ancestors against the colonisers. The abuelas or *jach'a mama* (grandmothers) say that the weavers who today live and reproduce their culture are the spirits of the ancestors who have come to continue resisting and protecting their knowledge.

The notion of communication in weavers is based on weaving and braiding. It is immersed in the craft of weaving, which is a tactile and visual narrative through the observation and action of the role played by the textile. Each weaver modifies her action according to the purposes she has as a person. Communication is tactile in that the information that transits is given through the fingertips. The first exchange of messages or production of meaning is between the weaver, an object (for example, the spinning wheel), and an observer (a girl who is learning). The way this relationship is conveyed is visual. It requires careful observation over a long period of time. Thus, a process of communication takes place between the forms of expression, the wool and the threads, the animals, and the actions of the people, all integrated in the context of life in the *Ayllu*.

The transit of information in the fabric is based on the sensitivity of the fingers. The training of the fingertips, with which one learns to read a thick yarn or a thin yarn, to touch the garment, is to acquire the sensitivity that passes through the body. The fingertips describe the world of the yarn that is being woven and braided. They perform a kind of scanning that provides the information necessary to produce a garment that carries a political, religious, and cultural meaning that is expressed in the iconography of the textile.

> The communication between a thick yarn and the fingers will be completely different, because the yarns are rustic. So I am not going to touch it with delicacy, I am not going to treat it like a fine thread, which I would have done with great delicacy. That communication between the object and the person is very difficult to transfer to a boy or a girl. So, for that reason, many times what is said is: "touch and learn", it is like "look and learn". So, when you say "watch and learn", you are observing and by observing, when it touches you, let's say by touching it, you are absorbing this information.
>
> *(Dialogues with women in the community,*
> *personal communication, 2017–2018)*

The notion of weavers' education is inspired by the visual and sensory education of Andean communities. It is a permanent instruction that is passed from generation to generation, from grandmothers to children. Learning to spin is very different from the common classroom experience of blackboard and screen because its logic does not match the community environment. The grandmothers' instructions for learning to spin are "watch the spinning wheel as it spins", "watch your fingers feel", "listen to your body as it receives", "listen to the spinning wheel as it spins and sings in your fingers", "let your fingers feed on the textures so you can identify things", and "listen to how the blood runs through your body as you spin". Everything is interconnected; learning from the wool, from the spinning wheel, and from your body allows us to share different actions that train us in skills to learn in a visual and sensorial way.

To transform wool into yarn, it is necessary to pass it through or route it with the spinning wheel, with the fingers, with the hands, and the movement of the body. Feeling the textures, smelling the wool, and thinking about the whole set of production actions enable multidisciplinary learning that allows you to feel and understand that the spinning wheel is not only an instrument, but a living being that inspires and guides you, to bring a thread to life.

> It is very broad because we are already talking from touch, not only from learning that enters through the eyes. Learning from that sensitive communication with the fingertips that scans. That sensation goes through your

body, it goes through your thinking, it goes through your feeling. Going through your feeling, going through your thinking, absorbing all that sensory communication, in the long run, makes you a master. You don't need a tool like a magnifying glass, like a microscope, for example. Automatically, you are detecting with your fingers what you have scanned with your own fingers. You already realise what kind of raw material we are talking about, what kind of fabric we are talking about, and how it is processed, also by its texture.

(Dialogues with women in the community,
personal communication, 2017–2018)

The communication-education process in the weavers of the Andes is visual, tactile, and sensorial. These are the way women weavers write and read the world and their way of producing knowledge. It implies a collective imagination and a cosmic intelligence. By this, we mean that the cosmos, humans, and other species count and have something to say—they produce senses. They communicate and offer an education different from that of the dominant colonial system.

The living textile, which becomes a person

Weavers produce life through their textiles. The textile is not only an object. It is about the gestation of life, as when a child is created from a union of thoughts and feelings, of love. "When you are pregnant . . .", the weavers say, "you are weaving life". The same happens with the life of the textile. They call it gestating the life of a textile.

When the weaver is pregnant, when she begins to have to gestate a life, it is forbidden to spin, forbidden to weave. Because it is said that you are weaving life, it is in your belly and you have to take care of it. That care is full, as much of the woman as of the man, and the same for weaving. We say gestating the life of a fabric.

(Dialogues with women in the community,
personal communication, 2017–2018)

The weavers take it very seriously to give life to their weaving, they take care of it, and they give it life. They point out that the textile becomes a person. The weaving is gestated with the care of the flock, the selection of the wool, the spinning, the winding, the twisting, and the weaving, especially the latter because the whole process of preliminary care is the stage before making a yarn. It is the transit of feelings between the person, the animal, and the wool. It is the connection of the gestation of life. It is the production of the wool towards the yarn, of the thread towards a fabric to weave a loom. It is like depositing the seed, engendering it. The umbilical cord would be the initiating and cultivating mother of the living being which, in this case, is the textile. Warping the umbilical cord gives the textile the most important sustenance of all the warps to be nourished with the weft.

Jaqichaña to gestate life
Jaqichasiña to build life
Taqikuna jaqichaña every life is gestated

> When we feed the weft, it will become a fabric, and when it becomes a fabric, it is a person. This person must have all the complements, just as we do in life after having gestated for nine months. When we are born, we need, for example, care, we need teaching and family education.
>
> *(Dialogues with women in the community,*
> *personal communication, 2017–2018)*

The weavers have the same conception of care that is given to the birth of an individual, to the care they give to a weaving. As the life of a baby is gestated, the life of the weaving is gestated. When a loom begins to gestate, it is fed with wefts and it is a subject that is being born. The weaving, like a child, requires more attention. In the case of weaving, this attention refers to the finish on the edge. When it is finished, we want that finish to be special (see Figure 2.3).

FIGURE 2.3   A woman's hands finishing the weaving process. Photograph by Elvira Espejo.

When the weaving is finished, the finish is special. It is of a special structure and technique. This finish gives a personality to the object, in this case, to the aguayo or poncho, so that it accompanies a person. It accompanies the person who has made the weaving or the person to whom it will be given as a gift. For that reason it is said "to gestate a person". It is not only making a weaving, but it is to gestate a person, a textile character. That textile character is going to accompany me in life, because you are going to wear it or use it as an accessory.

(Dialogues with women in the community,
personal communication, 2017–2018)

When the garment is worn on the body, the fabric is warm and caring, not only because it is a garment but also because of everything that is included in the process of making it: the wool of an animal, which gives it so that the fabric protects that person from the cold, and the care that the weaver offers to gestate the life of the fabric so that it lives in the body and is a companion of life for a long time. The textile ceases to be an inert object, as it is considered in the West, to become a living object that communicates care and generates joy. The iconography of the textile also provides information. Through the colours, it is possible to identify the community to which the textile belongs, the geographical location, and the religion it professes.

Weaving produces meaning through the sharing of life and mutual care between the Aymara and other species. This process of weaving is what is called mutual nurturing, and this refers to Buen Vivir, Good Living (Mora, 2020). The Andean good living has to do with raising life in a multispecies family, which has consciousness and cosmic intelligence, which is interconnected with life and is the possibility of creating knowledge and daily life in the territory. It is also connected to a network of links to create places of well-being and happiness, where food is produced, children are raised, and people live connected to the earth. The daily practices of women weavers are in balance and harmonious relationship for a good and beautiful life for everyone.

Note

1. Reexisting is a way of living that accounts for personal self-determination and a community that has traditionally been violated, giving a central place to respect, dignity, and the value of shared memory and history. Thus, a new meaning is given by weaving and creating a community that resists oppression, to occupy a space in a territory and in history, despite colonialism, racism, classism, and machismo (Botero & Mora, 2018).

References

Arnold, D. Y., y Espejo, E. (2013). *El textil tridimensional: La naturaleza del tejido como objeto y como sujeto* (p. 379). Fundación Interamericana/Fundación Xavier Albó/Instituto de Lengua y Cultura Aymara.

Arnold, D. Y., y Espejo, E. (2019a, Diciembre). *Ciencia de las mujeres: Experiencias en la cadena textil desde los ayllus de Challapata*. ILCA: Serie Informes de Investigación, II, N° 6. Segunda Edición.

Arnold, D. Y., y Espejo, E. (2019b, Diciembre). *Ciencia de tejer en los Andes: Estructuras y técnicas de faz de urdimbre*. ILCA: Serie Informes de Investigación, II, N° 7. Segunda Edición.

Botero, P., & Mora, A. (2018). Comunidades en Resistencias y Reexistencias: Aporte a los Procesos de Comunicación Popular. In G. Muñoz (Ed.), *Re-visitar la comunicación popular: ensayos para comprenderla como escenario estratégico de resistencia social y re-existencia política*. Corporación Universitaria Minuto de Dios. https://repository.uniminuto.edu/handle/10656/7153

Espejo, E., Arnold, D., y Yapita, J. D. (2008). *Hilos sueltos: Los Andes desde el textil*. Plural e IleA.

Huanacuni Mamani, F. (2015). *Vivir bien/buen vivir: Filosofía, políticas, estrategias y experiencias de los pueblos ancestrales* (6th ed.). Coordinadora Andina de Organizaciones Indígenas.

Mora, A. I. (2016). Vivir bien/Buen vivir con los otros: perspectiva política de la comunicación-educación en la cultura. In A. I. Mora (Ed.), Comu- nicación educación en la cultura para América Latina, desafíos y nuevas comprensiones. Uniminuto. https://repository.uniminuto.edu/bitstream/10656/5392/1/Comunicacion%20educacion%20en%20la%20cultura%20para%20America%20Latina.pdf

Mora, A. I. (2018). Elvira Espejo una Mujer de Resistencias y Re-existencias de los Andes. En *Revista Nómadas*. Universidad Central.

Mora, A. I. (2020). *Buenos Vivieres y Transiciones: La vida dulce, la vida bella, la vida querida, La Vida Sabrosa: Convivir en armonía*. UNIMINUTO.

Sánchez Riaño, F., & Mora, A. I. (2019). Epistemologías del fuego, una propuesta a partir del pensamiento Ancestral. *Misión Jurídica*, *12*(16), 281–308. https://doi.org/10.25058/1794600X.995

3
PROMOTING NONVIOLENT COMMUNICATION FOR A HARMONIOUS COMMUNICATION ECOSYSTEM

Vedabhyas Kundu

Introduction

This chapter explores the value of nonviolent communication for the strengthening and expansion of the pluriverse. It shows that, in the face of a systemic context of conflict and violence, the teachings and practices of Gandhian nonviolent communication provide a toolbox for promoting communicative justice and conflict resolution. Communicative justice, as a dimension of pluriversal justice, is key for the development of a harmonious and peaceful communication ecosystem, which can facilitate the relations that are needed for different human agents to communicate and act with dignity, plurality and respect, appreciation, and love towards other humans as well as towards nonhuman agents. Thus, communicative justice is understood as fundamental to building social and environmental justice. This chapter focuses specifically on the learnings from the training and teaching experiences of the author with police officers, members of the judiciary, and educational institutions.

Our contemporary society is hungering for peace. Conflicts of different kinds and at different levels hog the headlines of different media across the world every day. Whether human–human conflicts or human–nature conflicts, including with animals, the range of conflicts accentuates both social and natural disharmony. While the world witnesses increase in polarisation, hate speech, radicalisation, intercultural tensions, and xenophobia, the unchecked march towards environmental destruction in the name of development further complicates the global scenario. On the one hand, while we grapple with the explosion of conflicts, on the other hand, we are left to fend for the unimaginable effects of climate change.

The new hypertechnological global communication architecture has made it easier to construct messages and make these viral within seconds. The agents

DOI: 10.4324/9781003316220-4

of disinformation can use these to spread hatred and pollute our communication ecosystem. Ikeda (2007), in this context, points out, "rapid advancement of media technologies has made it possible for religious and ethnic hatred to be broadcast around the globe in the blink of an eye".

In the same way, powerful corporations across the world in the pretext of fast-tracking development are destroying habitats, forests, sanctuaries, and precious water bodies. Communication is central in all these adventures or misadventures that humankind is presently involved in. Though there may be contentions and contestations on the role of communication, in its parlance, it may be said that our communication ecosystem is increasingly becoming violent. This could range from human-to-human communication to human-to-nature and human and all other living beings' communications.

The challenge before the global human community hence is to urgently address the effects of an increasingly violent communication ecosystem. The need, therefore, is to promote a pluriversal communication ecosystem that is nonviolent in nature and contributes to a spirit of dialogue, tolerance, empathy, compassion and mutual respect. The aim is also how the communication ecosystem promotes respect to ideas of the pluriverse, particularly peaceful transaction of diverse approaches and views.

As there are concerns that unprecedented technological advancements have taken away the heart from our communicative efforts, the goal of the pluriversal communication ecosystem should be to encourage soul-to-soul communication and emotional bridge building. It should also address the issues of social and environmental justice. In fact, the soul-to-soul communication should not be limited to communication between human beings but all other living beings and nature at large. It is only then we can grapple with the problems of climate change, extinction of many flora and fauna, and the increasing conflicts between human beings.

One of the powerful approaches for a harmonious, pluriversal communication ecosystem is nonviolent communication. As it promotes soul-to-soul communication and encourages empathetic connections, compassion, and mutual respect, nonviolent communication is that centrifugal force which if practiced by the human community can help stem the rise of conflicts. It offers a critical tool in the hands of citizens across the world to use to counter the effects of hate and destructive communication. By imbibing the elements of nonviolent communication, human beings can find new and innovative ways of peaceful communication with nature and all other living beings in the context of the pluriverse.

For a holistic healthy communication ecosystem in our societies, nonviolent communication should be integrated into the entire architecture of the pluriverse. Be it the civil society, civil servants, judiciary, police, educational institutions, the medical community, and all other settings in our societies, a harmonious coexistence can be ensured when each member of these settings and institutions as a whole practice the art and science of nonviolent communication.

FIGURE 3.1   Training of judicial officers on promoting nonviolent communication for meaningful interaction between the bar and the bench. Credit: Gandhi Smriti and Darshan Samiti.

This chapter will be looking at how nonviolent communication which promotes the ideas of pluralism, diversity and mutual respect has been part of Indian tradition. It will delve into the approaches of Mahatma Gandhi, one of the greatest proponents of nonviolent communication in the modern times, and his followers like Natwar Thakkar who gives a nuanced understanding of the subject. Using this, the chapter aims to capture different perspectives on the practical use of nonviolent communication from the author's own work—training, workshops, lectures, and writings to look at how it can be replicated at the global level to contribute towards a culture of peace and nonviolence. Working as Programme Officer of Gandhi Smriti and Darshan Samiti, the national memorial of Mahatma Gandhi in New Delhi, the author has been extensively involved in research, writings, and practical training in different dimensions of nonviolent communication in different settings like the judiciary, police, and educational institutions.

Nonviolent communication in Indian tradition

To understand the depth and gamut of ideas that constitute nonviolent communication, it would be pertinent to look at the expansive explanation given by senior Gandhian, Natwar Thakkar (Kundu, 2018):

> To me nonviolent communication literacy would mean how our communication efforts should be nonviolent; how our ability and capacity to

communicate not only with ourselves but with our family and society be nonviolent in all aspects and overall how the entire process of communication whether between individuals, groups, communities and the world at large should be nonviolent in nature. This would entail deep understanding of the art and science of nonviolence and its centrality in all our daily actions. It's not just verbal and nonverbal communication, nonviolent communication literacy would also include whether our thoughts and ideas are nonviolent or not. This would also mean how we can rid of our preconceived notions of individuals or groups with whom we want to communicate and stop evaluating them to suit our own ideas. More than often we are attuned to think in terms of moralistic judgments which may be our own constructions. By developing deep understanding of the art and science of nonviolence and integrating it in our communication practices we could get over with biased and moralistic judgments; this in turn could contribute to emotional bridge building.

While Thakkar talks about the essence of understanding the art and science of nonviolence to be able to practice nonviolent communication, he looks at it holistically involving verbal and nonverbal communication and all our thoughts and ideas. It is critical as our thoughts and ideas constitute the primary form of communication and it has been said that what we communicate as thoughts gets reflected outside. He also warns of how individuals get entrapped into issues of stereotypes and get judgemental. The core is the necessity to ensure nonviolence in all aspects of our communication. Thakkar further underlines the importance of respect and understanding and how communication should be a catalyst for emotional bridge building. His perspectives encompass how nonviolent communication is a critical pillar of the pluriverse.

Thakkar uses the Gandhian approach of nonviolent communication to develop his understanding of the subject and echoes with the deep traditions of how different dimensions of nonviolence have been an important part of the cultural ethos. The Indian communication system reflects its syncretic traditions and the spirit of genuine pluralism. It helped people from different backgrounds and communities come together to search for shared values and practices thereby contributing towards harmonious intercommunity interactions.

The importance of thoughts and the essence of pluriversality in the communication process have been well captured by this verse from the Rig Veda (1.89.1): *Aano bhadra krtavo yantu vishwatah* (many noble and auspicious thoughts come to us from all over). In fact, the quest for truth in our communication process through a reconciliation of different ideas and views has been an integral part of the Hindu thought. The essence of harmonious dialogue in arriving at the truth has also been underlined in several writings like this proverb, '*vade vade jayate tattvabodha*' (through continuous dialogue alone one arrives at the truth).

The importance of words that we use has been aptly stressed in Maitri Upanishad which says, "Words cannot describe the joy of the spirit whose spirit is cleansed in deep contemplation, who is one with his/her own Spirit (of Ahimsa). Only those who experience this joy know what it is".

The sacred Hindu scripture, Bhagwad Gita offers important insight into the importance of speech. In Chapter 17, Stanza 15, it says:

anudvega-karaṁ vākyaṁ satyaṁ priya-hitaṁ ca yat
svādhyāyābhyasanaṁ caiva vāṅ-mayaṁ tapa ucyate

It essentially means,

> austerity of speech consists in speaking in a manner that will not agitate the minds of the listeners or enkindle the base emotions of the listener or his passion; the communication should be true, it must be beneficial to the listener and also pleasant. One should also engage in self study.
>
> *(Balakrishnan, 2013)*

The essence of nonviolent communication has been eloquently put together in one of Buddha's eight-fold paths, the right speech (*sammāvācā*). Its importance can be emphasised by the fact that the Buddha mentioned it in his very first *sutta* after awakening, "the Discourse on Turning of the Wheel of Truth" (*Dhammacakkappavattana Sutta*). What then constitutes right speech? Magga-Vibhaṅga Sutta (SN 45:8) explains it, "And what is right speech? Abstaining from lying, abstaining from divisive speech, abstaining from abusive speech, abstaining from idle chatter".

Meanwhile, the *Subhāsita Sutta* says, "that word only should one speak by which one would not torment oneself nor harm others. That word indeed is well-spoken". This is definitely an important foundational stone of nonviolent communication.

The Jain doctrine of *anekantvada* (many-sidedness or relative pluralism) also echoes the pluralistic tradition of the Indian communication ecosystem. This Jain doctrine helps us understand the principles of pluralism and the significance of multiplicity of viewpoints. The principle also teaches us that reality can be perceived and interpreted differently from diverse viewpoints. It helps us in realising that no single view is a complete truth.

Thirukkural is one of the most important texts in Tamil written by Thiruvalluvar. In one of the texts, Thiruvalluvar says that a person should never employ a bad or filthy language to address another person. The language that we use, according to the text, should be pleasing for people to listen to. He devotes a complete chapter of 10 couplets to the importance of learning by listening, an important element of nonviolent communication.

Echoing the Indian tradition of nonviolent communication, Swami Vive-kananda in his seminal speech, *The Cosmos: the Microcosm*, delivered on 26 January 1896, in New York noted,

> the infinite future is before you, and you must always remember that each word, thought, and deed, lays up a store for you and that as the bad thoughts and bad works are ready to spring upon you like tigers, so also there is the inspiring hope that the good thoughts and good deeds are ready with the power of a hundred thousand angels to defend you always and forever.

Here Swami Vivekananda stresses on the essence of good thoughts and good deeds which are an integral part of a nonviolent communication ecosystem.

The contemporary foundation of nonviolent communication was laid by Mahatma Gandhi. His approach to nonviolent communication stems from his five basic principles of nonviolence: respect, understanding, acceptance, apprecia-tion, and compassion (Gandhi, 2017).

Gandhi's vision of a nonviolent society was based on the "cosmocentric view of human beings". Parekh (1997) explains the notion of cosmocentric view as followed by Gandhi:

> The cosmos was a well-coordinated whole whose various parts were all linked in a system of yajna, or interdependence and mutual service. It con-sisted of different orders of being ranging from the material to the human, each governed by its own laws and standing in a complex relationship with the rest. Human beings were an integral part of the cosmos and were tied to it by the deepest bonds. In Gandhi's favourite metaphor, the cos-mos was not a pyramid of which the material world was the base and the human beings the apex, but a series of ever-widening circles encompassing humankind, the sentient world, the material world, and the all including the cosmos.

According to Parekh, Gandhi was clear that a nonviolent society, "as human beings were interdependent, should discourage all forms of exploitation, dom-ination, injustice, and inequality . . . and should find ways of institutionaliz-ing and nurturing the spirt of love, truthfulness, social service, cooperation and solidarity".

Parekh (1997) further delves into Gandhi's prescriptions of a nonviolent soci-ety that should "cherish epistemological pluralism". He notes:

> It should appreciate that reason, intuition, faith, traditions intergeneration-ally accumulated collective wisdom, and emotions are all valuable sources of knowledge, and make their own distinct contributions to understanding and coping with the complexities of human life. The good society should

encourage dialogue, a creative interplay between them, and not allow one of them to acquire a hegemonic role or become the arbiter of all others.

The Gandhian framework of nonviolent communication is based on the aforementioned cosmocentric view of human beings and his vision of a nonviolent society. The volume and expanse of Gandhi's nonviolent action and his prescriptions for a society based on equality, justice, and a nonexploitative paradigm can be understood as fundamental tools to favour social and environmental justice in the pluriverse.

Gandhi's approach to communication was to not just reach out to the masses but also adroitly engage them in constructive work. The tools of communication were used to wake the millions out of their slumber and prepare them for one of the most powerful nonviolent struggles in the world's history; the aim was to fearlessly face the exploitative British Raj and demand for political, social, and economic justice. The constructive work which aimed at emancipating the poorest of the poor in the country was an integral part of his strategy of nonviolent communication. Using his method of nonviolent communication and constructive work, he was able to develop a massive network of people across the length and breadth of India to oppose the British.

The essence of constructive work to reach out to the last person of the society has been aptly captured by Gandhi himself (Collected Works of Mahatma Gandhi, Vol. 38, pp. 311–312):

> The volunteers are called upon to enlist themselves in order to do village reconstruction work, and this village reconstruction work is nothing but the organization of the peasants and workers on an economic basis. We want to enter into the hearts of the peasants. We want to identify ourselves completely with the masses. We want to make their woes our own. We want to feel with them in everything in order to better the lot of those on whose toil we the people of the city are really living. We must therefore make common cause with the workers.

In order to reach out to the people, Gandhi used the strategies of padyatras or walking pilgrimage. This method of communication was actually an effort to encourage solidarity and struggle for justice through nonviolent means. During his lifetime, he and his followers undertook a large number of padyatras to connect with the masses.

The Gandhian principles of Satyagraha offer the guiding principles of nonviolent communication. The principles of Satyagraha necessitate that adversaries were never considered as eternal enemies but actually as potential friends. For a Satyagrahi, the object was "not avoidance of all relationship with the opposing power" but the "transformation of relationship". Reaching out to one's opponents or those with whom we disagree is important when we think of resolving differences through strategies of nonviolent communication. In Gandhi's Satya-graha, in situations of dispute or differences, the aim should be to see the validity of the opponent's position and not push only one's point of view. The essence is to be empathetic in resolving differences. In Young India (19–3–1925), the Mahatma writing in this context says:

> Immediately we begin to think of things as our opponent thinks of them, we shall be able to do them full justice. I know that this requires a detached state of mind, and it is a state very difficult to reach. Nevertheless, for a satyagrahi it is absolutely essential. Three-fourths of the miseries and mis-understandings in the world will disappear, if we step into the shoes of our adversaries and understand their standpoint. We will then agree with our adversaries quickly or think of them charitably.

In fact, the Gandhian model of nonviolent communication rests on the signifi-cance of nonviolent persuasion. This was an important attribute of Gandhi's *satya-graha* for reaching out to the adversaries. Here it would be pertinent to look at what nonviolent persuasion really constitutes, and in this context, Pelton (1974) noted,

> an essential ingredient of nonviolent persuasion is the honest and straight-forward dissemination of information . . . the withholding of information, the making of unsubstantiated charges . . . the packaging of an issue, and appeals to greed, prejudice and hatred cannot under any circumstances be reconciled with the philosophy of nonviolence.

Gandhi's communication principles have been well captured by Dr. Rajendra Prasad, the first President of India who in his Introduction to the Collected Works of Mahatma Gandhi, paying homage to the Mahatma writes ("Homage", Collected Works of Mahatma Gandhi, Volume 1):

> Here are the words of the Master covering some six decades of a superbly human and intensely active public life -words that shaped and nurtured a unique movement and let it to success; words that inspired countless individ-uals and showed them the light; words that explored and showed a new way of life; words that emphasized cultural values which are spiritual and eternal, transcending time and space and belonging to all humanity and all ages.

Meticulous use of nonviolent symbolism also formed part of Gandhi's communi-cation strategy. In order to remain disciplined in his search for truth and ahimsa, Gandhi took a vow to observe silence every Monday of the week. On the impor-tance of silence, he notes in his *Autobiography*, "proneness to exaggerate, to sup-press or modify the truth, wittingly or unwittingly, is a natural weakness of man and silence is necessary in order to surmount it. A man of few words will rarely be thoughtless in his speech; he will measure every word".

Another powerful technique of nonviolent communication which Gandhi used was fasting. It was an effective method of nonviolent nonverbal persuasion. Used as a means of self-purification, he used this tool to convert the heart of the offender and also as a method to do penance for any wrongdoing. Merriam (1975) talking on this nonviolent persuasion method points out,

> Of all his techniques of symbolic action, the fast or hunger strike most typified Gandhi's character and temperament. Fasting afforded a method of influencing political policy and social attitudes by creating an emotional impact difficult to achieve through ordinary speech and negotiation. It also provided a source of spiritual renewal for a man dedicated to controlling his senses and desires.

In the context of the aforementioned understanding of the expansive nature of the Gandhian approach, his model of nonviolent communication can be encapsulated as an all-encompassing process. This includes:

I.   His model of nonviolent communication entails nonviolence in all aspects—verbal, nonverbal, thoughts, and how the mind, heart, and body remain disciplined at every stage.

II. Importance of nonviolent persuasion as an attribute of nonviolent communication process.

III. Essence of nonverbal symbolism that aims at encouraging self-introspection and self-discipline, struggle for justice, and emotionally connect with the people even the adversaries.

IV. Gandhi's model of nonviolent communication encompasses principles of human interdependence and underlines the importance of the cosmocentric approach to human nature.

V.   His strategy involved in reaching the hearts of the masses through constructive work for social and economic emancipation. For instance, his Talisman is a powerful statement of how each individual needs to introspect on what they are doing for the last person of the society—the essence of empathetic connections.

VI. His five basic pillars of nonviolence—respect, understanding, acceptance, appreciation, and compassion can be considered as a foundational architecture of a nonviolent communication ecosystem.

VII. The Gandhian model entails the evolution of an individual to a higher plane of values and ethics and respect for human dignity.

VIII. His communication model underlines the importance of being morally disciplined, strictly adhering to the principles of ahimsa and truth, meticulous planning, creative and innovative, and open and flexible.

Senior Gandhian Natwar Thakkar, who used the Gandhian praxis of nonvio-lent communication to reach out to the people of the Indian state of Nagaland, talked about the role of communication in emotional bridge building, especially between people from diverse groups and communities. Throughout his life, he was trying to do the work of emotional bridge building between the people of the North East of India and the rest of the country. He stressed on the role of communicators which should be to challenge attempts to divide people on the basis of case, religion, race, and ethnicity. Thakkar (Kundu, 2018) notes, "the communication education to my mind should integrate the values of pluralism, mutual respect and inclusivity. It should not be a vehicle to sensationalize or incite passion but a lesson to practice self-restraint and principles of nonviolence in all aspects".

Using the understanding of nonviolent communication as espoused by Gandhi and his followers like Natwar Thakkar, this chapter will explore how communica-tion messages can be constructed which are nonviolent in nature. This Gandhian model of nonviolent communication needs to be integrated into the working and action of different pillars of democracy so that the democratic process can be strengthened. It can help in greater participation of the citizenry including the marginalised to contribute towards holistic and sustainable frameworks by trying to incorporate their voices.

Using the author's own experience of training judicial officers, police, teach-ers, and students in nonviolent communication, the aim is to put together and advance an argument of why nonviolent communication should be an integral part of structured curricula in the education system. The following discussion also delves into the need for incorporating its training for different stakeholders like police, judicial officers, and teachers.

Practical applications of nonviolent communication

The following is an excerpt from an observation of a police officer, Shri Khudmukhtiar Dev Singh in a training programme organised by Gandhi Smriti and Darshan Samiti with the Jammu and Kashmir Police Academy on 5–8 February 2018. Mr. Singh shared his experience of having worked with a Station House Officer (SHO) at a police station in the initial stages of his career. This case study explains how an SHO can promote nonviolent communication in policing. He said:

i. Ease of accessibility: Anyone in distress who would approach the police sta-tion would not find any difficulties in meeting the SHO. Right from sentry to beat constable, all would ensure that the person was at ease when they approached the police station. Openness and approachability are important issues in nonviolent communication.

ii. When the person would meet the SHO, he would be asked politely to sit down. The SHO, showing full interest, would ask about the concerns and problems. This explains the importance of right attitude and behaviour which are crucial for nonviolent communication. The body language of the SHO was friendly and affable.

iii. The SHO would then call the waiter to serve water to make the person more comfortable. Again this is a case of right attitude and behaviour and essence of human dignity.

iv. One of the important attributes of nonviolent communication is active listening. Mr. Singh said the SHO possessed enormous patience and listened attentively to the problem.

v. Nonviolent communication also demands sincerity in addressing others. The SHO would then call the Investigating Officer and ask him to seriously work on the complaint.

vi. Mr. Singh also narrated how the SHO in the evening always made it a point to go around the area under his charge and meet his beat constables posted in different places. This is an important attribute of a good team leader and how a leader reaches out to his subordinates.

vii. The SHO also would reach out to people of the area; this was a confidence-building measure with the public. This was also an important strategy for crime prevention as in case of any untoward incidents, the public could immediately reach out to the police.

FIGURE 3.2 Training of police officers in nonviolent communication. Credit: Gandhi Smriti and Darshan Samiti.

One of the biggest hurdles in police–public interaction is the notion of hegemony and power that the police think rests with it. The foundation of Gandhi Smriti's intervention is what Mahatma Gandhi underlined on the policing system:

> The police of my conception will, however, be of a wholly different pattern from the present-day force. Its ranks will be composed of believers in nonviolence. They will be servants, not masters, of the people. The people will instinctively render them every help, and through mutual co-operation they will easily deal with the ever-decreasing disturbances.
>
> *(Harijan, 1–9–1940)*

The Gandhian perspective underlines the importance of shifting away from the traditional notion of policing which relies on retributive practices and use of power over the people. Its approach to justice is essentially retributive justice, whereas Gandhi stresses that police should be reformers. The Gandhian approach builds on mutual trust and harmonious engagement between the police and the public using the strategies of nonviolent communication.

In another instance, a participant of the Delhi Home Guards in a feedback session after a month when a workshop on nonviolent communication and nonviolent conflict resolution was organised shared the following experience: One of the home guards narrated an incident that happened in the police station where he was posted. Two groups had surrounded (*gheraoed*) the police station and there was every possibility of the situation going out of hand. The participant said he was reminded of the efficacy of engaging opposing parties through dialogues, an important outcome of using nonviolent communication. The SHO was convinced and leaders of the two conflicting parties were invited to the police station to resolve their issues. The participant shared how through intense dialogue, within an hour, the entire mob got dispersed without the police resorting to the lathi charge.

During various workshops, police officers indeed felt the need for integrating nonviolent communication into their work so that the trust deficit between the police and people can be bridged. Also, it was felt that this can actually aid in crime prevention. When the common people trust the police, they can actually support in preventing crimes in the neighbourhood.

An important arena that needs integration of nonviolent communication is institutions of education, be it schools, colleges, and universities. For peaceful educational institutions, it is critical to encourage a nonviolent communication ecosystem. For instance, in the context of schools, our traditional approaches are firmly framed in institutional power dynamics. The teacher–student relationships are still based on the principles of hegemony with students having limited autonomy in their educational journeys.

The aim of the workshops that the author has been conducting for teachers focuses on replacing retributive practices with restorative practices. The thrust has been to encourage effective classroom management practices using strategies of nonviolent communication. Here it would be pertinent to point out the different elements of nonviolent communication:

- Nonviolence in our speech, action, and thoughts
- Use of appropriate words and language
- Understanding self and ensuring constructive inner dialogue and self-talk
- Avoiding moralistic judgements
- Avoiding negative evaluative language
- Avoiding stereotypes
- Realising the power of empathy
- Promote compassion
- Connecting with the needs of others
- Expressing gratitude
- Importance of flexibility and openness in our communication process
- Importance of active and deep listening

While the goal of every educational institution is to encourage greater learning outcomes, the aim should also be to provide an opportunity for the students to harness their skills in creativity activities and ensure their holistic development. When the communication ecosystem in the educational institutions is nonviolent in nature and with the interplay of the different elements of nonviolent communication, it is much easier for these institutions to move towards their goals.

During the sessions with teachers, it was felt that constructive resolution of differences in school settings becomes easier when nonviolent communication is used and it also encourages peer mediation. In fact, some teachers felt that nonviolent communication helps in team building and leadership development amongst students. They felt it helped students forge deeper connections and develop a greater understanding of each other's perspectives. This helped in developing cohesive teams of students and aided in a greater sense of belonging to the educational institution.

For instance, student S. Saba noted that,

> By practicing tools of nonviolent communication, we students are able to engage in dialogues more efficiently. Whether within the group or while reaching out to other students and the community the ability to engage in efficient dialogues are critical . . . So even if some conflict arises in our group, engaging in dialogues using nonviolent communication techniques helps us resolve these. These also help us to develop better relationships with the communities in which we work.
>
> *(Kundu, 2018)*

Another student, Shazaf Masood Sidhu of The Peace Gong, pointed out how deep understanding and respect are crucial ingredients of nonviolent communication and young people can value the unique qualities of each member of their team through mutual respect. She argued that nonviolent communications can help in developing relationships despite differences and diversity (Kundu, 2018).

During a feedback session, one of the teachers shared how pro-social behaviour of many of her students was enhanced and they were taking part in many community volunteering initiatives. This is in sync with several psychological studies which show that compassionate behaviour leads to the enhancement of pro-social behaviour. Also, the teachers felt practicing different elements of nonviolent communication was associated with cognitive benefits for the students. For instance, in an empathetic classroom, students were more open-minded and developed a critical understanding of diverse perspectives. One of the biggest drawbacks in many educational settings was that they limited the critical capacities to look at an issue from different angles and plurality in our thoughts and ideas.

The judiciary is an important pillar of any society. The thrust of any egalitarian democratic society is the promotion of restorative practices instead of being retributive. Reformation of an individual who may be on the wrong side of the law should be the key goal. Here Gandhi's nonviolent communication can provide an important guiding post in the functioning of the judiciary. He writes in his *Autobiography, My Experiments with Truth* (1927):

> I had learnt the true practice of law. I had learnt to find out the better side of human nature and to enter men's hearts. I realized that the true function of a lawyer was to unite parties riven asunder. The lesson was so indelibly burnt into me that a large part of my time during the twenty years of my practice as a lawyer was occupied in bringing about private compromises of hundreds of cases. I lost nothing thereby—not even money, certainly not my soul.

When Gandhi says the true function of a lawyer was to unite parties, his underlying message is that adversaries need not further drift apart; instead, the effort should be to use the strategies of nonviolent communication to help them resolve their disputes. This has to be the basis of all alternate dispute resolution approaches.

Gandhi also stressed the importance of linking his notion of nonviolence to justice. He notes, "the first condition of non-violence is justice all round, in every department of life" (Mahatma, Vol. 5 by D. G. Tendulkar, p. 278). Nonviolence was not possible without practices of justice.

As part of the initiatives with the judiciary, the author has been taking sessions on how nonviolent communication can promote meaningful interaction between the bar and the bench. For instance, when lawyers learn the art and

FIGURE 3.3   Training of judicial officers on promoting nonviolent communication for meaningful interaction between the bar and the bench. Credit: Gandhi Smriti and Darshan Samiti.

science of nonviolent communication, they are able to use this technique when dealing with clients and also during cross-examination. Important elements of nonviolent communication like empathy, mutual toleration, and respect, critically trying to understand the other's point of view from a needs level, practicing active and deep listening skills, flexibility in one's approach, and compassion if practiced can help in creating a better client–lawyer relationship. It can also help in creating a congenial environment between two opposing parties thereby opening the doors for dialogue and mediation.

There could be situations when judicial officers while passing orders could use harsh words. Here again sensitivity towards the use of nonviolent communication amongst judges could assist in using words that are nonviolent in nature. This will open space for mediation and could stop further review petitions in higher courts.

Conclusion

The chapter has developed an understanding of different approaches to nonviolent communication according to Indian tradition as a key aspect to expand the pluriverse. Specifically, it has elucidated the Gandhian approach to nonviolent communication. It has looked from the author's own practical work with the police, educational institutions, and the judiciary system at how critical is the integration of nonviolent communication in the pluriverse for a harmonious coexistence. More fundamental interdisciplinary research needs to be done on the significance of nonviolent communication and how people at large can make it part of their daily habits. Also, different stakeholders need to ensure training in nonviolent communication as part of their training curriculum. Most importantly, the chapter has underlined the essence of introducing nonviolent communication as part of life skill education in schools so that future citizens of the world can imbibe it.

Reference list

Balakrishnan, T. S. (2013, September–October). Effective executive communication, the Bhagavad Gita way. *IOSR Journal of Business and Management, 13*(4), 26–29.
Gandhi, A. (2017). *The gift of anger.* Penguin Books.
Gandhi, M. K. (1927). *An autobiography or the story of my experiments with truth.* Navjivan Publishing House.
Ikeda, D. (2007). *Interaction of civilizations leads to a flourishing culture of humanity.* Acceptance speech of honorary doctorate in communications in the University of Palermo.
Kundu, V. (2018). The role of nonviolent communication in teambuilding in youth volunteer groups. *International Journal of Peace, Education and Development, 6*(2), 63–69.
Merriam, A. H. (1975). Symbolic action in India: Gandhi's nonverbal persuasion. *Quarterly Journal of Speech, 61,* 290.
Parekh, B. (1997). *Gandhi: A very short introduction.* Oxford University Press.
Pelton, L. H. (1974). *The psychology of nonviolence.* Pergamon Press.

4

VOICES WITH PURPOSE

Lessons learned from the South–South
collaboration between Latin America
and Africa for the strengthening
of communication capacities
in social organisations

*Jair Vega-Casanova, Rafael Obregón Gálvez,
Sara-Nathalie Brombart, and Gabriel Baglo*

Introduction

Capacity building has been at the core of international development initiatives for
several decades. The 2005 Paris Declaration´s focus on the centrality of strengthening local capacities to accelerate development initiatives provided a tremendous
boost to capacity development. That impetus was subsequently reinforced by
global initiatives such as the Millennium Development Goals and the Sustainable
Development Goals, including their emphasis on South–South cooperation. As
a result, efforts to build and strengthen capacities in health, nutrition, education, and many other development themes and topics have grown over the years,
many of which have been gradually inserted into development programs and projects. For example, significant investments have been made to strengthen existing
capacities at regional and national levels to increase access to and provide a better
quality of social services, develop research competencies, or improve the institutional capacities of government and civil society organisations.

Building and strengthening capacities in strategic communication, communication for development (C4D), social and behaviour change communication (SBCC),
and similar communication concepts, however, have not necessarily received a similar type of support or investments, or, at the very least, those efforts have not been
sufficiently documented in the scarce literature available in this area. While many
communication initiatives do consider capacity development components, these
are often limited to the development of training materials and resources, and to
the implementation of training activities. They tend to be short-lived or lack substantial investments for long-term actions, follow-up, and sustainability over time.

DOI: 10.4324/9781003316220-5

Many international development agencies and organisations argue that the implementation of SBCC initiatives and projects inherently carries a capacity-strengthening component but even if that were the case, it is not necessarily driven by a coherent approach with clearly defined competency, behavioural, and social change outcomes. The primary assumption is that the implementation of SBCC strategies and campaigns will contribute to improving the skills and competencies of organisations and individuals involved in development projects, which in turn should contribute to improved development-related outcomes.

Another tendency is that SBCC initiatives often draw on approaches and models developed in specific cultural contexts, typically developed in the global north or in the global south with a significant level of resources, which are then applied universally in other contexts. The fact that communication processes are strongly linked to local cultural contexts and dynamics makes it very challenging to follow universal models and approaches for the design, implementation, and evaluation of SBCC strategies. While key principles and processes generated through decades of research and practice in SBCC are pivotal to capacity development and strengthening efforts, we posit that SBCC capacity building must be situated within the framework of differentiated cultural contexts, processes of social and community empowerment, and the strengthening local voices.

In this chapter, we document the implementation of Voices with Purpose, a case study of South–South collaboration supported by the *fesmedia* Africa of the Friedrich-Ebert-Stiftung (FES) to strengthen local capacities in SBCC in sub-Saharan Africa. This initiative was developed based on a similar previous experience implemented in Latin America. In reflecting on Voices with Purpose, we draw on key concepts central to the driving tenets of this book, including capacity building on communication from a decolonial perspective in a South–South dialogue, capacity building on communication, ecologies, and pluriverses, as well as communicative justice and capacity building on communication. Lastly, we also draw on the feedback provided by 10 facilitators from several countries in Africa, who participated in Voices with Purpose, about their experience conducting training with social organisations over the past few years.

Next, we provide a brief introduction to capacity development, including an organisational framework that guides our analysis, followed by a description of Latin American and African experiences, including observations from participants in these processes. Finally, we present key lessons learned and recommendations in line with the driving concepts of this book.

A decolonial perspective of the generation of capacities in communication

Capacity development has been defined in a multiplicity of ways by several authors and organisations. In fact, there is no standard or common definition of capacity development. However, capacity development efforts have distinct characteristics and components that are emphasised, depending upon the intended outcomes.

First, all forms of capacity development, for example, typically involve some form of competency and skills development, transfer of knowledge, and expected improvements in the achievement of specific results. Also, capacity development efforts can focus on individuals, teams, organisations, institutions, networks, and sectors, amongst others, or on a combination of them. Time and resources are also important variables in capacity development efforts. The effect of capacity development can hardly be seen overnight. Depending on the complexity of the issues, the existing capacities, and the enabling organisational, policy, and financial factors, capacity development can move at a faster or slower pace. And lastly, regardless of those considerations, capacity development requires political commitment, adequate resources, and optimal time frames.

Obregon and Lapsanski (2022) discussed the experience of the United Nations International Children's Emergency Fund (UNICEF) in building its organisational capacity in C4D (a concept often equated to SBCC). Obregon and Lapsanski argued that the UNICEF experience demonstrated that building capacities across different levels of a large organisation is feasible, can be done in adaptable and flexible ways, and requires substantial political support, financial investments, and time commitments. The UNICEF experience included a wide range of components, ranging from the development of a competency framework, training resources and platforms, and training activities across all levels (technical, managerial) to partnerships with academic centres and local civil society organisations (CSOs), to name a few elements.

In the context of this book, our focus on an SBCC capacity development initiative is highly relevant because it provides an opportunity to examine not only the most known characteristics of capacity development as described earlier but also how an SBCC capacity-building initiative can lead to South–South dialogue and engagement, leading to the questioning, refinement, and adaptation of communication concepts, models, and practice. More importantly, the latter also allows us to examine this SBCC experience through the notion of the pluriverse, decoloniality, and communicative justice, the guiding concepts of this book.

While several capacity development frameworks have been developed and applied globally, for the purpose of our analysis, we draw on the conceptual framework on capacity development that Crisp et al. (2000) developed to assess progress in capacity development in the health sector. While these authors recognise that capacity building can take many forms and can target different groups—from individuals to organisations to nations—they choose to focus on organisations as their unit of analysis. Therefore, Crisp and colleagues' framework is highly relevant to our analysis as the primary focus of the FES *fesmedia* Africa experience emphasises the development of capacity building within organisations as opposed to individuals.

The framework developed by Crisp and colleagues includes four approaches: (a) a top-down organisational approach, which emphasises changes in policies and practices in institutions often through vertical directives that are implemented over time but with a clear timeframe, (b) a bottom-up organisational approach that focuses on training or skill-building activities of individuals within an organisation which can gradually transform the organisation's practice, (c) a partnership approach that seeks to strengthen connections and collaborations between organisations, especially through horizontal learning and sharing, and (d) a community organising approach that aims to connect community members with organisations through collaborative initiatives that often bring community members into the organisations or can lead to the formation of new community organisations.

While each of these approaches has its own characteristics, they also can be highly complementary to each other. As we discuss later, although bottom-up, partnership, and community organising approaches seem to lend themselves better to the notion of South–South collaboration, arguably, the implementation of the FES *fesmedia* Africa capacity development initiative in SBCC reflects two or more of those approaches.

Approaching capacity building on communication from a decolonial perspective in a South–South dialogue implies assuming a central concern for the oppressed, especially the subaltern, and a critique of the dominant paradigm that seeks to universalise and homogenise not only the conception of communication but also individual and collective communication skills, regardless of context. From this perspective, the critique of colonialism, which includes both knowledge, communication, and power (Fals Borda, 1987; Santos, 2016; Torrico-Villanueva, 2017), implies transcending communication skills focused on control of processes and outcomes towards the generation of capacities that contribute to emancipation and autonomy.

Likewise, understanding the generation of communication capacities from an ecology (Santos, 2007) and pluriverse (Escobar, 2018) perspective implies assuming the recognition of the existence of multiple worlds and interconnected knowledge in various ways but also differentiated. Some examples include potential connections between Latin America and Africa from the contexts of exclusion and marginality, and others between social movements that organise advocacy processes to generate transformations towards a dignified life, however, always considering their well-differentiated social and cultural histories and processes. Drawing upon the communicational capacities from the ecologies proposed by Santos, it is about not only the capacity to produce and circulate messages, but also, above all, the capacity to trigger processes of political impact. These processes are based on the recognition of the plurality of heterogeneous knowledge and their interconnections, while understanding that this knowledge is always generated in collective processes.

Finally, the relationship between cognitive justice (Visvanathan, 2006), communicative justice (a concept discussed in the first chapter of this book by

Herrera-Huérfano, Pedro-Carañana, and Ochoa-Almanza) and the generation of communication skills is examined. The perspective of this book assumes that communicative justice starts by questioning the monoculture of modern communication as one of its strongest limitations. To this end, the communicative capacities generated in social organisations must, on the one hand, strengthen the critical analysis of the dominant media systems and, on the other, critically energise the sociopolitical processes, the technological communicative practices that are at the core of the autonomy of peoples and communities, as well as making visible forms of communication marginalised by the large conglomerates.

Torrico-Villanueva's (2018) proposal on thinking about the decoloniality of communication from the perspectives of Latin America compared to the dominant European and North American tradition in social studies could be incorporated as a framework to address communicative justice from communication skills.

We believe that the examination of a capacity-building initiative in SBCC that builds on South–South collaboration and dialogue between Africa and Latin America provides a unique window into the dynamics of pluriverse dynamics and decolonial relationships, and thus contributes to the knowledge base on communicative justice. In the next section, we describe and discuss the process that led to the FES *fesmedia* Africa initiative, starting with a key workshop on strategic communication that led to a series of dialogues on the relevance of building communication capacity and the need to rethink key communication concepts, paradigms, and ways of SBCC practice.

MUSAVIA: the connection between "official" culture media and alternative and community media

In 1999, the Musavia Project facilitated in Antigua, Guatemala, the "Communication Strategies" workshop with the purpose of improving the effectiveness of the strategic communication work of several women's NGOs. Participant organisations identified the need to frame their communication work and practices in a more strategic manner, which would provide answers to the dilemma of how to issue transformative messages and communication processes using the media of the "official" culture, but also by using alternative media. The workshop resulted in an enriching experience that, at the time, Mara Girardi, director of the Musavia Project, summarised as follows:

> The combination of knowledge that has taken place in this workshop has allowed participants to reap very significant results. This would not have been possible without the will of women to enter new areas of knowledge, communication theories, semiotics, signs, meanings and signifiers, as well as the availability of the expert to discuss her own approaches, confronting them with this collection of experiences brought by the participants.
>
> *(Rodríguez, 2000, p. 5)*

Following the success of the workshop, the Musavia Project made the decision to turn the experiences of the workshop into a manual on communication strategies that could be used not only by women's organisations but also other national and international organisations interested in supporting women's movements. The manual edited by Musavia in 1999, based on the workshop developed by professor and researcher Clemencia Rodríguez, had a strong gender perspective, evidenced in some of the conceptual and methodological elements outlined throughout the document as well as through the examples used in the text.

In a dialogue with the women participating in the workshop, two elements were critical. First, the universal and instrumental concept of communication, understood primarily as the transmission of information and as an "external tool" that can be used indiscriminately to generate any change, was questioned and discussed. Such a unidirectional approach to communication is not only often used by officials or professionals from different organisations in charge of training social organisations in C4D, but it also has been assimilated in that way by the communities themselves. The need to understand the communication process in a different way was possible through a dialogue that allowed the identification and critical questioning of the conceptions that the participants had about communication. They then critically examined commonly used approaches in C4D such as persuasion models and social marketing strategies.

Second, even though participants recognised that it is frequently assumed that only the culture of the "official" media can facilitate social change, the importance of valuing one's own voice and one's own communication process was emphasised as fundamental to change. Likewise, and although this aspect was not included in the first manual, participants highlighted the relevance and contributions of the community and alternative media to processes of engagement and change.

This Communication Strategies workshop with the Musavia Project covered key content that later served as the basis for the subsequent manuals initiated by the FES on the subject. The first manual, Communication Strategies for Social Change (2002), was produced in Spanish and the later adapted versions of the manual Voices with Purpose: A Manual on Communication Strategies for Development and Social Change (Obregón & Vega, 2019a) were produced in English, French, and Portuguese and in 2022 in Spanish. These different manuals became a key resource for the workshops organised for civil society organisations in Latin America and Africa over the years.

"Communication strategies for social change": a perspective from Latin America

Given the useful communication strategies and concepts elaborated in the manual based on the Musavia experience, the FES sought to broaden its focus to address other social issues in addition to gender, and other organisations interested in generating processes of social transformation through communication. For this reason, the version entitled Manual on Communication Strategies for Social Change (Rodríguez et al., 2002) was published by the FES Latin American Media Project. The fundamental conceptual elements included in the previous publication were maintained, but several important modifications were made.

First, a shift from a gender-centred approach to a much broader approach both at the thematic level (health, democracy, education, conflicts, and children's rights, among others) and at the level of communication strategies (in addition to enriching the primary strategy included in the first edition, known as edutainment, other strategies such as media advocacy, civic journalism, mechanisms in search of consensus, and social mobilisation were included).

Second, conceptual aspects related to the understanding of communication were updated and broadened. In the first edition, approaches to communication as transmission of information and communication as dialogue were discussed, while in the second edition, the perspective of communication for social change was included, an approach that currently dominates much of the academic debate and practice in communication. Additionally, important differences were established around the implications of the use of the terms strategy, campaign, and product. Likewise, in addition to the psychological, constructivist, and pragmatic models of communication, the culturalist model of communication was incorporated as a perspective that allows visualising communication as a permanent process of resignification and creation of meaning.

Third, the second edition of the manual sought to broaden its scope to include citizen participation and social mobilisation. It incorporates conceptual and practical elements with examples of processes related to the construction of the public agenda, social mobilisation, and participation of citizens in democratic processes through communication, increasingly crucial aspects in Latin American societies of this new century.

Finally, the importance of research, to inform strategy design and to monitor and evaluate its impact, was reinforced. Indicators of communication for social change were included to strengthen the monitoring and evaluation components. This manual supported the subsequent implementation of FES communication strategies for social change workshops for members of social organisations in Latin America. Their purpose was to strengthen the internal and external communication strategies and advocacy capacities of trade unions, indigenous, women's, LGBTI, and afro descendent organisations, among others.

This diversity of organisations involved in these capacity-building initiatives provided insights into the role of communication in social organisations. First, it was observed that many of the social organisations held expectations about how the use of communication strategies could affect their external ("outwards") positioning in society, without considering how a transformative approach to communication could also affect their organisations internally ("inwards") and in turn strengthen and democratise their own internal processes and working relationships.

Second, in line with the previous point, the importance of strengthening communication capacities for social and behaviour change in social organisations through "*dialogue of knowledges*"[1] and social and cultural perspectives emerged as a key issue. This contrasted with the more common and dominant approaches that often understand strengthening of communication capacity primarily as communication training for social and behavioural change based on vertical and behavioural communication perspectives.

Third, the need to understand and build upon existing forms of communication that are unique to local contexts and communities was very much valued. This is an important consideration when it comes to, for example, indigenous and Afro peoples, who have longstanding traditions, not only cultural but also communicative. This implies that there are different communication skills typical to different social and cultural contexts, which must be considered in conjunction with other skills that are proposed in capacity development initiatives.

Voices with purpose: from the Latin American context to sub-Saharan Africa

In the last decade, it was increasingly clear that civil society actors in Africa were gradually finding more opportunities to promote citizens' participation in public programs and in initiatives aimed at fostering social change. Yet, it was also clear that many of these civil society actors lack the experience and capacities to communicate their efforts effectively and on a greater scale. To confirm this empirical observation, FES *fesmedia* Africa, conducted a feasibility study in 2015 which assessed whether, and if so how, civil society organisations integrate communication strategies into their work. The research found that many African civil society organisations and communication experts were eager to gain a comprehensive vision and understanding of the benefits of communication planning.

To support the African CSOs' need for effective strategic communication skills, FES *fesmedia* Africa launched the program "Communication Strategies for Social Change" in 2017. Its primary objectives were to: (1) enable civil society actors to articulate, represent, and advance their interests and causes to effectively impact policies and policy-making and (2) guide CSOs in using modern communications methods to broaden opportunities for sociopolitical participation and social change.

Through the *fesmedia* Africa Project, the Friederich-Ebert-Stiftung, sought to strengthen the capacity of social organisations in Africa, especially on the appropriate use of strategic communication actions for social change. This initiative was based on the assessment of the experience developed in Latin America and built upon the previous versions of the manual. The first step in that process was the adaptation of the manual on Communication Strategies for Social Change produced for a Latin American audience. While this may be perceived as a simple process, as part of the South–South collaboration, considerable effort went into the exchanges between the authors and African and Latin American communicators and into content refinement. Next, we describe this process.

After a two-year process of drafting, validating, and refining, the manual for Africa was published in 2019 with the title: *Voices with Purpose. A manual on communication strategies for development and social change.* Unlike the Latin American version, the manual included three modules: a conceptual module (Obregón & Vega, 2019a), a practitioner module (Obregón & Vega, 2019b), and a facilitator module (Obregón & Vega, 2019c). The manual was initially published in English and then translated into Portuguese and French, taking into account some of the mainstream languages spoken in the region.

The process developed for the writing of Voices with Purpose included:

1) An assessment of the use of the first manual in different capacity-building activities in Latin America.
2) Elaboration of a first draft of the manual for Africa based on the experience in the Latin American region and on current trends in the field.
3) A workshop with social organisations from the Caribbean region of Colombia in which 24 members from 12 social organisations participated, including neighbourhood and community leaders, victims of the armed conflict, journalists and community radio broadcasters, youth, human rights defenders, women activists, peace builders, and LGBTI leaders, amongst others. In this workshop, the draft manual was validated in terms of its relevance for social organisations, the language and clarity of the concepts used, and the ease of understanding the methodological steps. Suggestions made during this workshop were incorporated into a revised version of the draft manual.
4) A collaborative process between the team in charge of drafting the manual and a group of communication experts who regularly work with civil society organisations across the African continent, and with in-depth knowledge and experience of the regional context. This group included 17 communication experts from Benin, Botswana, Cameroon, Kenya, Madagascar, Mozambique, Namibia, Senegal, South Africa, Togo, United States, Zambia, and Zimbabwe. Likewise, there was substantive engagement and participation of members of ACTION Namibia, a coalition formed in 2012 by organisations and activists intent on putting access to information (ATI) on the Namibian political, policy, and governance agenda.

Interviews were conducted with the participating communication experts that would later act as facilitators for subsequent capacity-building activities accross the sub-Saharan region. The interviews revealed significant weakness and strenghs in communication practices.

With regard to weaknesses, participants indicated that social organisations often incorporate communication tools, including media release skills, without a clear communication plan to effectively deploy them. Among the obstacles that the group of facilitators identified in relation to the communication processes applied by social organisations, the following can be highlighted: (a) limited resources to develop them, (b) lack of knowledge, skills, and management capacity for implementing a communication strategy, (c) divergent views in the implementation, (d) unrealistic expectations about the results of the communication processes, (e) barriers to reach populations with different languages, (f) weak management support, insufficient prioritisation of communication, (g) tendency to develop desk-based strategies, that is, not needs based, (h) strategies developed to please donors, and (i) sometimes monitoring and evaluation frameworks that were not clear from the onset about what the strategy seeks to achieve.

Likewise, very relevant strengths were identified by the group of facilitators who participated in the interviews. These included: (a) deep knowledge of the social and cultural context of the organisations in the different countries, (b) great experience in terms of years dedicated to the facilitation of communication processes with social organisations, (c) extensive knowledge and skills related to communication in local contexts learned from experience, (d) extensive knowledge of communication, culture, and social change product of prior training and studies, including at university level.

A key component of this process was the review and validation of the draft training manual and supporting resources for the implementation of this programme. Recommendations from this review informed the final version of these resources. A five-day review and validation exercise took place 3–8 September 2017 in Windhoek, Namibia. The objectives of this workshop were the following: (a) validate and make recommendations to Voices with Purpose: "Manual on Communication Strategies for Development and Social Change", including a two-day hands-on exercise using the handbook to accompany ACTION Namibia in formulating an outline of a communication strategy, (b) consolidation of a pool of highly capable facilitators to deliver skills-building workshops; and (c) development of a common workshop training methodology.

Two years later and after incorporating the contributions of the first workshop, the "II Workshop: A Facilitator's Training on Communication Strategies for Development and Social Change" was held, 8–11 April 2019 in Windhoek, Namibia, this time with the purpose of validating the adjustments made to the first draft of "Voices with Purpose" and continue with the training of facilitators to improve their workshops aimed at strengthening the strategic communication skills of social organisations in their countries.

The knowledge and expertise of the participants were critical to providing relevant feedback and recommendations for the manual's content which contributed to its adaptation to the African context and to strengthening regional and local capacities in the application of communication for social change principles.

This process of adapting the manual developed for Latin America for use in different African contexts involved several important changes.

First, content updates included: (a) the role of communication within social organisations, (b) a reflection on the different paradigms used in the field of C4D and social change, (c) approaches to the concepts of individual and social change, (d) new communication planning models such as SBCC (which was then taken as the basis for the methodological proposal of the manual) and the integrated communication model that outlines a more participatory process, (e) communication strategies such as the use of digital media and community and citizen media, (f) a more detailed perspective of research in communication strategies, with emphasis on formative research, monitoring, evaluation, and systematisation; and (g) the development of a significant number of case studies, including, of course, several from the African context.

Before projecting communication processes "outwards", social organisation must critically reflect upon their own conceptions on communication. Are their conceptions and definitions on communication consistent with the logic of the expectations and objectives of the organisation or movement? On many occasions, for example, initiatives based on vertical and unidirectional communication approaches appear contradictory when their commitment is to a democratic and inclusive society.

The different paradigms, models, and strategies used in the field of C4D and social change are presented not simply as a technical tool box but also as a means to critically reflect on their perspectives, uses, and implications. This responds to the persistence of more universalistic approaches to communication planning, including expectations to control both processes and desired changes in people. Also, other approaches highlighted start with the challenge of defining with the participants the characteristics and meaning, not only of the changes that are desired but also of the communication strategy that is going to be implemented (Servaes, 2000). These paradignms, models and strategies are presented rather as a necessary debate in which participants of an organisation must engage when designing and planning their communication strategies.

In general, many manuals on communication and development start from a universal conception of development as a unidirectional, preestablished, progressive process towards which all communities, territories, and countries should aspire. In contrast, this manual presents a discussion about this conception, highlighting different paradigms from which this perspective of the future has been approached, under the understanding that it should be defined based on the characteristics of each context and by the communities themselves (Waisbord, 2001). In fact, conceptions are incorporated from those debated by Rogers (1976) in the 1960s and 1970s, to approaches from Latin America such as the "*Buen vivir*" perspective (Gudynas, 2011).

Arguably, it is very common that debates on topics such as social change, individual change, and culture, amongst many others, are considered only in the field of academics or by communication professionals. In the development of the manual, we assume that an important aspect of the approach to generating communication capacities in social organisations is the critical appropriation of these concepts which underlie communication processes.

Generally, when social change approaches are not discussed, it is assumed that there is only one approach, which equates individual change with behavioural approaches. However, understanding these different approaches allows for the inclusion and emphasis on social change from participatory perspectives which define the direction of change (Obregón & Mosquera, 2005). Likewise, understanding that the mere fact of assuming that a communication strategy is based on culture is not enough to differentiate when culture is assumed instrumentally based on the expected changes or, on the contrary, when the expected changes are based on the meanings that underlie the culture (Dutta, 2007).

One of the key aspects of the African version of the manual was the adaptation of the conceptualisation to the socio-political contexts of this region, understanding that concepts such as democracy and citizenship do not have the same connotations in all countries and that organisational and political structures have particularities that challenge their own constructions of meaning. For this reason, they are not presented as simple definitions, but as scenarios for debate and reflection.

Finally, it is also assumed that research and knowledge generation for and from communication processes is not an exclusive activity of academics nor that practice is the only contribution expected from social organisations. Based on this consideration, elements are included in the manual to understand research as a supporting tool for understanding the reality that is intended to be transformed. This is an important condition for an adequate communication strategy. Likewise, it is considered that monitoring and evaluation do not necessarily have to be external activities carried out by experts, but are also important as part of the empowerment of members of organisations and communities regarding their communication processes. In the same sense, it is also important to consider community involvement in processes such as the systematisation and generation of knowledge about the communication strategies implemented by their organisations as part of empowerment (Vega-Casanova, 2021).

At the beginning of the year 2022, a consultation was held, which was attended by 9 of the facilitators who participated throughout the entire process of co-creating "Voices with Purpose". Some of them highlighted the following aspects from their experience of using the manual: (a) the theoretical frameworks and defining the concept and process of communication are useful, (b) the tools present a holistic approach to communication for change, (c) comprehensive and user friendly, especially when it comes to strategies and group work, and (d) in terms of the overall performance, the manuals and tools provide the missing link trainers and organisation need in the South—South Cooperation.

Regarding knowledge exchange networks and collaborations that were strengthened or created in the course of ensuing workshops and in the use of the manual, facilitators have: (a) maintained contact with the group that consolidated the manual and share experiences or materials on an ad hoc basis, and (b) trained and/or advised other civil society organisations and networks such as trade unions, associations of street vendors, childrens's rights groups, as well as media, peace and environmental sustainability organisations, (c) trained other organisations such as a pan African organisation for the promotion of peace, (d) worked with media partners in Malawi, Zambia, and Namibia, and (e) collaborations with the trade unions movements and journalists movements.

In comparison to the types of materials and processes coming from the Global North, facilitators found that both the consolidation of the manual and the exchange process within the FES workshops had a differential perspective based on South-South cooperation. They pointed out that: (a) the discussion, development and engagement was very rich and fruitful, (b) the examples, processes, and strategies from the Global South were not only useful and differed from other methods but were validating, (c) the workshops focused on capacity-building rather than on geostrategical considerations, (d) both the manual and the workshops were developed in the right context, namely by designing them in the South rather than in the North, and finally (e) there was a feeling of ownership of the ensuing trainings by both the facilitators and the beneficieries.

The facilitators made some recommendations to continue developing and replicating South–South cooperation actions to strengthen communication and social change processes: (a) more training initiatives and opportunities from an assessment of training needs and topics related to development cooperation, (b) regular exchange forums, (c) spaces to build this collaboration between facilitators, (d) building of a community based around the aggregated ideals of the global South, (e) update the manual after a few years so that it factors in new developments and experiences, (f) consider how to use elements of the manuals in online training/self-learning sessions, and (g) lobby the donor community to financially support these workshops to achieve greater impact in their programmes.

Among the critques, the facilitators consider that the content of the Manual must be adapted for people without literacy or auditory skills. They also suggested that more spaces are needed for contact between facilitators interested in generating further capacities in communication for social and behaviour change. In this sense, in line with the partnership approach to capacity building, it is suggested to further strengthen the network of facilitators as some feel that a critical mass of people with the right skills in this field has not yet been reached.

Reflections on the experience of co-developing content for capacity building in SBCC

Content adjustments made to the manual "Voices with Purpose" responded not only to the necessary updates due to developments in the field of communication over time but also to the thematic challenges depending on the social, cultural, and political contexts in African countries. In any case, although in general common challenges and agendas between Latin America and Africa were identified, different developments were also evident in terms of the conceptualisation and use of communication, as well as the priorities and emphasis required to work in each country.

The methodological adjustments included the division of the manual into three parts: (1) One part is oriented to the participants of a given organisation with a step-by-step orientation accompanied by specific activities and matrices on how to design a communication strategy; (2) The second part describes different conceptual foundations necessary for the formulation of a communication strategy, and (3) a thrid part offers facilitators session by session guidelines for conductiong workshops with organisations. The three parts of the manual are connected through indications that refer in a complementary way to each other.

Although in principle the process of adapting the manual was considered a more technical process, the dynamics of drafting a new manual, its validation first as a pilot with social organisations in Colombia and then with a set of communication experts from across the African continent revealed several considerations not only cultural but also political of this type of South–South collaboration.

The draft and final Manual were used in the course of 2018 and 2019 to conduct training workshops in Namibia, South Africa, Zambia, and Zimbabwe. The facilitators remarked that the participatory methodology used in this Manual, unlike other methodologies, allowed the participants to take into account their political, economic, social, technological, legal, and environmental contexts and thus craft specific tools and inputs useful in achieving an effective communication strategy. The facilitators also remarked that the final communication strategy developed in the course of a given workshop felt "owned" by the participants and their organisation. While they are being trained to develop a communication strategy, they are also building capacities to train other colleagues. From his point of view, at the end of the day, the communication strategy that is developed through the workshops is owned by the participants and their organisations.

The communication experts that participated in the two initial FES training workshops expressed that the horizontal approach experienced and transmitted by the communication experts from Latin America was innovative and was well appreciated, in the sense that every person was considered to have the knowledge of their own context to work out the appropriate solutions to the problems affecting them. The role of the facilitator, educator, or mentor is to adopt the appropriate tools and pedagogy to lead the trainee to the solutions.

This approach widely used in Latin America has allowed civil society organisations, NGOs, and other nonstate actors to reach out to a wide range of grassroots and beneficiaries of their programmes to address development, human rights, elections, climate change, and other subjects. This horizontal and bottom-up approach to addressing the trainee's needs highlighted the teaching approach of the Brazilian educator Paulo Freire in his "Pedagogy of the Oppressed" that among others, proposed a new relationship between the trainer, the trainee, and the society. Freire calls the vertical or traditional pedagogy the "banking model of Education" because it treats the student as an empty vessel to be filled with knowledge, like a "piggy bank". He argues that pedagogy should instead treat the learner as a cocreator of knowledge.

To advocate sociopolitical and cultural justice as a dimension of the pluriverse raised by Arturo Escobar (2012), implies addressing the possibility of dialogues on commonalities and differences between Latin America and Africa in relation to communitarianism, communalisms, networks, and ties of cooperation and solidarity. It considers the characteristics of plurinational states seen from their own diversities, history, culture, interculturality, and relationships from the local to the global.

In this sense, thinking about the South–South relationship then implies, as Escobar (2012) suggests, starting from the need to think of places and communities within networks of relationships and forms of power that extend beyond the local, understanding that these places are always places not only of roots to a territory but also of negotiation and continuous transformation. "Thus, plurinationality and interculturality must be explicitly analysed as spatial processes that range from local to global, and from human to non-human" (p. 200).

Lessons learned and recommendations

Understanding the importance of generating elements that enable a better understanding of the challenges we have in fields such as the strengthening of the agency of social organisations in South–South cooperation, based on the Voices with Purpose experience, we put forward several lessons learned:

1) The elaboration of the first manual developed for Latin America, was initiated by Sara-Nathalie Brombart, the then director of the FES Latin America Media Project, and carried out by the authors, who in turn facilitated various training processes in Latin America. The Manual served as a platform to introduce decolonial perspectives into the writing of these resources.

2) Similarly, the elaboration of the second Manual updated and adapted to an African context, was initiated by Sara-Nathalie Brombart, the then director of fesmedia Africa of the FES, and carried out by the authors, who in turn were facilitators of the validation process. From the very beginning of this process, the African communication experts became co-producers of the content of the Manual.

3) This experience also illustrated the challenges and potential evidenced through the South–South collaboration for the strengthening of the agency and advocacy capacity of social organisations, mainly through the strengthening of their capacities in the use of communication strategies for social change. The challenges are not surprising—limited buy-in by donors, short-term time frames, limited resources of social organisations—but they do reiterate the need to invest more seriously and long term in capacity-building strengthening. The potential is clearly about how this experience shows that South–South collaboration in capacity-building strengthening can open up spaces for pluriverse dynamics and communicative justice in communication.

4) Arguably, the *fesmedia* Africa capacity-building initiative can be characterised primarily as a partnership approach given the multiple points of engagement of several actors from Latin America and Africa, the close collaboration required to adapt and refine the manuals, the inherent codesign process throughout the entire experience, and amalgamation of resources, experiences, and perspectives in the resource packet developed for the implementation of the initiative. Yet, it is also true, based on the feedback provided by the facilitators in their experience conducting workshops with civil society organisations in Africa, that the political commitment, and to a certain extent, the required resources, are not yet at the level that they should be in order to ensure sustained capacity-building.

5) The dialogue generated through the South–South collaboration served as a platform for a pluriverse that put in dialogue key communication concepts and paradigms. The engagement of African and Latin American practitioners contributed to the creation of a dialogue of knowledge rarely seen in the communication field. The appropriation of critical perspectives in both directions shows that South–South collaboration in SBCC capacity development is often a missed opportunity.

6) Assuming capacity-building processes from the notion of the pluriverse, in the sense of "Voices with Purpose", allows communication to be considered from a perspective that becomes political rather than technical, which makes it possible to question existing inequities and asymmetries to enable an authentic intercultural dialogue (Dussel, 2004) that contributes to systemic justice. As noted in the introduction to this book, "the pluriverse aims to foster dialogue and understanding in fair conditions by prioritising grassroots voices. These voices, capable of both expanding understanding

and generating conflict, are precisely those that liberal pluralism has marginalised" (Herrera-Huérfano, et al., 2022, p. 8).

Much remains to be done. One of the main challenges is to engage the donor community and decision makers for their buy-in process and to support sustained capacity-building efforts in SBCC and Communication for Social Change and Development. Meanwhile, the South–South cooperation and experience sharing must be pursued and strengthened for the sake of the pluriverse and its benefits, especially following the lessons learnt from the COVID-19 pandemic and in view of the ongoing Russia–Ukraine war.

Note

1. "Dialogue of knowledge" is the translation of "diálogo de saberes", a very common expression in Latin America to refer to different methodologies created to enable dialogue on equal terms between knowledge from different origins. Within them can be included the academy, the ancestral knowledge, the practice, and the experiences accumulated by the communities, among others. It is the closest materialization of what Santos (2016) calls "ecology of knowledge".

Bibliography

Beltrán, R., y Vega, J. (2012). Aprendizajes sobre la evaluación del diálogo y el debate en estrategias de comunicación y cambio social. El caso de la estrategia de eduentretenimiento + movilización social = cambio social. *Investigación & Desarrollo, 20*(2), 390–415.

Crisp, B. R., Swerissen, H., & Duckett, S. J. (2000). Four approaches to capacity building in health: Consequences for measurement and accountability. *Health Promotion International, 15*(2), 99–107.

Dussel, E. (2004). Transmodernidad e interculturalidad (Interpretación desde la Filosofía de la Liberación). En R. Fornet-Betancourt (Ed.), *Crítica Intercultural de la Filosofía Latinoamericana Actual* (pp. 123–160). Editorial Trotta. Retrieved April 23, from https://enriquedussel.com/txt/Textos_Articulos/347.2004_espa.pdf

Dutta, M. J. (2007). Communicating about culture and health: Theorizing culture-centered and cultural sensitivity approaches. *Communication Theory, 17*(3), 304–328.

Escobar, A. (2012). Más allá del desarrollo: Postdesarrollo y transiciones hacia el pluriverso. *Revista de Antropología Social, 21*, 23–62.

Escobar, A. (2018). *Otro posible es posible: Caminando hacia las transiciones desde Abya Yala/Afro/Latino-América.* Ediciones desde abajo.

Fals Borda, O. (1987). *Ciencia propia y colonialismo intelectual: Los nuevos rumbos* (3rd ed.). Carlos Valencia Editores.

Gudynas, E. (2011). Buen vivir: Germinando alternativas al desarrollo. América Latina en Movimiento. *Alai, 462*, 1–20.

Herrera-Huérfano, Pedro-Carañana, and Ochoa-Almanza. (2023). Dialogue of knowledges in the pluriverse. Pedro-Carañana, Herrera-Huerfano & Ochoa-Almanza (Editors). *Communicative Justice in the Pluriverse.* An International Dialogue. Routledge.

Obregon, R., & Lapsanski, C. (2022). Building capacity in communication for development and health promotion. In S. Melkote & A. Singhal (Eds.), *Handbook of communication and development* (pp. 262–283). Elgar Publishing.

Obregón, R., & Mosquera, M. (2005). Methodological challenges in health communication research. In O. Hemer & T. Tufte (Eds.), *Media and glocal change: Rethinking communication for development* (pp. 233–246). Nordicom Review.

Obregón, R., & Vega, J. (2019a). *Voices with purpose—a manual on communication strategies for development and social change: Conceptual module*. Friedrich Ebert Stiftung—Media Project for Southern Africa.

Obregón, R., & Vega, J. (2019b). *Voices with purpose—a manual on communication strategies for development and social change: Participant's module*. Friedrich Ebert Stiftung—Media Project for Southern Africa.

Obregón, R., & Vega, J. (2019c). *Voices with purpose—a manual on communication strategies for development and social change: Facilitator's module*. Friedrich Ebert Stiftung—Media Project for Southern Africa.

Rodríguez, C. (2000). *Estrategias de Comunicación*. Musavia.

Rodríguez, C., Obregon, R., y Vega, J. (2002). *Estrategias de Comunicación para el Cambio social*. Proyecto Latinoamericano de Medios de Comunicación, Friederich Ebert Stiftung.

Rogers, E. M. (1976). Communication and development the passing of the dominant paradigm. *Communication Research, 3*(2), 213–240.

Santos, B. (2007). Beyond abyssal thinking: From global lines to ecologies of knowledges. *Review (Fernand Braudel Center)*, 45–89.

Santos, B. (2016). Epistemologies of the South and the future. *From the European South: A Transdisciplinary Journal of Postcolonial Humanities, 1*, 17–29.

Servaes, J. (2000). Comunicación para el desarrollo: Tres paradigmas, dos modelos. *Temas y Problemas de Comunicación, 8*(10), 5–27. Retrieved April 6, 2022, from http://www.infoamerica.org/selecciones/articulo2.htm.

Torrico-Villanueva, E. (2017). La rehumanización, sentido último de la decolonización comunicacional. *Rev aportes de la comunicación, 23*, 31–38.

Torrico-Villanueva, E. (2018). La comunicación decolonial—Revista latinoamericana de Ciencias de la Comunicación. *Alaic, 15*(28). www.Alaic.Org/revista/index.Php/alaic/article/view/1150

Vega-Casanova, J. (2021). Disenchantment as a path toward autonomy: Orlando Fals Borda, participatory action research, communication and social change. In A. C. Suzina (Ed.), *The evolution of popular communication in Latin America: Palgrave studies in communication for social change* (pp. 109–128). Palgrave Macmillan.

Visvanathan, S. (2006). Alternative science. *Theory, Culture & Society, 23*(2–3), 164–169.

Waisbord, S. (2001). *Family tree of theories, methodologies and strategies in development communication*. Rockefeller Foundation.

5

CONSERVING THE MANGROVES? SOCIAL AND ENVIRONMENTAL CONFLICTS IN THE GULF OF GUAYAQUIL

The Case of Puerto El Morro, Posorja, and Isla Puná

Karen Andrade Mendoza and Galo Plaza Vanegas

Translated by: Catalina Campuzano Rodríguez

Context

The situation of the ecosystems and protected areas in the Gulf of Guayaquil[1] reflects a plurality of visions and actions. Some actions are for the use and others for the conservation of the area's natural resources. Thus, throughout the territory of the estuary, there are different activities such as industrial, maritime, tourism, agriculture, aquaculture, fishing, crustacean, and mollusc harvesting, among many others.

Mangroves are natural spaces that provide many key services to the ecosystem, ranging from sediment capture to coastal protection to producing a large amount of wildlife. Mangroves are freshwater and saltwater floodplains that regulate the salt concentration in estuaries, as well as protect coastlines. They are dominated by soft, nutrient-rich soils. Ecuador has 161,835 hectares (ha) of mangroves. Of these, 68,161.59 (ha) are under community control and are managed through the Agreements for Sustainable Use and Custody of Mangroves (Ministry of Environment of Ecuador, 2017).

In the early 1990s, the reduction of mangrove areas in the Gulf was intensive. A push for regulatory reforms sought to protect them through the creation of protected areas and protective forests (Jama & Coronel, 2019). However, since then, "Ecuador has lost approximately 27% of the original mangrove forest, especially due to aquaculture production, urbanisation, and natural resource extraction in this region" (Zhiminaicela-Cabrera et al., 2020, p. 274). The main cause of this loss was the conversion to build shrimp farms and urban areas, which generated

DOI: 10.4324/9781003316220-6

environmental, social, and institutional effects/impacts (Bravo, 2019). Environmental degradation has effects not only on nature but also on societies. Such degradation produces a deep environmental injustice because it increases poverty and increases corruption in public sectors. Hence, it is important to involve all social actors in conservation, including the Autonomous Decentralised Governments (GADs) (Carvajal & Santillán, 2019).

The Gulf of Guayaquil is extensively populated, with recurrent natural resource exploitation since the 18th century. Timber extraction, agriculture, aquaculture, and fishing are activities with a strong environmental impact. The area is of central interest to the shrimp industry, a situation that threatens the preservation of mangroves outside protected areas. Today's world is at a crossroads for peasant and Indigenous communities, even more so if their way of life is directly connected to the preservation, protection, and use of nature in the framework of the pluriverse. These communities that protect nature are continuously confronted with the interests of the capitalist world system and its dynamics of large-scale industrialised production as a model of development. Such dynamics are characteristic of the Monoculture of productivity, represented by industrial conglomerates, which are generally supported by the government.

Dynamics and social conceptions on development, progress, and coloniality imposed by the Western world remain as they are underpinned by patriarchal capitalist thinking where nature is separated from humans (Shiva, 2019, p. 6). The demand for resources from industrialised countries has an impact on people's lives in the south. Ecuador has a strong dependence on the extraction and commercialisation of natural resources for the generation of economic and financial resources. Several actors are involved: the government and its institutions, private enterprises and industries, environmental organisations and social activists and local communities, their representatives and leaders. These last actors are confronted with the Monoculture of capitalist productivity centred on economic benefits, private property, and fast economic production versus the need for habitat conservation and preservation of the territory and the cultural heritage.

For many decades, the communities and families of the Gulf of Guayaquil have recognised themselves as ancestral inhabitants of the region. During the 20th century, the original inhabitants of the Gulf of Guayaquil integrated with the peasant population of the area and identified themselves as Cholos Mestizos, although a Huancavilca ancestry is also recognised in the Gulf. However, at the beginning of the 21st century, a process of reethnicisation has strengthened their identification as a Punae people,[2] especially on Puná Island, according to the testimony of Vicente Quinde (Personal Communication, 3 June 2019).[3] In their daily activities, they express a deep connection with nature. From the Comuneros' point of view, "the defence of mangrove resources is essential for their survival", it provides the livelihood of their families through the practice of collecting crabs, which is an ancestral tradition.

The overlapping of protected natural areas with areas of aquaculture production and maritime activities complicates the possibilities for conservation of the Gulf's biodiversity and the preservation of traditional community practices. In addition, communities face the weakness of state institutions to exercise control and compliance with public policies. There are continuous tensions between the communities surrounding the mangrove swamp and the aquaculture industry and government authorities, both in the fisheries and conservation areas.

The purpose of this chapter is to deepen our understanding of the multidimensionality of environmental conflicts and their impact on the lives of the populations in the area of the Gulf of Guayaquil, which reveals a plurality of dynamics and knowledge around conservation -some of which are connected to alternatives to development and the urgency that communities have of developing a general framework of communicative justice in which they can reclaim their cultural baggage and their demands are attended. This work is based on ethnographic research carried out over three years in the Gulf of Guayaquil, in the communities of El Morro, La Puná, and Posorja. The authors interviewed around 20 activists and community leaders and reviewed media and documentary information. In addition, we visited the Gulf of Guayaquil to recognise and expose the multiple dimensions of the environmental problems in the area and the role of communication. The investigation highlights the difficult panorama for the conservation of biodiversity and the pressure exerted by economic sectors on natural resources and recognises the importance of communication as a conciliatory tool between community and industrial activities in the area.

Environmental justice in the conservation of natural and cultural heritage

Latin America is a diverse space, both socially and culturally. This implies a multiplicity of uses and forms of exploitation of nature by social and community groups. Ecuador controls the use of natural resources with a broad regulatory framework. The processes of appropriation and exploitation of ecosystems and their resources are tied to coloniality of power (Quijano, 2000), which is visible in the distinction imposed by the state regarding the priority sectors of the economy. This makes the growth of the aquaculture industry possible at the cost of a reduction of natural areas.

Environmental studies involve incorporating a wide variety of sociological, political, economic, cultural, biological, and ecosystemic sustainability knowledges. The pluriverse seeks to recognise and interpret all alternative realities to development (Escobar, 2012, 2018). The pluriversal perspective seeks to understand the diversity of realities and the confluence of cultures and interdependent relationships with the habitat in opposition to the prevailing industrial pressure on communal territories and conservation areas. Thus, this view is an alternative to the hegemonic paradigm of modernity.

From a Latin American political ecology perspective, it is important to expose the power relations surrounding nature, its control, and appropriation by social actors, as well as the need to preserve resources in the face of the interests of a multiplicity of sociopolitical agents. "Nature is socially constructed" and "nature . . . is a universal means of production" that relies on modern science for the accumulation of capital (Escobar, 1999, p. 7, 1996, p. 46). Latin American ecological policies have not favoured the dialogue of knowledges between science and popular wisdom. On the contrary, popular knowledge is often neglected in the design of public policies because it is considered less relevant under the pressure of economic development currents (Alimondia et al., 2017; Leff, 2017; Delgado Ramos, 2017; Alimondia, 2001).

Pressure on ecosystems originates from different sectors, both from the industrial sphere and from the populations surrounding conservation areas. Conflicts are multiplying and although solutions can be observed, there is little will on the part of political and economic elites to promote timely and appropriate solutions. There is evidence of the expressions and expectations emerging from "the rhetoric of development, sometimes called developmentalism" (Kothari et al., 2019, p. 35), where there is an ideological and cosmological imposition of the modern capitalist world, with a great affectation of the cultures and societies subordinated to a process of coloniality (Escobar, 2010, 2015; Quijano, 2000).

Community issues move in different temporalities, in the face of capitalist production based on power disputes. They express alternative systemic processes based on the protection of land and territory (Santos, 2009). Through self-management, cooperative organisation, and solidarity, narratives are woven as a commitment to communicative justice, which make visible human relations connected to the rights of nature, based on the idea of environmental justice (Escobar, 2018).

Environmental justice implies the right to environmental protection, the application of laws related to public health, and sharing of the externalities and costs of pollution in an equitable manner (López, 2014). In this case, it is the Gulf communities who suffer the consequences of pollution and ecosystem degradation. Environmental justice is fully in line with social justice that seeks a fairer ordering for society, where there is a possibility of decent human survival, key features of nature whose loss would be irreversible are protected, and the historical and idiosyncratic character of sustainability is valued (Riechmann, 2003, p. 104). Sustainability fought for by community members and peasants in the face of shrimp farms

On the other hand, environmental injustice is centred on inequalities that affect human well-being and duties towards nature. Here, environmental discrimination against indigenous or vulnerable peoples is added to the environmental impact of productive activities, limiting the use of environmental benefits (Hervé Espejo, 2015). This explains why over the last 20 years the area has experienced multiple dispossessions of its communities.

Environmental issues show deep sociocultural differences between local actors and trends in the exercise of power from the elite sectors. Several economic and industrial sectors find development niches in natural ecosystems, such as aquaculture, fisheries, and maritime activity. Changes in the ecological distribution of environmental conflicts and their spectrum of incidence on the economic status, ethnicity, and identity of peoples and their territorial rights must be expressed in collective terms of environmental justice (Martínez-Alier, 2019, p. 183). But this idea is continually not incorporated into the analysis of environmental conflicts, let alone in the search for solutions.

Pressure from the economic, financial, and industrial sectors on forests and wild ecosystems threatens the very preservation and sustainability of endemic species. They also continually transform the lives of nearby human communities. This leads communities and their activists to "promote a viable alternative against ruthless capitalist expansion aimed at reaffirming the knowledge, power, and nature of coloniality" (Escobar, 2015, pp. 264–265). Aquaculture and industrial fishing are economic sectors of great impact in the Gulf of Guayaquil. This development model responds to a global strategy of persistent exercise of domination and control over subaltern social sectors, as is the case of the communities in the area.

Each territorial space, based on its cultural cosmogony, seeks environmental awareness in recognition of rights and demands the protection of the habitats that surround them. The pressure exerted by capital and the extractive tendencies imposed by neoliberal modernity subordinates the very survival of social groups to a constant struggle to sustain their ways of life, territories, identities, and practices for the conservation of natural and cultural heritages (Kothari et al., 2019; Escobar, 2014, 2018).

The social struggle from local human groups makes visible the importance of the territory as an object of ecological and cultural transitions. This struggle is centred on demands for the indigenous and peasant control of the territory, to confront the multiple ecological and social crises (Escobar, 2014). In the Gulf of Guayaquil, different communities and ethnic groups coexist with wild ecosystems. They possess ancestral knowledge and traditions that are attached to their relationship with the habitats that surround them. An important part of their cultural heritage has transformed over time, but a relationship of interdependence with the mangrove ecosystems persists.

Control of the territory is not possible without the existence of norms and policies in accordance with the needs of the different sectors. Government institutions and civil society should play an important role in the formulation and implementation of environmental projects, since "there is no conservation without control of the territory and any conservation strategy must be based on the knowledge and cultural practices of the communities" (Escobar, 2014, pp. 78–80). The territory should be conceived as the place where people's capacities are enhanced through inclusive projects. Conservation processes are evidenced through the "Mangrove User Agreements", which are attached to the territory as a "source of culture and identity" (Escobar, 2015, pp. 266–267).

The local inhabitants of the Gulf of Guayaquil seek the vindication of their cultural and territorial rights, based on the recovery of their cultural baggage and their local representations of social life, which is, in turn, based on the direct relationship they maintain with the ecosystems in which they live. For this reason, organisations must be strengthened through participatory communication and the appropriation of the territory. The communities demand attention to their requirements from the Ecuadorian State. Based on the notion of *Buen Vivir,* they propose an exercise of social–political–economic autonomy within their territories and decoloniality of the power of the economic elites (Chuji et al., 2019; Quijano, 2014).

In this case, it is evident in the environmental and economic pressure exerted by the shrimp industry and the colonialist state on the communities and human populations of the Gulf. Capitalism adapts and reshapes traditional patterns of daily life. In response, struggles and both positive and negative experiences emerge aiming to promote a diversity of alternatives, some of which "come from Indigenous peoples, such as *Vivir Bien*" (Solón, 2016, pp. 8–9).

From the indigenous cosmovision, everything is connected in *Buen Vivir.* The imposition of models that are not in line with their worldviews and the exploitation of natural resources drives "the defence and recovery of ancestral lands and territories", as well as the strengthening of their organisational processes (Rodríguez Salazar, 2016, pp. 84–85). In 2008, the concept of *Sumak Kawsay* (Good Living) was incorporated into the Political Constitution of Ecuador, based on a principle of reciprocity, a proposal to recover the identity of peoples and reconciliation with nature (Macas, 2011). This constitutional protection, although systematically violated, also provides a useful tool for environmental justice.

Local populations require autonomy to develop their projects and initiatives and to reflect on the proposals generated by the government and the private sector, both in the productive-economic sphere and in the conservation of natural areas. At the same time, a continuous interdependence between the community and modern society is evident. The provision of basic services is not the only demand of communities; crucially, they defend their capacity to sustain their territories and build their ways of life.

Environmental conflicts and the demand for communicative justice

This section describes how the environmental complexity in the Gulf of Guayaquil demonstrates the need and demand for communicative justice from the communities in the rural parishes of El Morro, Posorja, and La Puná. This communicative justice is necessary to face external agents such as private companies, governmental and nongovernmental organisations, and the Ecuadorian state.

Mangroves and coastal zones are spaces for human development, which need to be protected and regulated in order to maximise their conservation. Government policy determines the use and exploitation of the territory. Mangrove ecosystems are essential for the protection of other surrounding areas, such as dry and fog ecosystems. Many species of fauna and flora converge in a humid and resource-rich ecosystem (Ministerio del Ambiente de Ecuador, 2014). Given this, constant monitoring and control of the sites by the Ministry of Environment are necessary, as restoration models for degraded ecosystems are a priority for their preservation (Negrete et al., 2019; Pozo-Cajas et al., 2019).

The Ministry of Environment is committed to socioenvironmental education, fisheries monitoring, and registration of crab catches in each of the communes that have concessions as mangrove users (Santillán & Rosero, 2019). In addition, sustainable mangrove management policies are applied, and workshops on fire prevention and management of agricultural products (such as cocoa) are provided. These activities are carried out in the communities or near the environmental reserves. Some of them are accompanied by nongovernmental organisations such as Conservation International (CI) World Wildlife Fund (WWF) and WildAid Ecuador and occasionally private companies. The results of these activities are socialised through digital social networks like Twitter and Facebook using hashtags such as *#ProtejemosElManglar* (WeProtectTheMangrove) and *#TusAreasProtegidas* (YourProtectedAreas).

These NGOs are part of activist networks with local leaders and environmental activists which is fundamental to consolidate, in order to promote causes and principles of conservation from a "rational understanding of their interests" (Escobar, 2010). These initiatives combine creativity, information, and media, as well as political processes with a vision of rights, and community traditions and customs (Escobar, 2018).

The figure of Custodians of the Mangrove[4] commits users to report any aggression, destruction, or affectation of the mangrove but does not guarantee compliance with the commitments or a response to the complaint. "The control bodies also face problems in carrying out effective monitoring of mangroves, among others, due to a lack of personnel, equipment (boats, fuel, and engines) and limited inter-institutional coordination" (Reyes-Bueno et al., 2019, p. 127). These factors intensify environmental conflicts, with various social and economic actors disputing access to the territory for its exploitation and use, with the continuous growth of shrimp farms and populated areas.

For environmental activists and academics, such as Irma Jurrius[5] (Personal Communication, 21 August 2019), Participatory community monitoring is essential for mangrove management. This process involves the evaluation and monitoring of the actions of the organisations working in the area and includes the whole community. This generates daily communication practices for care and conservation. This is a response to the need for a strategy to raise people's awareness to bring about changes in behaviour in favour of the rights of nature.

There is an urgent need for greater communication between the actors involved in the territorial conflicts in the Gulf of Guayaquil, to generate trustworthy channels of communication and facilitate political mobilisation to "defend the life project of the communities". Information becomes an important element to be shared and at the same time to generate communication channels that enable greater connectivity between the different social and community networks existing in each community.

Communication must be present in the development and execution of public policies and compliance with norms, to enhance the well-being of citizens and society (Torrico-Villanueva, 2017, 2016). Communication is necessary to enact public policies for the visibility of organisations, the circulation of discourses, and the dialogues between diverse cultural, social, economic, and political actors.

Communicative justice makes visible a plurality of practices and forms of communication that provide alternatives to traditional media and digital social networks. It implies an exercise of autonomy in decision-making and the circulation of information among the members of each community, within the framework of the rights to communication and information. Communicative justice recognises community knowledges (Santos, 2010, p. 200). It understands the human experience in relation to its history and its territory based on four axes connected with the philosophy of *Buen Vivir*. These are the land, the assembly (family, community), work (as a pillar of life, collectively), and the philosophy of enjoyment (celebration) (Martínez Luna, 2015).

Communicative justice draws on the four principles of communication based on *Vivir Bien*: (i) to know how to listen; (ii) to know how to share; (iii) to know how to live in harmony; and (iv) to know how to dream of a future that announces the good news of life in its fullness (Contreras Baspineiro, 2021, p. 210). All this implies considering the variety of worldviews and relations with nature of the actors converging in the Gulf.

The reproduction of traditional and sustainable ways of life on the Island would surely benefit from a wide application of the principles of *Buen Vivir*. As developed next, communities aim to practice harmonious communication and relations among members and with nature, but the broader economic model and communicative relations hinder the possibilities of Goof Living.

Huancavilca leader, Agapito Riscos,[6] says his ancestors were born in the Gulf of Guayaquil and explains that the economic well-being of each of the families in the region is tied to nature (Personal Communication, 18 September 2019). Many families keep transmitting culture from generation to generation regarding the care and use of biodiversity. Ancestral activities are encouraged by the Custodians of the Mangrove programme, a strategic governmental denomination for directing "economic benefits" to the communities.

On the Ecuadorian coast, the consumption of mangrove crustaceans and molluscs is common. Crabs and black shells are considered a delicacy by many people, which generates an economic circle of consumption and production. It is estimated that in the Gulf of Guayaquil at least 150,620 units of red crab are extracted in a given day (Ministry of Environment, 2018, July 28). Despite these figures, collecting families have not improved their economic conditions. Intermediaries limit their capacity to commercialise the products and obtain benefits (Mendoza et al., 2019). For this reason, associations and communities in the Gulf of Guayaquil seek to get organised to eliminate intermediaries. Currently, one of the main objectives of social organisations is to strengthen the artisanal and sustainable market, as well as unity between communities in the Union of Associations, which is a regulatory body. Some of their struggles have had positive results. For example, the Ministry of Environment granted a concession of 10,800 hectares to the Mangrove Users Association of the community of Cerritos de Los Morreños in 2011.

The Decentralised Autonomous Government (GAD, in Spanish) of El Morro is the entity that maintains direct relations with the Ministry of Environment, Water and Ecologic Transition (MAE, in Spanish). In this town, there are five organisations of artisanal fishermen, who are regulated and trained through conferences given by representatives of the MAE and by members of international organisations such as WildAid and CI. In El Morro, mingas[7] are held every month to collect rubbish along the riverbanks, with the participation of the women of the community. These activities maintain the dynamics of collective work through communication for *Buen Vivir*, that is, by learning how to live in harmony.

Since 1990, the dolphin population has been reduced by almost half in the Puerto El Morro area. The reasons are related to bycatch, boat strikes, pollution, and habitat degradation (Félix & Burneo, 2020; Félix et al., 2017). Alex Escalante[8] says this problem affects the life of the El Morro[9] population, as it is becoming increasingly difficult to encounter dolphins on sightseeing trips and this reduces visitor interest in the area (Personal communication, 16 June 2019). In response, the villagers are promoting initiatives for shellfish production and mangrove conservation linked to their cultural background and in the frame of living in harmony. Nonetheless, they feel their efforts are insufficient.

Negative environmental and social impacts highlight the need for communicative justice associated with knowing how to dream of life to the fullest. For example, Diana Panchana,[10] considers that the Deepwater Port affects not only wildlife and mangroves but also the daily life of the people (Personal Communication, 29 April 2022). Likewise, Jorge Banchón[11] points out that the population of Posorja is undergoing a strong social, economic, and cultural transformation due to the growing presence of the fishing industry and high port activity (Personal Communication, 5 June 2019). These and other industrial activities impose impediments to fulfil *Buen Vivir* and the communities' ability to dream life accordingly.

In the last two decades, mangrove concessionaires have filed complaints against shrimp farmers, demanding fines and surveillance by the authorities, without positive results in most cases (Zhiminaicela-Cabrera et al., 2020; ASAMBLA, 01/2021). Such is the case of the Asociación Río de Agua Viva, which denounced the deforestation of mangroves in its territory, without adequate attention from the authorities. This situation is evidence of a communication monoculture of large industrial conglomerates and state organisations that violate the sense of "knowing how to listen" of the communities that are heirs to the dynamics of *Buen Vivir*.

According to Xavier Flores,[12] social networks have made conflicts and complaints in the area visible (Personal Communication, 21 September 2019). However, litigation for nature fails when it is too big and is not accompanied by popular mobilisation. Tarcisio Granizo[13] argues that the Ministry of Environment is showing its weakness in the application of public policy, given its lack of action on the shrimp farmers' infractions (Personal Communication, 16 January 2020).

Collaboration between communities and sectional autonomous governments is occasional and rarely translates into results. The population aspires to improve their living conditions and expects support from the authorities. The difficulty lies in achieving long-term results and not depending on political will. In addition, the presence of political parties generates conflicts over natural resources and land concessions, which have a strong impact on the communities. Growing tensions between organisations and government authorities are intensified by the insecurity suffered by artisanal fishermen and crabbers.[14] Feeling abandoned and neglected by government actions is a recurrent sentiment often leading to despair.

The environmental problems in the Gulf of Guayaquil receive very little coverage in the Ecuadorian and international media. Internationally, Guayaquil is barely represented. The human catastrophe experienced by its inhabitants during the COVID-19 pandemic was shown around the world lacking context and explanation. At the national level, information is occasional and depends on specific events such as complaints about environmental damage and contamination, mangrove clean-up campaigns, possible tourism promotions, and political management. Some print[15] and digital[16] media have exposed the situation of the population of Puerto El Morro and other communities surrounding the mangrove ecosystems of the Gulf of Guayaquil to the public. However, there is no evidence of concrete actions by authorities or public opinion to raise awareness among the population and the sectors in power. Scarce and biased media treatment, as well as lack of media public policies and social mobilisation in support of communities, reflect the hegemonic monoculture of communication. Based on corporate and political control, monocultural communication permeates into societies and communities and makes it more difficult to engage in processes of communicative, environmental, and economic justice. Its main features are inattentiveness and unresponsiveness.

The leaders of the Artisanal Fishermen's associations and the inhabitants use social media to publicise problems that arise in their communities and in the wilderness areas. However, there is little internet coverage in the area. Currently, the accelerated advance of digital technologies allows the incorporation of new models and mechanisms of information sharing based on interactivity and participation of most actors, which promotes greater collaboration, participation, and plurality (Escobar, 2018). Thus, diversity, justice, and equity must come together to promote the Good Living of populations and their societies. Above all, they must guarantee the autonomy and sufficiency of the social groups surrounding sensitive ecosystems, such as mangroves. It is, thus, key to encourage a transition from the monoculture of communication based on not listening and not responding to pluriversal communicative justice. Cooperation for environmental and economic justice faces impediments established by monoculture, while processes of communicative justice aim to foster it. There are limitations to fair communication practices, which make communicative injustice still prevail. However, applying the learnings of communicative justice can contribute to overcoming such limitations.

The greatest strength of communicative justice lies in "knowing how to listen" through face-to-face contact and the permanent promotion of dialogue between members of the communities. These personal and assembly-based communications maintain solidarity networks, which are activated when the issue is of general interest. During the COVID-19 pandemic, community members opted to meet on Zoom, but by 2022, it has reverted to fortnightly meetings in most locations. Communication through digital media is limited, due to a lack of efficient internet coverage throughout the Gulf area.

The evidence of a communication monoculture in the area and, therefore, the communication injustice it entails is visible on the Facebook pages of the local governments of El Morro, Puná, and Posorja. They post about activities related to their competencies, but very little information regarding the follow-up of environmental complaints. In addition, there are few digital media in the area: Primicias TV managed by the Municipality of Guayaquil, and TV Mar Posorja managed by the parish government. In both cases, the participation of representatives who do not identify politically with these organisations is censored.

The leaders of the communes and their associations complain about the lack of coverage of the problems of their communities by the national and local media. There are very few reports on the area each year, which is evidence of a communicative injustice. This leads to a feeling of abandonment, which they try to counteract by increasing the exposure of their social dynamics through daily community solidarity and, more recently, using digital social networks. Communities intend to strengthen the internal communication of members with the use of WhatsApp., They also aim to communicate with the broader public opinion through their Facebook and Twitter accounts.

In each of the community associations, the leaders maintain personal contact with each of the other members. The leaders of these associations verbally pass on information about the progress of the assembly issues or news of community interest. Face-to-face relations are indispensable to sustain the bonds of solidarity and trust between members. In localities where there is internet service, calls for meetings are made by WhatsApp message, and in those where there is no service, calls for meetings are made through flyers. Aspects of communicative justice are slowly being reestablished, based on "knowing how to share". It is in the community assemblies where community members analyse their problems and try to find solutions based on their worldviews and daily life. This dynamic engages each of the members in a democratic exercise of participation for the formulation of agendas and action plans for conflict resolution.

Digital social networks have made it possible to make visible and inform about the assembly processes, especially about the crab ban controls, in which the Unión de Cangrejeros del Golfo De Guayaquil (Guayaquil Gulf Crab Fishermen's Union) participates with other associations. These digital social networks use videos to denounce the invaders who violate the closed season regulations, carry out fishing practices with trammel nets, deforest or invade and expropriate different resources from protected areas, and reserve zones through the figures of mangrove custodians. They are also used to inform the public about the progress of complaints about mangrove logging, training, or information events to be held by the GADs or nongovernmental organisations, as well as their results.

On several occasions, the leaders of the associations of mangrove users have protested about the impact of shrimp farms, the bans on crab fishing, and the treatment they receive from environmental authorities. Between 2019 and 2020, several mobilisations were carried out in the city of Guayaquil by crab farmers' organisations. In addition, actions to demand protection from the increasing insecurity in the Gulf of Guayaquil and the need for conservation were presented to the authorities, at both the local and national levels. Given the strength and wide dissemination of the monoculture of communication, local media did not echo these mobilisations. The media decided to show those issues that were useful for the economic elites and rendered invisible the daily struggles of the affected population. These exercises of denial are clearly an attack on the communities' right to communication, thus increasing communicative injustice, preventing their demands for the protection of the mangrove and the maintenance of their traditional practices of care and preservation from being heard.

Conclusions

The development of the shrimp industry in Ecuador overrides the principles of conservation of mangrove resources. The hegemonic discourse of the monoculture of capitalist development productivity is dominant in the country and calls for an intensification in productive areas, even when this increases the impact on wild areas and breaks with the principle of "know how to live in harmony" as a fundamental key to *Buen Vivir* and systemic justice. Under this criterion, nature is transformed into goods and commodities, making it difficult to sustain environmental justice procedures.

Indigenous, fishermen, peasant, and other local communities advocate for communicative justice among them and with political authorities and economic elites. The proposal of communication for *Sumak Kawsay* or Good Living is of particular relevance. However, communities feel ignored and, thus, demand communicative justice.

The relationship between shrimp farmers and mangrove users is tense. Community members report frequent clashes with shrimp farmers but do not find adequate responses from the environmental authorities. Many community members and leaders claim that the shrimp farmers do not listen to their demands and do not support the communities but only pollute and destroy the mangrove, resulting in environmental and communicative injustice. This situation is replicated in their feelings towards local government authorities and public institutions. This practice is contrary to the principle of "knowing how to listen", which is part of communication for *Buen Vivir*.

The communities of El Morro, Posorja, and La Puná are resisting this domination through denunciations and social mobilisations that demand answers from the authorities. The community members and guardians of the mangrove adhere to the Custody Agreements, as these reflect their ancestral practices of using the resource within the framework of "knowing how to live in harmony" and "knowing how to share". Community leaders implement communicative and noncommunicative actions such as *mingas*, encounters for the cleaning, care, and protection of crustaceans, reinforcing the collective bonds of the communities settled in the gulf. Their forms of assembly communication maintain the bonds of solidarity and are the means for the exercise of the right to communication, self-determination in the territory, and the preservation of social organisation through the artisanal fishermen's associations.

The communities embrace the conservation issues imposed by the government and nongovernmental organisations, to bring sustainability to their way of life. Their lives preserve traditional cultural features consistent with coexistence and respect for the mangrove. For this reason, their notion of Good Living is related to living in harmony in a healthy environment with the capacity to provide communities with the resources for their survival, in addition to sustaining their territorial autonomy and their capacity for self-management.

Local actors seek to make their problems visible, but the local and national media say little about their situation. The media discourse tends to promote a conception of capitalist development that is alien to the traditional practices of mangrove resource use. This is evidence of a communitarian injustice since the communities have no influence on the dissemination of formal information and are only now taking steps towards the appropriation of digital technological resources.

Social networks are an accessible dissemination space to sustain communication outside the communities. However, other forms of communication are essential in areas with little internet coverage such as coastal towns or Isla Puná. Limited internet coverage affects the ability of local organisations to maintain contact not only with the outside world but also with local populations.

Other limitations come from external actors who impose their notion of natural resources on the communities, measuring and shaping the worldview of the population regarding these resources. Private enterprises, international environmental organisations, state institutions, and sectional bodies (prefecture, municipality, etc.) examine nature as resources that can be exploited and commercialised for their economic value. On the other hand, communities and their leaders promote the conservation of their natural and cultural heritage, based on innovative ideas and life projects. For this reason, they demand spaces for continuous participation in actions implemented by state and government bodies.

The difficulty in making the voices of local communities visible and heard translates into a communicative injustice, making the communities' pluriverse invisible and their demands unheard. Communication for Good Living demands: To be heard, to have the capacity for self-management and organisation, and communal solidarity ties through which "a future that announces the good news of life in its fullness" (Contreras Baspineiro, 2021) can be projected in coherence with the expectations of its inhabitants. These qualities are made invisible by the dominant economic and political actors, which hinders local actors in their possibilities of generating sustainability and conservation of the mangroves.

Notes

1. The Gulf of Guayaquil is the largest of the Pacific coast of South America with 230 km, named after the Guayas River. It is home to 13 islands and a few islets. La Puná is the largest island in mainland Ecuador, followed by Santa Clara and Isla del Muerto.
2. The Confederation of Indigenous Nationalities of Ecuador (CONAIE) accompanied, on two occasions, the Congress of the Punae People of Ecuador. At the organisational level and in the face of the economic crisis in the territories, it ratified the unity of peasants, fisherfolk, community members, and organisations (II Congress, October 2021, Puná Island).
3. President of the Puna Association
4. Art. 103 of the Organic Environmental Code, Registro Oficial No. 983 of 12 April 2017.
5. Consultant for the German Technical Cooperation—GIZ and Technical Advisor of the Universidad Técnica Particular de Loja (UTPL).)
6. President of the association of crabbers and fishermen *Por la Gracia de Dios*, and president of the Punta de Piedra commune in the Gulf of Guayaquil.
7. Refer to collaborative work in the indigenous perspective.
8. President of the Ecoclub Delfines. Tour operator in Puerto El Morro.
9. Approximately 50 families have been working there and have formed four tour operators for 20 years.
10. President of the Citizens' Assembly of Posorja
11. Former President of the Association of Artisanal Fishermen of Posorja
12. Constitutional Lawyer, Guayaquilian, environmental activist.
13. National Director of World Wildlife Found—Ecuador
14. This is due to the steady growth of crime in the area.
15. Journalist Blanca Moncada, from the newspaper El Expreso del Ecuador, has carried out several reports on the subject between 2019 and 2020.

16. Most public institutions, private and nongovernmental organisations, as well as social and political leaders have and use social networks on the internet to communicate and publicise their actions, such as Facebook, Twitter, Instagram, and WhatsApp.

References

Alimondia, H. (2001). *La naturaleza colonizada*. CLACSO.

Alimondia, H., Toro Pérez, K., & Martín, F. (Coords.). (2017). *Ecología Política Latinoamericana: Pensamiento crítico, diferencia latinoamericana y rearticulación epistémica*. CLACSO.

ASAMBLA. (2021, January). *Actualización de la evaluación de impacto social participativo de la camaronera PUNÁ, Isla Puná, Parroquia Puná Cantón Guayaquil Provincia del Guayas*. Asesores Ambientales Latinoamericanos Cía. Ltd.

Bravo, M. (2019). Los acuerdos para el uso sustentable y custodia del manglar: Una estrategia de conservación, comanejo y asignación de derechos de uso. In N. Molina Moreira & F. Galvis (Comps.), *Primer Congreso Manglares de América*. Universidad Espíritu Santo. Samborondón-Ecuador.

Carvajal, R., y Santillán, X. (2019). *Plan de Acción Nacional para la Conservación de los Manglares del Ecuador Continental*. Ministerio del Ambiente de Ecuador, Conservación Internacional Ecuador, Organización de las Naciones Unidas para la Educación, la Ciencia y la Cultura (UNESCO) y la Comisión Permanente del Pacífico Sur (CPPS). Proyecto Conservación de Manglar en el Pacífico Este Tropical. http://conservation.org.ec/wp-content/uploads/2019/07/PAN-Manglares-Ecuador.pdf

Contreras Baspineiro, A. (2021). Communication and Vivir Bien/Buen Vivir: In the care of our common home. In *The evolution of popular communication in Latin America* (pp. 209–227). Palgrave Macmillan. https://doi.org/10.1007/978-3-030-62557-3_12

Chuji, M., Rengifo, G., y E. Gudynas. (2019). Buen Vivir. En A. Kothari, A. Salleh, A. Escobar, F., Demaria, & A. Acosta (Coords.), *Pluriverse: A postdevelopment dictionary*. Icaria Antrazyt.

Delgado Ramos, G. C. (2017). Hacia la conformación de nuevas perspectivas socio-ecológicas: Una lectura desde el caso de la Ecología Política. En H. Alimondia, K., Toro Pérez, & F. Martín (Coords.), *Ecología Política Latinoamericana. Pensamiento crítico, diferencia latinoamericana y rearticulación epistémica*. CLACSO.

Escobar, A. (1996). Constructing nature: Elements for a post-structural political ecology. *Elsevier Science, 28*(4), 325–343.

Escobar, A. (1999). After nature: Steps to an anti-essentialist political ecology. *Current Anthropology, 40*(1), 1–3.

Escobar, A. (2010). *Territorios de diferencia: Lugar, movimientos, vida, redes*. Envión.

Escobar, A. (2012). Más allá del desarrollo: Postdesarrollo y transiciones hacia el pluriverso. *Revista de Antropología Social, 21*, 23–62.

Escobar, A. (2014). *Sentipensar con la Tierra: Nuevas lecturas sobre desarrollo, territorio y diferencia*. UNAULA.

Escobar, A. (2015). *Ecología Política de la Globalidad y la Diferencia*. CLACSO.

Escobar, A. (2018). *Designs for the pluriverse: Radical interdependence, autonomy, and the making of worlds*. Duke University Press.

Félix, F., & Burneo, S. (2020, September 3). Imminent risk of extirpation for two bottlenose dolphin communities in the Gulf of Guayaquil, Ecuador. *Frontiers in Marine Science*. https://doi.org/10.3389/fmars.2020.537010

Félix, F., Coronel, A., Vintimilla, M., & Bayas-Rea, R. (2017, June 2). Decreasing population trend in coastal bottlenose dolphin (*Tursiops truncatus*) from the Gulf of Guayaquil,

Ecuador. *Aquatic Conservation: Marine and Freshwater Ecosystems*, *27*(4), 856–866. https://onlinelibrary.wiley.com/doi/abs/10.1002/aqc.2763

Hervé Espejo, D. (2015). *Justicia Ambiental y Recursos Naturales*. Ediciones Universitarias de Valparaíso.

Jama, B., & Coronel, J. (2019). Detección de cambios en manglares de la Isla Puná a través de sensores remotos durante el periodo 1985–2019. In N. Molina Moreira & F. Galvis (Comps.), *Manglares de América*. Universidad Espíritu Santo.

Kothari, A., Salleh, A., Escobar, A., Demaria, F., & Acosta, A. (Coords.). (2019). *Pluriverse: A postdevelopment dictionary*. Icaria Antrazyt. www.ehu.eus/documents/6902252/120 61123/Ashish+Kothari+et+al-Pluriverse+A+Post-Development+Dictionary-2019. pdf/c9f05ea0-d2e7-8874-d91c-09d11a4578a2

Leff, E. (2017). Las relaciones de poder del conocimiento en el campo de la Ecología política: Una mirada desde el sur. En H. Alimondia, K. Toro Pérez, & F. Martín (Coords.), *Ecología Política Latinoamericana: Pensamiento crítico, diferencia latinoamericana y rearticulación epistémica*. CLACSO.

López, I. (2014). Justicia ambiental. *Revista Eunomia*, *6*, 261–268.

Macas, L. (2011). El Sumak Kawsay. En G. Weber (Coord.), *Debates sobre cooperación y modelos de desarrollo. Perspectivas desde la sociedad civil en el Ecuador* (pp. 47–60). Centro de Investigaciones Ciudad-Observatorio de la Cooperación al Desarrollo en Ecuador.

Martínez-Alier, J. (2019). Environmental justice. En A. Kothari, A. Salleh, A. Escobar, F., Demaria, & A. Acosta (Coords.), *Pluriverse: A postdevelopment dictionary*. Icaria Antrazyt.

Martínez Luna, J. (2015). Conocimiento y comunalidad. *Bajo el Volcán*, *15*(23), 99–112. www.redalyc.org/pdf/286/28643473006.pdf

Mendoza Avilés, H. E., Betancourt Vera, A. S., & Murillo Erazo, F. Y. (2019). Factores productivos que inciden en el desarrollo económico y comercial de la Asociación de Cangrejeros 6 de Julio en el Golfo de Guayaquil. *Universidad y Sociedad*, *11*(2), 387–394. http://rus.ucf.edu.cu/index.php/rus

Ministerio del Ambiente. (2017). *Guía de derechos y deberes de las organizaciones custodias del manglar*. Ministerio del Ambiente de Ecuador, Conservación Internacional Ecuador, Instituto Humanista para la Cooperación con los Países en Desarrollo, Organización de las Naciones Unidas para la Alimentación y la Agricultura y Fondo para el Medio Ambiente Mundial. www.proyectomarinocostero.com.ec/wp-content/uploads/2020/02/Guia-de-derechos-custodios-de-manglar.pdf

Ministerio del Ambiente. (2018, Julio 28). *Comunidades se sumaron a la minga de limpieza en los manglares del Golfo de Guayaquil*. Ministerio de Ambiente. www.ambiente.gob. ec/comunidades-se-sumaron-a-la-minga-de-limpieza-en-los-manglares-del-golfo-de-guayaquil/

Ministerio del Ambiente de Ecuador. (2014). *Guía de la Reserva Ecológica Manglares Churute. Ministerio del Ambiente Ecuador*. http://areasprotegidas.ambiente.gob.ec/areas-protegidas/reserva-ecol%C3%B3gica-manglares-churute

Negrete, J., Varela, J., Heras, E., Alcívar, M., & Rosero, P. (2019). Estrategias implementadas para la recuperación del Estero Palanqueado, ramal interior de la reserva de producción de fauna manglares El Salado. En N. Molina Moreira & F. Galvis (Comps.), *Primer Congreso Manglares de América*. Universidad Espíritu Santo.

Pozo-Cajas, M., Ramírez, N., & Cobos-Pazmiño, P. (2019). Propuesta de Restauración del Ecosistema de Manglar en la Reserva de Producción Faunística de Manglares El Salado en el Cantón Guayaquil, Ecuador. En N. Molina Moreira & F. Galvis (Comps.), *Manglares de América* (p. 37). Universidad Espíritu Santo.

Quijano, A. (2000). Colonialidad del poder, eurocentrismo y América Latina. En E. Lander (Coord.), *La colonialidad del saber: Eurocentrismo y ciencias sociales. Perspectivas Latinoamericanas.* CLACSO.

Quijano, A. (2014). ¿Bien vivir?: Entre el 'desarrollo' y la Des/Colonialidad del poder. En *Cuestiones y Horizontes: De la Dependencia Histórico-Estructural a la Colonialidad/Descolonialidad del Poder* (pp. 847–860). CLACSO.

Reyes-Bueno, F., Jurrius, I., Astudillo, D., & Ramirez-Moreina, L. (2019). MANGLARAPP: Una herramienta tecnológica de gobierno electrónico que facilita la comunicación entre usuarios del manglar y entes de control sobre las amenazas socioambientales en los manglares. En N. Molina Moreira & F. Galvis (Comps.), *Manglares del Ecuador* (p. 126). Universidad Espíritu Santo.

Riechmann, J. (2003). Tres principios básicos de justicia ambiental. *Revista internacional de filosofía política, 21*, 103–120.

Rodríguez Salazar, A. (2016). *Teoría y práctica del Buen Vivir: Orígenes, debates conceptuales y conflictos sociales. El Caso de Ecuador* [Trabajo Doctoral, Universidad del País Vasco]. https://addi.ehu.es/handle/10810/19017

Santillán, X., & Rosero, P. (2019). Proceso histórico de creación del Plan de Acción Nacional para la conservación de los manglares del Ecuador continental como herramienta de gestión. En N. Molina Moreira & F. Galvis (Comps.), *Primer Congreso Manglares de América.* Universidad Espíritu Santo.

Santos, B. (2009). *Epistemología del Sur: La reinvención del conocimiento y la emancipación social.* Siglo XXI, CLACSO.

Santos, B. (2010). *Descolonizar el saber: Reinventar el poder.* Montevideo. Ediciones Trise.

Shiva, V. (2019). Development—for the 1 per cent. En A. Kothari, A. Salleh, A. Escobar, F. Demaria, & A. Acosta (Coords.), *Pluriverse: A postdevelopment dictionary.* Icaria Antrazyt.

Solón, P. (2016). *¿Es posible el Vivir Bien? Reflexiones a Quema Ropa sobre Alternativas Sistémicas.* Fundación Solón.

Torrico-Villanueva, E. (2016). La comunicación en clave latinoamericana. *Chasqui, 132*, 23–36.

Torrico-Villanueva, E. (2017). La rehumanización, sentido último de la decolonización comunicacional. *Aportes de la Comunicación, 23*, 31–38.

Zhiminaicela-Cabrera, J., Quevedo-Guerrero, J., Lalangui-Paucar, Y., Mogro-Mendoza, M., Astudillo-Herrera, J., & Barzallo-Encalada, X. (2020). Mapeo multiespectral del impacto de piscinas camaroneras al ecosistema de manglar del Golfo de Guayaquil, Ecuador. *Manglar, 17*(3), 269–274. http://dx.doi.org/10.17268/manglar.2020.039

6

REVERSE MEDIA POLICY

Challenging empires, resisting power

Des Freedman

Introduction

This chapter explores communication activism and media policy reform as fundamental processes for the development of communicative justice in the context of the pluriverse. It argues that structural change based on anticolonial and anticapitalist struggles is needed for building just communicative systems in which those who have been silenced or unheard can effectively transform the media and become protagonists.

Radical social change has always had its mediated element whether it is pamphleteers calling for the abolition of absolute monarchy, independent journalists campaigning against abuses of power, community media practitioners participating in social justice campaigns, filmmakers celebrating revolutionary upheavals, illegal radio stations supporting anti-colonial struggles or bloggers organising pro-democracy movements. The problem is that contemporary media systems—and in particular the policy processes that circumscribe them—all too rarely accommodate radical voices and perspectives. This chapter argues that we need to learn from a tradition of media activism—one that includes everything from purposeful struggles against inequality and injustice to more recent attempts to challenge unaccountable power and to diversify the media beyond a narrow and depoliticised centrist consensus—that can inform and inspire an activist and expansive approach to media policy.

Media policy ought not to be the dry and technocratic application of a highly rationalised and instrumental approach to decision-making (Freedman, 2008). Media policy should also not be restricted to facilitating the circulation of a handful of liberal democratic catchphrases such as the need to promote "a marketplace of ideas" and to secure "media freedom" when these are based primarily

DOI: 10.4324/9781003316220-7

on neoliberal economic assumptions and not collectivist or progressive criteria. Media policy should not be confined to a commitment to "promote competition" and "protect the public interest" when our media landscapes are already characterised by huge concentrations of power presided over either by unaccountable conglomerates or authoritarian regimes. Neither should models of media policy travel unidirectionally from North to South and West to East; they should not emanate in London and Washington DC and migrate to the rest of the world. Indeed, media policy should not emerge out of cloistered and privileged spaces—in any country—that are inaccessible to the citizens who are then reduced to the status of mere spectators: "publics" who are sometimes recognised (most often either as consumers or voters) but largely ignored in relation to a capacity to shape the policy agenda.

Instead, a radical media policy should, quite simply, animate media technologies, platforms, institutions, and actors to secure the objectives that Bertolt Brecht outlined back in 1930 in relation to radio: that our media could be

> the most wonderful public communication system imaginable . . . if it were capable not only of transmitting but of receiving, of making the listener not only hear but also speak, not of isolating him but of connecting him. This means that radio would have to give up being a purveyor and organise the listener as a purveyor.
>
> *(Brecht, 1983, p. 169)*

Media policy should focus on how to embed progressive values and principles into our communications systems and networks; it ought to draw on sets of ideas that dramatise the democratic potential of mediated interactions and design institutions that reflect these ideas. Above all, an activist media policy should aim to combat the antidemocratic and unequal relations of power that are only intensifying with the emergence of big tech companies that are impervious to the timid attempts to regulate them. In the context of this collection, we should speak of a "pluriversal media policy" that is based on a deep commitment to secure "social justice, the radical equality of all beings, and nonhierarchy" (Escobar, 2018, p. xvi).

This chapter highlights two orientations that I believe have been central to an activist understanding of media policy: anticolonial and anticapitalist perspectives that have, at times, been used by popular movements to confront media injustices as part of their wider challenges to exploitative and oppressive social systems. The chapter proposes a concept of "reverse policy transfer" in which, instead of the usual circulation of functional models from the wealthiest to the poorest countries, we see ideas of participatory communication, social movement activism, and class struggle inform the values and politics of those in the imperial centre. This does not involve fetishising the adoption of models from the Global South for their own sake. Instead, the chapter suggests that we can learn from activists and theorists, no matter their geographical origin, who help us to understand how best to resist elite power. Just as the "East" was never a unified sphere of a monochrome Western imagination, neither is the West a singular space but one, like the East, marked by division, inequality, and resistance.

Finally, the chapter briefly considers the communications activism of the UK-based Media Reform Coalition (MRC) from the perspective of one of its founders. It explores the internal dynamics of its coalition politics and the external shaping of the possibilities for radical change given the rise of antiausterity and social justice movements and a growing anger about media concentration and bias. It reflects on the significance of rituals such as the annual Media Democracy Festivals and the impact of "routine" reform-minded activities such as parliamentary submissions and lobbying in attempting to hold mainstream media to account and to pose alternatives to the current system.

The chapter is based on the notion that even the most sophisticated understanding of the cultural, political, economic, or philosophical dynamics of media institutions and practices can't guarantee change unless it is complemented by—and feeds into—a wider political strategy aimed at reconstructing our social systems along more democratic lines. This is a form of activism that both engages with the shortcomings of existing structures and seeks to replace them with models that more effectively represent and involve the publics to whom they are supposed to be accountable. If another media is not only possible but also essential, then it will have to feature as a meaningful part of a broader grassroots challenge to unequal and undemocratic societies.

FIGURE 6.1 Media Democracy Festival 2020. Credit: Media Reform Coalition (2020) (no copyright).

Media policy transfer

Transnational dimensions and movements of media policy are often seen in terms of notions of "policy transfer". This refers, as Dolowitz and Marsh put it in a classic political science exposition (1996, p. 344), to "a process in which knowledge about policies, administrative arrangements, institutions etc. in one time and/or place is used in the development of policies, administrative arrangements and institutions in another time and/or place". Specific policy tools, let alone entire cultures of decision-making, are copied or adapted to fit local circumstances in order to save the "recipient" nation or region the bother of developing its own approach to policy formation and implementation. Transfer is likely to include the adoption of similar policy frames, topics, and objectives in different circumstances, the participation of key international actors across different continents, the use of similar patterns of cultural diplomacy, and, finally, the "rise of similar policy models and regulatory authorities despite cultural and institutional differentiations" (Sarikakis & Ganter, 2014, p. 19).

The problem is that the underlying principles, key actors, preferred venues, and chosen mechanisms are far more likely to emanate from, and reflect the interest of, the influential policy communities of North America and Europe (with the occasional reference to Japan) than they are to come from more disadvantaged parts of the world. Policy transfer in an unequal world is an asymmetrical process whereby developing countries are likely to be its "beneficiaries" rather than its "hosts". Despite Dolowitz and Marsh's insistence that policy transfer is, above all, a process "by which actors borrow policies developed in one setting to develop programmes and policies within another" (1996, p. 357), these are effectively *interested* flows of power and not benign or charitable exchanges as indeed Dolowitz and Marsh recognise in their discussion of "coercive policy transfer". Indeed, far from equalising the balance of power between different policy communities or expanding networks of influence beyond the West, policy transfer—with its pluralist roots and positivist assumptions—is more likely to cement the "power of a relatively small circle of actors who consistently draw lessons from each other" (1996, p. 355).

Analyses of policy transfer in the field of media and communications tend to confirm this finding (for example, Harcourt, 2003; Humphreys, 2002; Prince, 2010; Sarikakis & Ganter, 2014) and to focus on the export of the idea of a 'converged media regulator' like Ofcom to other parts of the world or the imposition of EU protocols on developing nations and smaller trading blocs. Policy transfer, therefore, is best seen as a process in which the models of the most powerful actors are reproduced by those with less capacity and fewer resources to develop their own. It constitutes, by and large, a hegemonic process which restricts the space for the development of policies that challenge the very power relations that structure policy transfer as it currently exists.

I want to propose a form of "reverse policy transfer" in the media landscape based on a rejection of these status quo arrangements. This is not simply about "contra-flows" or "subaltern flows" (Thussu, 2016) in which countries like Brazil, Nigeria, China, and South Korea are brought into the global circuit of cultural trade as significant market players. Instead, this refers to the circulation of ideas and practices that seek to inspire purposeful challenges to unequal power flows both between and within individual nation-states. In that sense, the flows are not just South to North or East to West but from the streets to the palaces, and from communities to legislatures, in whatever country in which they take place. Reverse policy transfer turns on its head the protagonists in the usual definition so that it is the publics and communities who become the "lenders" and elite groups and institutions who become the (reluctant) "borrowers".

Anticolonial and anticapitalist inspirations for media reform

There is a rich tradition of media critique, policy, and activism from the global South that has been central to securing decolonisation, sustaining indigenous cultural movements, challenging the corrupt relationships between private media groups and autocratic regimes, and providing emancipatory accounts of the possibility of mass media. These initiatives, often emerging from community movements or popular insurgencies, go well beyond formal supranational processes like the New World Information and Communication Order (NWICO) and the World Summit on the Information Society (WSIS) and are in direct contrast to state-supported development projects that are run on a "modernizing" logic that "static societies are brought to life by outside influence, technical aid, knowledge, resources and financial assistance" (Golding, 1974, p. 43). Instead, they are based on *struggles*: active campaigns and mobilisations for national liberation, collective representation, land reform, and workers' rights and in opposition to dictatorship, oligopoly, violence, and poverty (Freedman et al., 2016; Mattelart & Siegelaub, 1983; Padovani & Calabrese, 2016).

Paula Chakravartty illustrates the contribution of "socialist, third-world feminist, civil rights and decolonization movements . . . that ultimately aimed for *liberated infrastructures* to combat colonial propaganda and build transnational circuits of transport and communication (radio and newspapers) in the service of the commons" (2019, p. 257). More recently, Latin America has perhaps led the way in pioneering a new form of media and digital activism: to challenge oligopolies and mobilise communities in realising new forms of democratic communications (Artz, 2017; Martens et al., 2020; Segura & Waisbord, 2016; Vinelli, 2014) and to engage in antiimperialist critique (most famously Dorfman & Mattelart, 2019). The campaign in support of the 2009 Audiovisual Communication Services Law in Argentina that promised to clamp down on the private media sector and to expand the opportunities for the public and community media sectors, together with the 2012 #YoSoy132 movement against concentrated media power in Mexico, are just two recent examples in which activists have been central to media policy debates (Abraham-Hamanoiel, 2016; Becerra & Mastrini, 2014).

The global North has much to learn from these struggles and campaigns but it is not the case that mobilisations for radical media reform have been absent from the radical movements in the West—whether this refers to the words quoted earlier from Bertolt Brecht to the emancipatory vision of Hans Magnus Enzensberger (1970) for a bottom-up, decentralised media system to the battle for media justice in the United States (McChesney et al., 2005). Radical media democracy, whether fought for on the streets of London, Los Angeles, or Lagos, has to be an essential demand of any progressive movement and this chapter now identifies two perspectives that may help us achieve this objective: anticolonialism and anticapitalism.

Anticolonialism

In recent years, anticolonial and antiimperial movements have been somewhat overshadowed (certainly in academia itself) by a conceptual shift towards postcolonialism—an increasingly popular academic discipline that is based on unsettling established western canons and on highlighting the contributions of voices representing marginalised communities. Leading postcolonial theorists, including Stuart Hall, Gayatri Spivak, and Homi Bhabha, urge readers to think about the ways in which the patterns of colonialism continue to persist and to challenge residual forms of colonial power and thought.

Yet postcolonialism is itself a contested term. Does it refer to a specific historical period, for example, the epoch after decolonisation and specifically the period from the 1960s following anticolonial revolts across the world? Or does it refer to an attempt to "consciously seek to push past and beyond the condition of coloniality" (Jazeel, 2019, p. 5). Given that colonial structures, legacies, and modes of thought are clearly still present and that we have not yet superseded colonialism as an ideological and political structure, and given that what Alhasssan and Chakravartty describe as "postcolonial media policy" is "deeply embedded in discourses and practices of development and modernization" (2011, p. 366), I want to put the focus back on anticolonial *struggle* as an inspiration for media activism. In particular, I want to briefly discuss the work of the activist and psychiatrist Frantz Fanon who wrote powerfully about the ways in which culture was a tool of both colonial and anticolonial struggles. Fanon has been hugely influential in identifying the lived experience of the colonised as well as reflecting on the technologies through which colonisers attempt to control the colonised.

Fanon was born in the French colony of Martinique, fought for Free French forces in World War 2, and moved to France after the war where his experience of racism as a black, colonial subject led him to write *Black Skin, White Masks*, first published in 1963. Much of Fanon's work is concerned with the scars of racism but, inspired by the anticolonial struggle in Algeria where he got a job as a psychiatrist in 1953, he threw himself into exploring the possibilities of resisting colonialism itself.

Fanon argues that the settler and colonised know each other well in the sense that "it is the settler who has brought the native into existence and who perpetuates his existence" (2004, p. 28) in a systematic and, for Fanon, violent, means of *misrepresentation*. There are a series of powerful binaries in the settler/colonised relationship: one is ethical, the other devoid ("the negation") of values; one is generative, the other "corrosive"; and one is of course civilised, the other "constitutionally depraved". No wonder that when, according to Fanon, "the native hears a speech about Western culture, he pulls out his knife—or at least he makes sure it is within reach" (2004, p. 33).

The colonised live in a world that is "divided into compartments" (2004, p. 29) beyond which they are not allowed to go—both physically *and* imaginatively. Instead, they are forced to dream of freedom: "the native never stops achieving his freedom from nine in the evening until six in the morning" (2004, p. 40). They imagine themselves as active, autonomous individuals who reoccupy the spaces that the colonisers have deprived them of. The internal life of the colonised is shaped therefore by the experience of oppression and managed by a range of symbolic practices that may help to flush out their anger but that are unable to compensate for the wider damage done.

Resistance to colonialism changes this situation and transforms all those involved.

> After centuries of unreality, after having wallowed in the most outlandish phantoms, at long last the native, gun in hand, stands face to face with the only forces which contend for his life—the forces of colonialism.
>
> *(2004, p. 45)*

Old habits start to change in the process of self-realisation and struggle. Whereas previously, the violence of colonialism was met with compensatory rituals, myths, and movement, and "in finding fresh ways of committing mass suicide, now new conditions will make possible a completely new line of action" (2004, pp. 45–46).

Fanon was particularly absorbed by the "imaginative" role played by radio in the unleashing of anticolonial revolt in Algeria. In *A Dying Colonialism* (originally written in 1959), he explores in detail how radio was transformed from being a tool of the coloniser to an essential part of the anticolonial struggle. In the early days of the revolt, Algerians refused to participate in this "world of signs", deliberately choosing not to buy radio sets as they were seen as enemy objects, as "civilising tools". This changed as a result of the revolts when French domination started to crack and when, as Fanon puts it, "the occupier's lie becomes a positive aspect of the nation's new truth" (1965, p. 76).

In 1956, the insurrectionary radio station, the Voice of Fighting Algeria, was launched and brought a level of self-consciousness and organisation to the people of Algeria. Having a radio now meant, as Fanon argued, "paying taxes to the nation" (1965, p. 84), and indeed, it became so popular that people actually *imagined* they had heard broadcasts even when they had not. Jammed by the French and constantly closed down, the Voice of Fighting Algeria nevertheless allowed Algerians to imagine the spreading of resistance: "behind each modulation, each active crackling, the Algerian would imagine not only words but concrete battles" (1965, p. 88). For Fanon, "having a radio meant *going to war*" (1965, p. 93).

In an anticolonial movement such as the one in Algeria, struggles over the production and distribution of media resources are vital in that they help to generate a sense of collective identity. They strip the occupier's voice of its authority and reassert the emerging power of the previously colonised. Indeed, they transform the media from a tool of oppression into one of potential liberation and this struggle creates the possibility of an entirely different conception of media policy: not as an unaccountable, technocratic rule-bound system but as a process that expresses the changing political dynamics of a combative population. Furthermore, turning to voices such as Fanon is particularly useful given that "anticolonial thinkers and writers were as concerned with re-writing histories from the perspective of the oppressed as they were in creating the terms for collective emancipation" (Chakravartty, 2019, p. 258). This is not so much, misquoting Paulo Freire, a pedagogy but the 'reverse policymaking' of the oppressed.

Anticapitalism

Anticolonial struggles have provided hugely important lessons about how to resist occupation and oppression and how to struggle for self-determination. Yet anticapitalist struggles, structured above all on the basis of class division and a resistance to exploitation, speak powerfully to the need to secure political, economic, and communicative economic equality. Karl Marx, as capitalism's first great critic, was captivated by its revolutionary innovations but horrified by the means in which it sought to reproduce itself and sought to identify some fundamental features of this dynamic but brutal social system.

He argued that, as opposed to earlier societies where any surplus was consumed by the ruling elite, capitalists need to reinvest this surplus in order to compete more effectively in a market. Capital, understood by Marx, as any accumulation of value that acts to increase its own value, "exists and can only exist as many capitals" (Marx, 1973, p. 414). The fetishising of competition, as embodied in the modern free market, is the DNA of this new social system, and innovation is therefore required to step up productivity, reduce labour costs, identify new markets, and increase the rate of profit—the ultimate goal of any zealous entrepreneur. Capitalists become wedded to the further competitive accumulation of capital to be able most effectively to achieve these aims: "Accumulate, accumulate! That is Moses and the prophets" (Marx, 1918, p. 606).

This means that capitalists will do everything they can to extract more value from the production process; that labour, once an essential part of human subjectivity, becomes something over which the labourer has little control; that objects that were previously enjoyed for their immediate and organic qualities become valued mainly for their ability to be exchanged and to secure a profit; and finally, that due to the lack of coordination in the economy, there will be a tendency towards crises of overproduction that will wipe out weaker firms.

These structural processes of exploitation, alienation, commodification, and concentration are, according to Marx, the terrible price to be paid by the majority of the people on the planet for the contradictory technological advances experienced under capitalism: for the vaccines that follow pandemics; for the developments in green energy that follow a climate crisis caused by fossil fuels; or for the innovative communications platforms that are used to fuel militarism, racism, and misogyny.

Mainstream media constitute a central way in which these hegemonic social norms are proposed, naturalised, and policed by elite interests. They constitute a regulatory force committed to upholding a status quo based on private property and the rule of capital. While they are not immune from the contradictions and tensions that are to be found in all societies (Freedman, 2014)—indeed, the most effective forms of media power are precisely those that provide limited expressions of discontent within a more general embrace of existing social relations—their loyalty is, above all, to a capitalist logic in which they are deeply embedded. Tech owners, media moguls, newspaper editors, senior broadcasters, advertising executives and media regulators, and policymakers are all partners—even if, at times, warring ones—in the management of media markets, the protection of private property, and the consolidation of unequal social relations. Their power increasingly depends on economic and political control of communications landscapes—a dominance that is scarcely comparable to the far more limited opportunities for individuals to use the media for progressive ends.

This points to a situation in which we face the challenge of a renewed *executive power* where elite groups deploy their resources—their access to capital, their political influence, and their ideological congruence—to dominate contemporary media systems. Marx wrote about the triumph of executive power over legislative power in relation to mid-19th century France in *The 18th Brumaire of Louis Bonaparte*. He described its "enormous bureaucratic and military organisation with its wide-ranging and ingenious state machinery" and condemned "this terrifying parasitic body which enmeshes the body of French society and chokes all its pores" (Marx, 1852). Of course, the context is radically different some 170 years on but are we really in a situation in which we are free of instrumental calculations, imperial ambitions, state machinations, and complicit relationships when we think of the role of, for example, Google and Glovo, Fox, and

Facebook? Indeed social media algorithms, state surveillance systems, and a "club culture" at the top of the media would suggest that this form of capitalist power is more deeply embedded than ever. It means that the struggle for a fully democratic media must be an anticapitalist struggle: one which challenges the profit motive of large sections of the media, contests its ideological basis that distorts its ability to make sense of the world, liberates it from authoritarian regimes, and generates a "social and productive process, the practical means of which are in the hands of the masses themselves" (Enzensberger, 1970, p. 15).

Militant media reform

By drawing on these two perspectives, the anticolonial and the anticapitalist, we can look to a form of militant media activism that is, as Bob Hackett and Bill Carroll once wrote, both "defensive and pro-active" (2006, p. 13). In other words, this is an approach to media policy that it is not only reform-oriented in practice but also revolutionary in spirit. A commitment to media reform involves an understanding of democracy that includes the right to share meaning as well as an increased emphasis on participation and equality through acts of media-making. Indeed, it is harder and harder to insulate media reform from political reform more generally in particular because of the lack of autonomy of the media "field" from the actions of the state and the market despite the fact that the media still retain the power to affect the operations of other social actors.

Robert McChesney in his work on media reform movements echoes this link between media and political reform as well as the need to connect together both the "insider" and "media justice" elements of media reform (McChesney, 2008). He argues that the 21st-century US media reform movement was triggered by the anticapitalist and antiglobalisation struggles that took place in the late 1990s and which raised serious questions about the incorporation of the right to communicate within neoliberal frames and policies. The movement had to "bed in" before taking to the streets but was also inspired by a radical critique of mainstream media performance (2008, p. 54). This is why media reform activists need to employ an "inside/outside" perspective—producing research, engaging in "official" lobbying, attempting to influence politicians and regulators—as well as applying external pressure and participating in direct action to transform the wider political climate.

What this means is that to secure a fundamental shift in media power, we need to engage in media reform but not from a reformist perspective. We can learn a lot from the German revolutionary Rosa Luxemburg who distinguished between "revisionist" strategies for reform which attempt to administer palliative care to the capitalist system and more radical strategies that seek to win reforms as a fundamental part of a revolutionary strategy to transform the status quo. While the former wants "to lessen, to attenuate, the capitalist contradictions" (1989, p. 51) in order to stabilise society and produce consensus, the latter approach engages in reform as part of a more widespread challenge to capitalist hegemony. The crucial point for Luxemburg however was that movements for reform were central to a more profound social struggle: "Between social reforms and revolution there exists for the revolutionary an indissoluble tie. The struggle for reforms is its means; the social revolution, its aim" (1989, p. 21).

Media reform, like all other forms of social reform, is a contradictory and uneven process in which different groups are involved and different strategies are involved. There is a world of difference between a reform campaign that calls on a handful of the "great and the good" to plead its case and one which seeks to mobilise greater numbers of people using all the tactics that are available—a difference perhaps between "reform from above" and "reform from below". You do not have to believe exclusively in parliamentary change to fight for reforms though it would be equally short-sighted to refuse to engage with parliamentary processes as part of a reform campaign. Just as there is little point in aiming only at the band-aid, there is also little point in refusing at least to treat the wound. There is a need to delegitimise and pose alternatives to the power structures that created these problems in the first place. Media reform allows us to do this *if* we build the necessary coalitions and *if* we pursue the right strategies.

Media activism focused on policy reform and structural change is, therefore, an essential part of any movement for meaningful democracy. It is not the case that communications activism *requires* a policy orientation given that other approaches—from scholarly critique of the social reproduction of power to the production of alternative and radical media—may feed into and inspire advocacy campaigns. However, this chapter adopts an understanding of policy that refers less to a bounded legal process than a highly contested field in which "a variety of ideas and assumptions about desirable structure and behaviour circulate" (Freedman, 2008, p. 13). In this context, a policy dimension will complement—and ideally strengthen—other areas of media activism.

This approach is not only organised around grasping the dynamics of media—its ownership patterns, regulatory regimes, legal frameworks, everyday routines, structural constraints, and contextual pressures—but it also seeks to intervene in these debates on the basis of normative attachments to principles such as equality, social justice, diversity, and participation. So just as it involves the patient work associated with media policy debates more generally—commissioning research, contributing to consultations, working with stakeholders, producing briefing papers, and evaluating policy initiatives—it simultaneously requires the integration of this work inside social movements and campaigning. Many academics already produce "helpful" information and "persuasive" evidence, but this counts for relatively little if it is not aimed at, and used by, social forces pressing for more deep-rooted change. As Joe Karaganis has pointed out, "systemic change requires a social movement capable of linking policy agendas with grassroots activism" (2009, p. 1).

The emphasis on "systemic change" is important. Media policy activism is aimed above all at structural, and not individual, transformation. After all, flaws in media content and governance are not due to the failures of individual journalists, programme-makers, regulators, or politicians but are a reflection of the highly unequal environments in which media content is produced, distributed, and consumed. This is a problem to do with sustained inequalities that are endemic to capitalism and that are reflected inside media institutions and processes. This means that activists need first to identify those policies and systems of thought that are constraining democracy, then to propose alternatives, and finally to bring to bear appropriate knowledge and resources in campaigning for meaningful change. In doing this, it is vital to draw on the resources that emerge from campaigns for democracy and social justice wherever they take place in the world—to "reverse" the normal flow of policy prescriptions from West to East and from "official" spaces down to publics and citizens. More than ever, activists need to borrow and adapt a wide range of social movement strategies such that policy transfer becomes less a technical matter than a militant programme of action.

This requires alliances both with civil society groups working on issues of media standards, economics, and ownership and with those outside the media—immigrant organisations, women's groups, and the antiwar and antiausterity movements—in order to mobilise the wider publics about the negative impact of existing media structures on public discourse and representation.

Media Reform Coalition

The MRC emerged in the United Kingdom out of the *News of the World* phone-hacking scandal in 2011, an abuse of media power at the heart of Rupert Murdoch's media empire and at the very core of the capitalist media system. This was not an exception to or a breakdown of professional journalism as practised in one of the world's oldest democracies but the logical outcome of a neoliberal order in which the public interest has been repackaged as salacious gossip and "insider" parliamentary politics. MRC grew out of a coalition of interests involving academics, activists, students, and trade unionists seeking both to democratise media from the inside and to apply the spirit of social movement activism to a more patient reformist politics. This is an uncomfortable and difficult balance that has marked its activities as it has campaigned on a range of issues including ownership concentration, anti-discrimination, independent journalism, platform democracy, and media diversity.

FIGURE 6.2 Media Reform Coalition. Credit: Media Reform Coalition (N.D) (no copyright).

MRC has organised noisy rallies and conducted quiet lobbying; it has not only produced a steady stream of submissions to official policy deliberations but also commissioned high-profile research into concentrated ownership and media bias against prominent progressive figures; it not only has drafted a parliamentary bill designed to support new journalism initiatives and to cap the power of the largest media companies but also organises the annual Media Democracy Festival which brings together academics, activists, and independent media producers. It is a space in which civil society groups can strategise around how best to counter media misinformation and how to develop an effective response.

There have been, of course, "necessary tensions" as Schlosberg and Brevini have called them (2016, p. 141): between strategies of productive engagement with the policy community and resistance to its core beliefs, between consensus building and holding firm to established principles, and between acting as a formal representative body and as a more ad hoc campaign. The MRC, by drawing on the (admittedly sometimes limited) autonomy of academics to conduct critical research that then feeds into advocacy campaigns, has been able to bridge the gap between higher education and a more activist orientation on political engagement and mobilisation. For example, its data on media ownership in the United Kingdom is now part of the secondary school media curriculum while its supporters are active in coordinating opposition on the ground to the worst excesses of media bias and distortion. Nowhere is this clearer than in its coordination of the opposition to the proposed takeover of Sky by 21st-Century Fox in 2017 where MRC was able to bring together a powerful group of traditional media activists and online campaigners.

MRC is far smaller than Free Press in the United States or OpenMedia in Canada and far more financially insecure than other reform groups in the United Kingdom like Hacked Off or the Open Rights Group in the United Kingdom. These are all organisations that are important stakeholders in the policy debates to which they are attached. But what MRC shows is how academics, with minimal resources and scarce amounts of time, can use their ability to carry out high-quality and *interested* research and advocacy in pursuit of meaningful media reform. Yet this is most effectively achieved only as long as they seek to highlight contributions and histories from outside their comfort zones—including the anti-colonial and anti-capitalist perspectives discussed earlier in this chapter—and to work with non-media-focused civil society groups in pressing for radical media change.

Conclusion

Unlike Arturo Escobar's preoccupation with securing the salience of "difference" in *Designs for the Pluriverse*—and making sure that difference is not "effaced or normalized" (2018, p. xvi)—this chapter is more concerned with *power* and how best to secure communicative reform as part of a wider challenge to existing social relations. This is not simply about celebrating difference but eradicating inequality; not just about welcoming diversity but challenging the relations of power that reduce "diversity" to an advertising slogan; not so much about the experience of the oppressed as what the struggle against oppression can teach those engaged in political activism more generally.

Media policy is usually an obscure and peripheral dimension of this struggle precisely because it is contained within technocratic and neoliberal assumptions of efficiency, competition, and accumulation. Its foundational principles are exported from richer to poorer countries and its processes involve a transmission of rules and regulation from the "top" to the "bottom" of society. This chapter has argued that we need to reverse the direction of travel: that media policy needs to be seen as a site of struggle over the distribution of crucial societal resources with its dynamic firmly grounded in a belief that all meaningful social change is not bequeathed by elites but won by mass movements. This process can be an effective way to build communicative justice at the same time that social justice is developed at a systemic level, thus favouring the much-needed strengthening of the pluriverse.

References

Abraham-Hamanoiel, A. (2016). A perfect storm for media reform: Telecommunications reforms in Mexico. In D. Freedman, J. Obar, C. Martens, & R. McChesney (Eds.), *Strategies for media reform: International perspectives* (pp. 123–137). Fordham University Press.

Alhassan, A., & Chakravartty, P. (2011). Postcolonial media policy under the long shadow of empire. In R. Mansell & M. Raboy (Eds.), *The handbook of global media and communication policy* (pp. 386–382). Wiley-Blackwell.

Artz, L. (Ed.). (2017). *The pink tide: Media access and political power in Latin America*. Rowman & Littlefield.

Becerra, M., & Mastrini, G. (2014). The audiovisual law of argentina and the changing media landscape. *Political Economy of Communication, 2*(1). www.polecom.org/index.php/polecom/article/view/31/213

Brecht, B. (1983 [1930]). Radio as a means of communication: A talk of the function of radio. In A. Mattelart & S. Siegalaub (Eds.), *Communication and class struggle. Vol. 2: Liberation, socialism* (pp. 169–171). International General.

Chakravartty, P. (2019). Media, "Race" and the infrastructures of empire. In J. Curran & D. Hesmondhalgh (Eds.), *Mass media and society* (pp. 245–261). Bloomsbury.

Dolowitz, D., & Marsh, D. (1996). Who learns what from whom: A review of the policy transfer literature. *Political Studies, XLIV*, 343–357.

Dorfman, A., & Mattelart, A. (2019 [1971]). *How to read Donald Duck: Imperialist ideology in the disney comic*. Pluto Press.

Enzensberger, H. M. (1970, November–December). Constituents of a theory of the media. *New Left Review, 64*, 13–36.

Escobar, A. (2018). *Designs for the pluriverse: Radical interdependence, autonomy and the making of worlds*. Duke University Press.

Fanon, F. (1965 [1959]). *A dying colonialism*. Grove Press.

Fanon, F. (2004 [1963]). *The wretched of the earth*. Grove Press.

Freedman, D. (2008). *The politics of media policy*. Polity Press.

Freedman, D. (2014). *The contradictions of media power*. Bloomsbury.

Freedman, D., Obar, J., Martens, C., & McChesney, R. (Eds.). (2016). *Strategies for media reform: International perspectives*. Fordham University Press.

Golding, P. (1974). Media role in national development: Critique of a theoretical orthodoxy. *Journal of Communication, 24*(3), 39–53.

Hackett, R., & Carroll, W. (2006). *Remaking media: The struggle to democratize public communication*. Routledge.

Harcourt, A. (2003). The regulation of media markets in selected EU accession states in Central and Eastern Europe. *European Law Journal, 9*(3), 316–340.

Humphreys, P. (2002). Europeanisation, globalisation and policy transfer in the European Union: The case of telecommunications. *Convergence, 8*(2), 52–79.

Jazeel, T. (2019). *Postcolonialism*. Routledge.

Karaganis, J. (2009). *Cultures of collaboration in media research*. https://papers.ssrn.com/sol3/papers.cfm?abstract_id=1485181

Luxemburg, R. (1989 [1899]). *Reform or revolution?* Bookmarks.

Martens, C., Venegas, C., & Tapuy, E. (Eds.). (2020). *Digital activism, community media, and sustainable communication in Latin America*. Palgrave Macmillan.

Marx, K. (1852). *The 18th Brumaire of Louis Bonaparte*. www.marxists.org/archive/marx/works/1852/18th-brumaire/ch07.htm

Marx, K. (1918). *Capital: A critical analysis of capitalist production* (Vol. 1). William Glaisher.

Marx, K. (1973). *Grundrisse: Foundations of the critique of political economy*. Vintage.

Mattelart, A., & Siegelaub, S. (Eds.). (1983). *Communication and class struggle. Vol. 2: Liberation, socialism*. International General.

McChesney, R. (2008). The U.S. media reform movement: Going forward. *Monthly Review, 60*(4), 51–59.

McChesney, R., Newman, R., & Scot, B. (2005). *The future of media: Resistance and reform in the 21st century*. Seven Stories Press.

Media Reform Coalition. (2020, May 27). *Media democracy festival 2020 moves online—watch it now!* www.mediareform.org.uk/blog/media-democracy-festival-2020-moves-online

Media Reform Coalition. (n.d.). www.mediareform.org.uk/

Padovani, C., & Calabrese, A. (Eds.). (2016). *Communication rights and social justice*. Palgrave.

Prince, R. (2010). Policy transfer as policy assemblage: Making policy for the creative industries in New Zealand. *Environment and Planning, 42*, 169–186.

Sarikakis, K., & Ganter, S. (2014). Priorities in global media policy transfer: Audiovisual and digital policy mutations in the EU, MERCOSUR and US triangle. *European Journal of Communication, 29*(1), 17–33.

Schlosberg, J., & Brevini, B. (2016). Between philosophy and action: The story of the media reform coalition. In D. Freedman, J. Obar, C. Martens, & R. McChesney (Eds.), *Strategies for media reform: International perspectives* (pp. 138–152). Fordham University Press.

Segura, M. S., & Waisbord, S. (2016). *Media movements: Civil society and media policy reform in Latin America*. Zed Books.

Thussu, D. K. (2016). Contra-flow in global media: An Asian perspective. *Media Asia, 33*(3–4), 123–129.

Vinelli, N. (2014). *La Televisión Desde Abajo*. Collectivo El Topo Blindado.

7

POPULAR MUSIC, GENDER, AND COMMUNICATIVE JUSTICE ON INTERNATIONAL WOMEN'S DAY[1]

Josep Pedro and Begoña Gutiérrez-Martínez

Introduction

This chapter explores the planetarisation of popular music by examining two emerging female bands—Quartetazzo and Ladies in Blues—in relation to their performances in Madrid, Spain, on International Women's Day (8 March 2019). Formed by diverse women from different national, cultural, and geographical backgrounds, Quartetazzo and Ladies in Blues present insightful and challenging case studies that inform us about the planetarisation of popular music and its significant role in communicative, cultural, and sociopolitical transformations. The daring flute quartet Quartetazzo expresses its singular voice based on the conscious exploration of popular music traditions such as jazz, blues, flamenco, chacarera, and forró. For their part, Ladies in Blues embrace an eclectic notion of the blues genre in relation to different subgenres, as well as to gospel, soul, and funk.

The selected case studies represent forms of communicative justice intimately related to the sociopolitical and cultural justice dimensions of the pluriverse (Escobar, 2012), as well as to the ecology of recognition and the ecology of transscales as the articulations between the local and the global (Santos, 2007). They present examples of cooperation, solidarity, diversity, female inspiration, and empowerment in the public sphere, and they illustrate the ways in which popular music and glocal music scenes stimulate intercultural and intergenerational dialogue. Thus, we are particularly interested in the combinations, interactions, and arrangements of multiple distinct voices that coexist and grow within a music group, both on and offstage.

Moreover, these case studies also relate to the political economy justice dimension of the pluriverse due to the focus on gender equality within a context associated with feminism, outsider lifestyles of popular musicians (Becker, 1997), and

DOI: 10.4324/9781003316220-8

their participation in an unstable and often misunderstood live music economy and profession. This dimension is also relevant because the participation in official acts framed within the International Women's Day (8-M hereafter) may involve more public attention, media appearances, work opportunities, and even some extra pressure for the participants.

By employing the concept of pluriverse to analyse the reality of popular music, gender, and communicative justice, this chapter examines two broad and complex dimensions of contemporary music scenes as sites for artistic experiences and intercultural encounters. The first one, associated with the sociopolitical and cultural justice dimensions of the pluriverse, relates to the ways in which music as a social practice helps to develop artistic alliances, unity within diversity, and a sense of camaraderie and community that nurtures the experiences of committed participants—musicians, producers, aficionados, and so on. It illustrates some of the most ideal and gratifying aspects of inhabiting a music scene—a dynamic, material, and symbolic everyday live construction that may be thought of as a developing pluriverse of coexisting, interconnected worlds converging around live music experiences. This involves acknowledging its collective nature, as well as the distinct contributions of multiple participants with different origins, lifestyles, and discourses. Potentially, their alliances transcend multiple barriers related to nationality, gender, race, and class, revealing alternative cultural practices and questioning hegemonic power structures in society and within the music scene.

The second key aspect of music scenes as observed from the pluriverse perspective relates to its political economy justice dimension. In contrast with performance and identity issues, which point towards the ecologies of recognitions and transscales, the live music economy of popular music scenes is marked by an uncertain and precarious situation within the capitalist system. Contemporary music scenes centred around live music continue to suffer from endemic problems linked to precariousness, as well as from more general and hard-hitting crises. The global financial crisis of 2008 and the COVID-19 pandemic mark two of the most recent and profound examples of crisis in many aspects of life, including the musical and cultural fields. The shifting economic and sociopolitical context impacts the everyday life construction and sustainability of popular music scenes, even if scene musicians and committed aficionados develop intimate bonds and group solidarity within their projects.

Following a long-term ethnographic approach towards the music scene and a specific orientation towards the role of women musicians, this chapter draws on participant observation conducted in the Madrid music scene between 2012 and 2020, as well as on in-depth face-to-face interviews with the members of Quartetazzo and Ladies in Blues. Strategic participant observation was conducted by both authors during the 8 March 2019 live music performances at Café Berlín, as well as at the Ladies in Blues' debut at the same venue on 10 December 2016. Moreover, the selection of these two bands was informed by previous knowledge, research, and fieldwork experiences regarding several band members. Interviews were conducted on 6 March (Ladies in Blues) and 7 March 2019 (Quartetazzo) at the rehearsal studios Ritmo y Compás and the proximity of the music school El Molino de Santa Isabel, respectively.

First, we will contextualise the planetarisation of popular music by conceptualising the Madrid music scene as a complex pluriverse that hosts multiple traditions, styles, and identities. We will then focus on aspects of identity, performance, and repertoire regarding Quartetazzo and Ladies in Blues. In this process, we will address the complex communicative justice aspects of popular music, gender, and institutional production around International Women's Day. Drawing on the discourses and experiences of the observed musicians, we will focus on the most gratifying and problematic aspects of participating in the live music scene and in the 8-M celebrations.

The planetarisation of popular music and the Madrid music scene

Researching a historically consolidated scene like the Madrid music scene implies entering a complex spatiotemporal glocal context defined by multiple musical and sociocultural experiences, which have been collectively developed across time. More particularly, we may emphasise the development of the highly-influential jazz and pop-rock music cultures. The former culture in Spain can be traced back to the 1920s and 1930s, when a wide definition of "jazz" began to be globally disseminated and appropriated. It included different types of African-American dances, blues, spirituals, and gospel, which coexisted along with the constant yet shifting influence of Latin American music—bolero, mambo, cha cha cha, tango, salsa, and so on—and the foundational baggage of national traditions as significant as flamenco and copla.

As for a pop-rock culture in dialogue with the rock "n" roll explosion, its reception and incipient scene took off approximately during the mid-1950s and early 1960s (see, for instance, the album El Rock and Roll de Los *Estudiantes*, produced by Phillips in 1959), developing multiple subgenres. Blues music also played a key role. As indicated elsewhere (Pedro, 2018, p. 195), "its musical language and social history background was present and was a decisive influence on Spain's changing soundscapes throughout the Francoist dictatorship (1939–1975) and the transition to democracy (1975–1982)". It actually operated frequently as a sign of authenticity. Moreover, the 1980s marks a differentiated stage of scene crystallisation that is remarkable due to the emergence of blues-specific bands, clubs, and audiences.

Marked by centripetal and centrifugal forces, a contemporary music scene such as the Madrid music scene is defined by its dynamic and collective nature, its pronounced hybridisation, and the constant movement of its participants. Hybridisation refers to "sociocultural processes in which discrete structures or practices that existed separately are combined to generate new structures, objects and practices" (García Canclini, 2009, p. iii). Furthermore, from Bakhtin's (1981) perspective, hybridisation is seen as an intrinsic quality of language, as any concrete discourse necessarily draws on and contests previous works, discourses, and voices from ongoing traditions.

Among the centripetal forces that affect the scene, we may stress the importance of continuous national and international migration, both temporal and permanent, as well as of the historic vibrancy and concentration of the music scene and industry in the Spanish capital. Like many populous capital cities, Madrid is associated with more opportunities, and the city plays its role in being host for many, a process that contributes to its changing face and identity.

Regarding centrifugal movements, touring is a constant and Madrid's central location allows multiple options and routes through the country, as well as to other parts of Europe, Latin America, or the United States. Moreover, movements towards the outside also speak about the challenges and difficulties of inhabiting the centres. As in other major cities, living in Madrid and being able to make a living out of music present a considerable economic challenge due to a multiplicity of factors, including high rents, gentrification, and extended low pay for popular musicians. In this regard, the Madrid music scene illustrates a growing global concern about the difficulties of becoming a professional musician or an artist in highly digitalised, contemporary western societies (for a further discussion, see Deresiewicz, 2020).

While Madrid is originally a peripheral geographical site for African-American music, Latin American music, and—to a lesser extent—flamenco, it also counts on a well-established, multicultural live music tradition that spans over many decades since the early 20th century. In fact, the idea of Madrid as a central melting pot is implicit in one of the city's traditional nicknames: *el foro* (the forum), which suggests geographical and political centrality, as well as an open conception of the city as a public space for interaction and dialogue with others.

Scholar Barry Shank (1994, p. 122) defines the music scene as "an overproductive signifying community; that is, far more semiotic information is produced that can be rationally parsed". Accordingly, music scenes remain a necessary condition for musical production to be able to transcend its local cultural character until questioning and transforming the dominant structures of identification. In other words, the music scene appears as a complex material and symbolic place for sociocultural encounter and performance, identification with artists, and identity experimentation and transformation. This confluent and dynamic nature of music scenes is intimately connected to the pluriverse, both as a theoretical framework and as particular sets of practices and realities.

The conception of the scene as a semiosphere (Pedro et al., 2018), in allusion to Yuri Lotman's (1996) discussion about these universes of meaning, is enriched with the perspective of the pluriverse. On the one hand, understanding the pluriverse as "a world where many worlds fit" (Escobar, 2012, p. 49) is in synch with the possible subdivision of scenes and semiospheres in different levels or dimensions. As expressed by Lotman (1996, p. 25): "each of them is, at the same time, both a participant in the dialogue [a part of the larger system that encompasses them] and the space of the dialogue [a complex whole]". Therefore, we could potentially approach the cases of Quartetazzo and Ladies in Blues as representative of the Madrid jazz and blues scenes as independent entities. Instead, a broader view of the Madrid live music reveals the stylistic range of subscenes and groups as part of a common heterogeneous construction. On this occasion, the scene's dynamics connect with a huge social demonstration dedicated to women, 8-M, and a highly significant social movement such as feminism.

The centrality of live music and face-to-face interaction lies at the centre of many music scenes, and this has favoured the role of ethnography as one of the key methodologies in popular music studies (Cohen, 1991; Shank, 1994; Bennet & Peterson, 2004; Llano Camacho, 2018; Pedro et al., 2018). Ethnographies of music scenes are generally enriched by repeated and prolonged participation, and these incursions open up multiple scenarios and potential research lines. Given the extraordinary occasion presented for the study of popular music, gender, and communicative justice, as well as the previous knowledge about the observed musicians, the venue, and the scene, in this particular investigation, we strategically selected these two case studies and live events, which marked a highlight in Madrid on International Women's Day.

Quartetazzo and Ladies in Blues performed in consecutive gigs at the well-known music venue Café Berlín as part of the publicly-funded *Ellas Crean* Festival ("They Create", Community of Madrid, 2019), which celebrated its 15th anniversary with an impressive music production around the city. According to the specialised music magazine and association *La Noche en Vivo* (2019, p. 4), which collaborates closely with the festival, there were more than 70 acts by female artists or groups throughout the month.

Quartetazzo is an innovative and eclectic flute quartet predominantly associated to jazz and flamenco. It was originally conceived in 2017 during a flamenco course taught by the legendary Spanish jazz and flamenco musician Jorge Pardo at Sanlúcar de Barrameda (Cádiz). It features Emilse Barlatay (Córdoba, Argentina, 1979), Trinidad Jiménez (Almería, Spain, 1984), Leticia Malvares (Río de Janeiro, Brasil, 1982), and Carmen Vela (Madrid, Spain, 1979). In order to cooperatively create their original compositions, they consciously embrace roots music and diverse popular traditions, assuming an enriching conception of hybridisation and interculturality.

Rather than a fixed and formally established group, Ladies in Blues is strictly a special reunion that brings together some of the leading female voices in the blues scene: Marta D'Ávilas (Madrid, Spain, 1979), Patricia Göser (Germany, 1976), Tatiana Firminio (Brasil, 1979), Laura Solla (Pontevedra, Spain, 1993), Laura Gómez Palma (Buenos Aires, Argentina, 1970), and Mariana Pérez (Bilbao, Spain, 1985). This superband reunion has been intimately linked to Café Berlín and to the producer Jorge Biancotti (former president of the Madrid Blues Society), whose original proposal was to dedicate an event to the pivotal role of women in the history of blues (see, for instance, Davis, 1999). In addition, the reunion has stimulated further female bands such as Bluesas—a pun between blues and goddesses—which features several of them. The line-up in the bands' first show at Café Berlin (10/12/2016) featured the established singer-guitarist Susan Santos and drummer Ezequiel Navas in place of Solla and Pérez.

The observed artists explained that their experience in female bands has been marked by a unique camaraderie, which positively affects the group's management, cohesiveness, and sense of direction. "Personally, what I like most is that we are all responsible in terms of rehearsal hours", admitted Emilse Barlatay. "Many things that sometimes are more difficult with groups of guys, when it comes to: 'come on, you do this, you do that . . .'". "Quick things are solved soon, practical things are also solved easily", summed up Leticia Malvares. While Malvares had played more with women than men in Brazil, her musical experience in Spain—like the experience of the rest of the band members—has been primarily associated with male colleagues. Quartetazzo has marked a change: "It is a haven of peace", said Carmen Vela:

> Nobody has to inform or remind anyone because we're all here. We are a train. And of course, as we are also used to pulling the wagon in other places, now we see ourselves as four engine drivers in the same train. Just imagine it.

In contrast with situations marked by a lack of group commitment or leadership, Vela summarised the union of strength and safety through the train analogy. She affirmed its horizontal nature, where the four members compose music and share responsibilities.

For their part, the musicians of Ladies in Blues explained that they were still in the process of getting to know each other better, as this was being an enriching, novelty experience. D'Ávilas pointed out that she felt very comfortable working among women and that the working dynamic was more productive. Mariana Pérez explained that "in the end you feel more like you're with family, like with your mother and sisters, your grandmothers. In a closer, more familiar environment". "There's a little bit more care", added Marta D'Ávilas.

However, the members of Quartetazzo and Ladies in Blues also insisted on the difficulties of generalising or making broad statements when describing both male musicians and women as a collective. They emphasised the importance of mutual respect, understanding, and diversity within unity. Furthermore, it is worth noting that these female musicians felt a much bigger distance regarding the social and professional worlds that lie outside the live music scene than regarding male musicians, many of which they saw as peers and companions. Therefore, occupation, lifestyle, and class become important variables that intersect with gender, ethnicity, migration, and cultural experiences.

On the other hand, the most problematic aspects of making a living as a female popular musician include not only ongoing challenges and concerns linked to participation in the scene, economic sustenance, ageing, and motherhood, but

also more specific conflicts that arise from work opportunities, often contributing to scepticism and disbelief towards institutions. Noting the multiple jobs held
by popular musicians, Laura Solla felt that "people from the outside understand
absolutely nothing of what happens in the music world. . . . There is also a kind
of secrecy. . . . They don't understand why you have to be in 10 bands to make
a living". Moreover, Trinidad Jiménez and Marta D'Ávilas coincided in point-
ing out that they had faced many judgements from people for the fact of being a
mother and still be playing music professionally. Together with working schedules
and travelling commitments, the unconventional lifestyle associated to popular
musicians also impacts affective relationships, as indicated by Leticia Malvares. "In
the end that's why we all wind up with musicians", laughed Emilse Barlatay. In
this process, the tension between economic autonomy as a female musician and
economic dependence regarding male partners is also key.

Based on her experience, Mariana Pérez critically reflected on the social interest in popular music:

> I notice that people in general don't like music at all, unless you are famous.
> For example, in my job everyone says, "oh, that's great! Let me know when
> you play . . ." And then . . . [laughs]. Never, nobody. No one has ever
> come to see me. Until the day you play in the Superbowl, at WeZink, [or]
> before Real Madrid . . . In the end you say: "nobody likes music, and I'm a
> fool . . ." Because we like music, and that's why we are here. But people
> don't give a damn.

Her discourse in relation to the everyday underground scene urges us to rethink
the value attributed to music in contemporary society, and how the degree of
fame or stardom influences it. "Ordinary people don't know about the underground circuit, which is what sustains the music in Spain", explained Laura Solla:

> Apart from music lovers, drunks and night owls—in the end we are among
> them . . . [laughs]. I go out every day, man. I mean, yeah. To jam sessions
> and all that. And there are people playing live every day, making a living
> every day in an unknown club.

Identity and performance

The observed case studies expose the cultural and political implications of popular
music, as well as its role in social change, public expression, and communicative justice. Along with the general strike and the massive demonstrations that
continue to grow over the last few years, we acknowledge the 8-M live music
celebrations as important cultural and sociopolitical achievements that contribute
to female visibility and empowerment. In this regard, not only is the personal
political but also the musical performance and festive celebration, which incorporates liberating and transformative elements of "the carnivalesque" (Bakhtin,

1984). Pop concerts tend to create for its audience a space for representation and experience. It is a similar time space to that of carnival, which is "both stage and life, game and dream, discourse and spectacle" (Kristeva, 1980, p. 79).

Both groups celebrate women's prominence in music, and they reflect on the importance of giving them a greater visibility during a day, the 8th of March, which has become a symbol of social struggle, equality, and freedom. Quartetazzo is a flute quartet formed in 2017 by instrumentalists Carmen Vela (C flute), Leticia Malvares (G and C flutes), Trinidad Jiménez (bass flute and C flute), and Emilse Barlatay (C flute). Originally launched in 2016 yet with less regular continuity, Ladies in Blues is a blues supergroup formed by Marta D'Ávilas (vocals), Patricia Göser (vocals), Laura Gómez Palma (bass), Tatiana Firminio (piano), Laura Solla (guitar), and Mariana Pérez (drums).

Quartetazzo

It's 8 March 2019 in Madrid. Almost 9.45 p.m., the lights of Café Berlin go out for the start of the show. Marked by an old theatre atmosphere, this venue hosts two musical performances as part of *Ellas Crean* festival. Quartetazzo and Ladies in Blues put the final touch to a day in which hundreds of thousands of women have fought for their rights and participated in a massive demonstration.

The stage presence of the flute quartet is surprising, as it is not common for flutes to be almost absolute protagonists. Jazz music was the starting common ground for these artists, who looked to develop their own eclectic and innovative sound by integrating swing, blues, flamenco, chacarera, forró, and other forms of roots music. In a creative exercise of intercultural encounter and dialogue, these artists develop their shared identities and experiences during their performances, which are open to improvisation. Together, they project an affective disposition of cheerful positivity and intercultural encounter, present in their discourses and images. For instance, the booklet of their CD *En el aire* (self-produced, 2019), which presents nine originals, includes poetic verses to introduce the compositions. The song "Quartetazzo" (Malvares) is framed as follows: "Universal music/ women-universe/flute love/solos".

The original line-up of Quartetazzo is marked by the arrangements of four flutes and singular voices, and these frameworks imply an expansion and repositioning of the roles usually performed in standard line-ups. Trinidad Jiménez, who earned a Ph.D. in musicology (University of Seville) dedicated to the music language of Jorge Pardo, explained the challenges and mutual enrichment associated to Quartetazzo:

> Undoubtedly, being a hardly explored formation, you have the uncertainty and the freedom to compose whatever you want. . . . It uses up our creativity to recreate textures that perhaps with other bands are much more established: the role of the bass is such, the role of the flute is such . . . Here, being

four flutes, we have to recreate all those parameters in a thousand ways. To that handicap, add the handicap of blending the styles that each of us brings. One has a way of saying on the flute that has nothing to do with another. For example, Leticia Malvares is super rhythmic. So you try to listen and learn horizontally from the partners and the way they understand the music.

Her statement illustrates how a musical project such as Quartetazzo involves role repositioning and constant search. In this process, reaching a higher degree of freedom and artistic achievement becomes a goal and group challenge, which is approached through cooperation, mutual understanding, and horizontal learning. Regarding the particularities of role redefinition, Jiménez explained that she had played bass flute in flamenco ensembles to bring a certain colour or melody to the song. Yet the novelty in Quartetazzo is that her "role is rhythmic, to sustain harmony, to direct the pulse".

The formation of Quartetazzo is intimately linked to music education, as the four flutists advanced into it during a flamenco course taught by the veteran Jorge Pardo. The musicians realised that, while they could all perform *falsetas* accurately, they articulated this type of flamenco phrase differently. "The sound was different", explained Vela:

Suddenly, we opened our ears to four personalities and four different ways of playing the flute; four paths already made. That was also very motivating when the four of us got together. Such different ways, and how I would like to learn from you.

Furthermore, Barlatay affirmed that not only is musical performance varied within the group but also musical composition: "it's cool because one of us brings a tune and we all try to listen, adapt, and make it sound good according to how it has been composed".

Quartetazzo's motto, "four women, three nationalities, a sea of styles", emphasises diversity in terms of gender, nationality, and style. The group illustrates the strong and profound bonds between Spain and Latin America, particularly Argentina (represented by Barlatay) and Brasil (Malvares). Moreover, the many influences that shape their dynamic "sea of styles" include swing, modern jazz, several flamenco styles or *palos*, Latin American music such as chacarera, forró, maracatu, bolero, and cha-cha-chá, contemporary music, and classic rock. Vela pointed out that their motto constitutes both enrichment and a challenge, particularly regarding the intercultural dialogues developed through music from the other side of the Atlantic. Malvares suggested that flamenco provides a common ground or meeting place for them, even if they are coming from different routes.

"Basically, I think it's a reflection of Madrid. . . . Due to how alive it is, how much music there is, people from everywhere. You always end up meeting someone", explained Barlatay. While nodding, Jiménez added: "The scene is like this in Madrid". The extensive stylistic range of Quartetazzo is far reaching. It avoids repetition and favours broadness and openness, yet the myriad of voices and styles come together in the singular sound of the line-up. "The timbre, the fact that it is all for flute quartet, unifies the repertoire", explained Jiménez. Occasionally, they are backed by percussionist Epi Pacheco, who contributes with a versatile rhythmic support.

The members of Quartetazzo also reflected on the role of women in the history of flamenco and jazz. Jiménez recalled that "the women who sing [flamenco] have always sung at home, and taught their children. They are the ones who have become professionals because they have gone out of the house to work, but the women stayed at home". She cited Camarón's relationship with her mother as an example. Vela referred to female jazz instrumentalists as a minority within jazz history and also to the additional challenge presented by racial barriers. Additionally, she explained that there are very few female jazz instrumentalists in Madrid, being a clear minority within the scene.

Again, their CD booklet illustrates the immersion and reinterpretation of cultural traditions in relation to their social and communicative environments. "Cholero" (Malvares) is described as a bolero that wants to cry, as a choro that wants to dance, and "Swinga" (Vela) refers to the urban tempo: "in the city everything runs fast. It's about walking with your own pace in the blue tangle of the city". As for "Preludio a marzo" (Jiménez), its verse shows the connection

FIGURE 7.1 Trinidad Jiménez, Leticia Malvares, Carmen Vela, Emilse Barlatay, Lisi Sfair, Gabriel Matías, and Epi Pacheco after the performance by Quartetazzo. Café Berlín, 8 March 2019. Photograph by Ferdi Pérez.

between the experimental artistic nature of the group and the moving inspiration they take from the air, the sea, and the seasons: "Stubborn knots push new searches. They are only seasons in transit, cycles that flow into the sea". With the addition of "Why not" (Michel Camilo) and "Atlántico" (Luciano Cámara), the live show is focused on the songs of their debut album, which also includes: "Raíz" (Malvares), "De arena" (Jiménez), "Paschi" (Barlatay), "Mirada de mono" (Barlatay), and "Cruzando el charco" (Vela) (see Figure 7.1).

Towards the end of the concert, Brazilian flamenco dancers Lisi Sfair Denardi and Gabriel Matías delight the audience with several unexpected appearances. Placed at the centre of the semicircle of flutes, the *bailaores* establish an effective and surprising communion with the flutists. Their flamenco passion enhances a show marked by movement, nuances, and contrasts. Their heels contrast and connect with the soft and high-pitched sounds of the flutes. We experience an emotional journey driven by the flute players; by the whisperings, screams, and blows of Quartetazzo.

Ladies in Blues

An explosion of dance energy is transmitted to the public as the Ladies in Blues burst into the stage at 11 p.m. With a cheerful and relaxed eclecticism that contests more purist approaches to the genre, the Ladies form a plural, experienced, and talented group. While all-men bands have been the general norm in the specialised scene since the 1980s, their all-female line-up is innovative both for its gender identity and for its particular appropriation of the blues tradition. As an eclectic urban blues sextet, their style is primarily based on African-American electric blues, rhythm & blues, gospel, soul, and funk, as well as ballads.

Accordingly, throughout the concert they perform songs associated with well-known female blues musicians such as Koko Taylor ("Voodoo Woman", "I Can Love You Like a Woman"), Ruth Brown ("Mama, He Treats Your Daughter Mean"), Etta James ("A Sunday Kind of Love"), and Sugar Pie Desanto ("Soulful Dress"), as well as covers of blues, jazz, and soul classics such as "Catfish Blues" (Robert Petway), "Summertime" (George Gershwin), "Bring it On Home to Me" (Sam Cooke), and "A Change is Gonna Come" (Sam Cooke). Furthermore, the repertoire includes renditions of "Each Day" (Ann Cole), "I'm a Little Mixed Up" (Betty James), "Misty Blue" (Dorothy Moore), "Won't Be Long" (Aretha Franklin), and "Big Bad Handsome Man" (Imelda May).

A reunion project such as Ladies in Blues demands a collaborative effort from the six musicians involved, who approach their rehearsals and performances as a way of getting to know each other better. In particular, drummer Mariana Pérez explained that this project posed an exciting challenge for her in relation to blues music performance, as she was more used to playing rock and punk. "Apparently it is a very basic basis, very simple to understand but not to interpret. That is very cool and I'm super happy to be a part of it", she affirmed (see Figure 7.2).

FIGURE 7.2   Tatiana Firminio, Laura Gómez Palma, Mariana Pérez, Patricia Göser, Marta D'Ávilas, and Laura Solla during a gig by Ladies in Blues. Café Berlín, 4 October 2019. Photograph by Jorge Biancotti.

Regarding the elaboration of the band's repertoire, singer Marta D'Ávilas explained that they have tried to select songs that were sung by women. "When I started with blues", she recalled, "all the suggestions I got were from guys [male singers]", despite the number of women artists in the blues tradition. She talked about the identification with female voices, yet she also emphasised her interest in the feeling of the voice, regardless of whether it is a male or female singer. In fact, she cited John Lee Hooker as one of her most important influences.

When asked about the role of women in the history of blues and the bond they feel with those figures, Patricia Göser responded that "the bond is the struggle". They all expressed admiration for their talent and for their braveness to perform as black women within a racist environment. "I think they were much braver than we can be now", D'Ávilas suggested. She insisted on the intimacy of singing and on how it involves opening up, revealing oneself, in front of audiences.

[Singing blues] is not about being a diva. It's about you being emotionally naked. So it seems to me that they were gals who were like,

> look, either I do this or . . . [I don't know what I'll do]. Shoot me if you want, I'm already messed up, I can't be any more messed up. That's where I really connect a lot. I feel like I connect with the feeling of what the blues is, rather than on whether it's a pure style or not. And more with slavery,

because this music comes from what comes. That's right, the bittersweet it has comes from there. That's the part that I connect more with in the genre. A lot of feelin'.

D'Ávilas discussion about singing the blues emphasises its link with certain life conditions and struggles, and it points towards the interconnection between gender, race, and class. She acknowledges the inspiration taken from legendary blues singers, and a metaphorical connection is traced in terms of maintaining a powerful, overcoming attitude.

On this occasion, the Ladies are joined on stage by Argentinean artist Marina Sorín, who plays the phonofiddle, an atypical stringed musical instrument that contrasts with the urban sextet during the performance of "Catfish Blues". The seemingly improvised encounter prompts the passionate applause of the audience, and it is the result of the constant mobility and interaction between musicians from different generations and geographical backgrounds. The Ladies intertwine their voices and immerse themselves into the cultural tradition of the blues, making it clear that they are ready to follow their own path.

This meeting of female musicians pays tribute to legendary artists while promoting the visibility of current female artists. Their performance during 8-M has received outstanding coverage in specialised news media outlets such as *Madrid en Vivo* magazine (2019), where they appear on the cover. D'Ávilas referred to the idea of women empowerment in relation to music: "When a woman is on stage, she has to empower those who are below it". The connection and the bond between musicians and their audiences are based on musical discourse and performance, on sharing the encouragement to undertake, get up, take control, and step forward. According to her discourse: "It's like 'I'm here and, if you want to, you can be here too'".

The Ladies in Blues expressed support and close familiarity with the specialised blues scene, yet they articulated a critique that focused on the way in which the highly complex and disputed notion of purism affects artistic judgements and, subsequently, job opportunities. In this regard, D'Ávilas expressed the difficulties she faced trying to pitch her project De Holidays—a guitar and vocals duo dedicated to jazz singer Billie Holiday—to some of the main venues of the blues scene, who had considered it off-limits for their productions. Moreover, Laura Solla expressed ambivalence regarding the younger generation of well-established blues musicians: "I love it. I'm at La Coquette [Blues Bar] all day. But I mean, they just call each other, you know?" Solla felt musical admiration for these players, but she lamented the limited rotation of players and reclaimed a higher participation.

Since the crystallisation of the blues scene in the 1980s, the dominant construction of authenticity has been strongly linked to a high, almost exclusive, degree of specialisation in blues music, often associated to the tag "blues bands". "We're a little like intruders sometimes, aren't we?", reflected D'Ávilas. "I never sold myself as someone who does just this [plays blues exclusively] and is a purist about it. Not at all. . . . I've had direct criticism and friends who have told me that. But for me it's not a criticism". "I don't understand that need for it to be . . . clean and pure", responded Göser. "What is clean and pure? For you it's one thing and for me it's another. Besides, why does it have to be clean and pure? What kind of bullshit is that?" Interestingly, the young guitarist Laura Solla rhetorically asked "how are you going to be pure if you are Spanish?"

Nonetheless, the most problematic aspect of participating in the festival *Ellas Crean* arised from the hiring for a brief promotional performance in the centre of Madrid, organised by the Women Institute for Equal Opportunities, a public organism of the Madrid community. Ladies in Blues agreed to perform a couple of songs, yet three days before the event celebration scheduled on 6 March, they were asked to perform "Ain't Got No Life" (Nina Simone). The band explained that this song was not in their repertoire and that they did not have enough time to rehearse it. They proposed other politically meaningful songs such as "A Change is Gonna Come", "I'm a Woman", and "Feelin' Good" (to accommodate the Nina Simone petition), but the representative of the public institution decided to cancel their participation one day in advance. The Ladies felt disappointed and disrespected due to the arbitrary decision and the imposition of vertical power over collaboration and rapport around such a celebratory date. In fact, some of them even lost money in the process, as they had cancelled classes to be able to perform. Ultimately, they were replaced by a female violinist.

Conclusions

The analysis of Quartetazzo and Ladies in Blues reveals the intimate bonds between communicative justice, the planetarisation of popular music, the collective construction of glocal music scenes, and the development of the pluriverse as a context for multiple interconnected worlds, identities, and artistic voices. The examination of the scene and the observed case studies from the pluriverse perspective brings further insights into its collective construction as a place for musical performance, social encounter, and alternative lifestyles. These female popular musicians tend to identify with the underground sphere, enacting the idea of "prestige from below" (Lipsitz, 2001). Furthermore, while contributing to the ecology of transscales through multiple dialogues between the global and the local, they exemplify the ecology of productivities marked by cooperative organisation and group solidarity.

Interrelated and in dispute, the existing tension between the sociopolitical and cultural justice dimension and the political economy justice dimension is generally addressed by musicians through the pursuit of multiple projects and strategies to gain visibility. Situated within Madrid's music scene, yet connected to multiple places through migrations and eclectic stylistic influences, Quartetazzo and Ladies in Blues provide inspiring examples of the planetarisation of popular music and the leading role of female musicians. By observing the intersection of gender, nationality, class, and race, the analysis brings further insights into the organisation and performance of female groups associated with popular music genres such as jazz, flamenco, forró, blues, soul, and funk, among others. Despite difficulties, specialised scenes provide orientation and comfort to committed participants, who tend to develop a sense of home within the underground sphere. Nonetheless, the unveiled discourses of female musicians also exemplify the presence of ongoing conflicts and debates within the scene, mostly related to competition, "purism" or stylistic disputes, and the social value of music in a particular territory.

Given the precariousness that affects popular music scenes and the minority character of the genres they represent, the ability to perform live music professionally, while contributing to enriching intercultural encounters, may be seen as one of the highest achievements and everyday challenges of the observed musicians. They participate in regular performances with different line-ups, and this involves multiple rehearsal processes and repertoires. Some of these artists teach music at schools and in private classes, and others combine their musical activity with different day jobs. Both groups acknowledged the celebratory, sociopolitical and cultural justice meanings associated with their musical performances on International Women's Day. However, it also became evident that both groups are defined by internal diversity in terms of geography, opinions, and perspectives—that there are multiple ways of being and expressing yourself as a female musician.

The artists were supportive of the women's movement and aware that their repertoire and physical participation in the scene may contribute to widening its scope and questioning its "purism". The expansion of certain identity and stylistic limits of the music scene as a pluriverse with porous frontiers also conduced to concerns regarding belonging, appreciation, and recognition within the scene and towards the bigger outside, mass culture audiences. However, the observed musicians were also critical about the lack of institutional support for popular music throughout the rest of the year. There was a common desire of normalising the presence of female popular musicians not only in the scene but in different arenas of the public sphere. Ambiguity, ambivalence, and uneasiness aroused with their potential exoticisation and disputed communication practices, as well as with the permanence of gender and cultural stereotypes. Performing on and offstage, they all saw the road as a work in progress.

Note

1. This chapter is framed within the research project "Public Problems and Controversies: Diversity and Participation in the Media Sphere" (Ref: CSO2017–82109R), funded by the Ministry of Science, Innovation and Universities, Government of Spain. The authors wish to express their sincere gratitude to the featured artists, Quartetazzo, and Ladies in Blues, for their attention, information, and welcoming disposition. Also, special thanks to the photographers Ferdi Pérez and Jorge Biancotti for the generosity.

References

Bakhtin, M. (1981). *The dialogic imagination: Four essays.* The University of Texas Press.

Bakhtin, M. (1984). *Rabelais and his world.* Indiana University Press.

Becker, H. S. (1997). *Outsiders: Studies in the sociology of deviance.* The Free Press.

Bennett, A., & Peterson, R. A. (Eds.). (2004). *Music scenes: Local, translocal, and virtual.* Vanderbilt University Press.

Cohen, S. (1991). *Rock culture in Liverpool: Popular music in the making.* Oxford University Press.

Davis, A. (1999). *Blues legacies and Black feminism.* Vintage Books.

Deresiewicz, W. (2020). *The death of the artist: How creators are struggling to survie in the age of billionaires and big tech.* Henry Holt and Company.

Escobar, A. (2012). Más allá del desarrollo: Postdesarrollo y transiciones hacia el pluriverso. *Revista Antropología Social, 21,* 23–62.

García Canclini, N. (2009). *Culturas Híbridas: Estrategias para entrar y salir de la modernidad.* Randon House Mondadori.

Kristeva, J. (1980). *Desire in language: A semiotic approach to literature and art.* Columbia University Press.

La Noche en Vivo. (2019, March). 15 años de visibilidad y creatividad musical. *Madrid en Vivo, 106,* 4–9.

Lipsitz, G. (2001). *Time passages: Collective memory and American popular culture.* University of Minnesota Press.

Llano Camacho, I. (2018). *La salsa en Barcelona: Inmigración, identidad, músicas latinas y baile.* Editorial Milenio.

Lotman, I. (1996). *La semiosfera I: Semiótica de la cultura y del texto.* Frónesis Cátedra, Universitat de València.

Pedro, J. (2018). Jazz's little brother: The origins of the Spanish blues scene. *Jazz Research Journal, 12*(2), 193–212.

Pedro, J., Piquer, R., & Val, F. (2018). Repensar las escenas musicales contemporáneas: Genealogía, límites y aperturas. *Cuadernos de Etnomusicología, 12,* 63–88.

Santos, B. D. S. (2007). Beyond abyssal thinking: From global lines to ecologies of knowledges. *Review, XXX,* 45–89.

Shank, B. (1994). *Dissonant identities: The rock 'n' roll scene in Austin, Texas.* Wesleyan University Press.

8

EXPLORING RESISTANCE TO DEVELOPMENT IN THE OKINAWA PLURIVERSE

Daniel Broudy and Ariko Ikehara

Introduction

Though Okinawa has long served as a vitally important strategic base of operations for the militaries and economies of two major world powers, the prefecture is not well understood broadly beyond the East-Asia region. Japanese and American influence in Okinawa before, during, and after World War II (WWII) has, in terms of culture, language, and history, been monumental and lasting. Despite this, local people have also successfully managed to give some direction to these powerful forces in important and surprising ways in the interest of cultural preservation as well as in revitalising what has been erased by practices of (neo)colonial development. The authors point to another, less well-known success in Okinawa based upon ethnographic studies. The island's resistance movements reveal that there remain relational worldviews and ontologies for which the world, according to Arturo Escobar, is always multiple—a *pluriverse*. The authors integrate C. Douglas Lummis' concept of "antidemocratic development" to also analyse the actions of people through grassroots movements in Okinawa's pluriverse. The aim of this chapter is to add another layer of understanding to the literature where Okinawa studies intersect with communication research for the benefit of advancing communication justice.

Enlightenment scholar Bernard Le Bovier de Fontenelle contemplates the power and origins of mythology as a communication medium,

> Why would they have bequeathed us a mass of falsehoods? What could this love of men for manifest and ridiculous falsehood, have been, and why did it not last longer? For the Greek fables were not like our novels, which are intended as stories and not as histories.
>
> *(1728, p. 329)*

DOI: 10.4324/9781003316220-9

De Fontenelle grapples with the larger meanings of myth to the concerned citizen who seeks to become enlightened, to understand present truths in light of the past, and what course ought to be carved out for a just society for all citizens. Much of the story of Okinawa (Ryukyu) today can be seen as a grasping effort among many outsiders to understand the purpose of myths reproduced in mainstream education and media for the benefit of a social, economic, and political order established by the Japanese prefecture and US interventionism in the wake of WWII.

Princeton historian Richard Falk attempted to cut through the most enduring myths about the region, noting that

> the tragic fate that has befallen Okinawa and its people results from being . . . a forgotten remnant of the colonial past. . . . In this respect, it bears a kinship with such other forgotten peoples as those living in Kashmir, Chechnya, Xinjiang, Tibet, Puerto Rico, Palau, and the Mariana Islands, among others.
>
> *(2016)*

Okinawa has been described variously as "Ryūkyū" (Minority Rights, 2018); as a "double colony" (Tokuyama, 2013); as "a colony in a postcolonial world" (Falk, 2016); as "the keystone of the Pacific" (Yoshida, 2008); as "a daughter sold to the US by Japan" (Takazato in Tanji, 2006, p. 159); as "an important strategic base of aggression for US imperialism" (FBIS, 1969, p. A6); as a "problem" that "is no problem" (Eldridge, 2012); and as a prefecture of the Japanese state whose "citizens" enjoy full rights "under the democratic peace constitution" (Komatsu, 2017).

It has been represented in media as an important "stepping stone" (Feifer, 2001, p. 411) to other major regions of East Asia; as a "land of immortals" (Talmadge, 2001) who live in "Shangri La" (ibid); as an "idyllic Oriental land of peace and tranquillity" (Smits, 2010); as *iyashionoshima* (a place of healing); and as an "orphan of conquest" (Mears, 1956). So important are myths to the propagation of existing social, economic, and political structures that scholars devote entire volumes to the explication of their power over thought and behaviour. In *Myth Protest and Struggle* (2006), political scientist Miyume Tanji, for example, explores how various resistance movements in Okinawa came to rest upon the politics of myth in the popular imagination. In his recent book, a probing reexamination of the history of Okinawa titled *Maritime Ryukyu*, historian Greg Smits encounters "a vast array of differing conceptions of early Ryukyu" (2019, p. 252). Indeed, as international relations scholar Robert Eldridge observes, "The fundamental issues (bases, economic development, social and administrative integration with Japan, relations with the central government) inherent in the problem can be seen across years and decades, forming seemingly endless cycles and patterns (2004, p. 1). Beyond the East-Asia region, the story of Okinawa remains a story not well understood, a place where people strive to preserve, recapture, or reassert remnants of their indigenous identity, unique culture, history, and languages (*Shimakutuba*). For the authors of this chapter, Okinawa is home—a place of ceaseless fascination and concern about the future of indigenous cultures and languages, not merely in the East-Asian archipelago, but throughout the world.

The discussion taken up herein offers a brief background of Okinawa, Japan, as a post-WWII project of Western development. It introduces the concept of "antidemocratic development" (p. 45) as elaborated by C. Douglas Lummis in *Radical Democracy* (1996) and considers how communication justice is managed and moderated in the face of popular movements resisting the latest forms of antidemocratic military-industrial development in the northern part of the island. The aim is to sketch a clearer picture of Okinawa's pluriverse where local people seek systemic justice through acts of public communication for the redress of grievances against prevailing power structures. Okinawa's recent past and present are explored from the perspective of activists and communities that face challenges in communication justice. Research strategies for this chapter include participant observation in data collection and data analysis methods within the critical discourse analysis tradition.

Local developments in antidevelopment sentiment

In *Radical Democracy*, Lummis demolishes prevailing positive concepts associated with programs of unceasing development in a world of finite resources. The extent of Okinawa's finiteness is especially evident to the casual observer surveying the landscape through the lens of US national defence imperatives: the main island comprises merely 0.6% of the entire Japanese landmass yet hosts over 70% of all US forces (Fujiwara, 2020). Lummis begins by presenting a little-known understanding of development by drawing upon its etymological roots. The English term has Italian forebearers found in the verb *viluppare*, "to enwrap, to bundle, to fold, to roll up" (1996, p. 62). Herein, we explore its opposite in *de*-velop. Freed from its ideological connotations, "development" does not necessarily signify natural and positive change since, for example, forest fires, invasions, diseases, and plots against people and their natural rights, among many other projects and processes, develop and progress.

Nevertheless, the ideology of development, the positive connotations of which have long been cultivated through public discourse in democratic capitalist societies, has become so tightly wound to rationality that "sustainable development", the latest neoliberal doublespeak, has morphed into a powerful myth normalising top-down forms of fiscal austerity, dispossession, and "coercion . . . repackaged as empowerment" (Morningstar, 2020). With the United Nations announcing its strategic partnership with the World Economic Forum in June 2019, UNSDG doublespeak shows how the pervasive "sustainable development" (Tedeneke, 2019) slogan, designed by the "transnational capitalist class" (Phillips, 2018, p. 24), means a sustained supply of natural and human resources freely available for extraction and investment from a fully marketised biosphere, while, for the masses, it means the protection and preservation of nature and the public commons from continued exploitation.

Within this ideology of development, Lummis observes that "the power of the metaphor is that it gives the impression that projects being carried out under that ideology are natural, inevitable, and bring about the proper and predestined future of the entity being developed" (1996, p. 63). We draw attention to a less well-known local achievement in Okinawa based upon long-term ethnographic, participatory research. Okinawa's anti-base resistance movements "show that there are indeed relational worldviews or ontologies for which the world is always multiple—a pluriverse" (Escobar, 2011, p. 139).

This multiplicity of ways in being can be observed in the daily actions of local people, many elderly, and some in their late 80s, who have since the 1990s been raising their voices through sit-in protests at the gates of various US military installations, and whose concepts of justice remain grounded in traditional local culture, wartime experiences, local agriculture and maritime biodiversity, indigenous language rights, and the reinvigoration of local arts. Since these ongoing movements confront power structures through public discourse and direct action, which aims to create new structures promoting the right to communication, we can see that local understandings of development have not been entirely coopted by transnational stakeholder capitalism. While local traditions of resistance to colonialism and antidemocratic development date back to the late 1800s, we confine the following analysis to the post-WWII era.

Okinawa as an American project of development

Since Japan's late-19th-century colonisation of the Ryukyu Kingdom—a veritable empire in Smits' analysis (2019, p. 178)—the Ryukyu archipelago renamed Okinawa prefecture has been relegated to an exotic, feminine, inferior, cultural backwater: that is, Japan's internal South, in the geographical, political, and socioeconomic sense. In the wake of the war, western interpretations of development began appearing in practices of dispossession when American base expansion plans necessitated access to local land and water resources. *New York Times* reporter George Barrett, dispatched to Okinawa in 1952 to describe the project, which for years prior had been unfolding, offered the most vivid account of the US military's efforts. In the title of his article "Report on Okinawa: A Rampart We Built", Barrett prepares his readers for a description of America's frontier activities in East Asia by alluding to the lyrics of the "Star Spangled Banner", and, thus, fusing the positive connotations of patriotism and national defence with the necessary spread of the American way of life.

> [L]iving down its reputation as an "outpost for the outcast", [Okinawa] is now a collection—almost a magical transplanting—of whole American communities, with several more still building. Some of these are already

complete, even to schools, department stores, theatres and suburban hous-
ing developments boasting winding roads, flagstone walks and "picket"
fences made of bamboo.

(Barrett, 1952)

The title of Barrett's article features an oblique reference to key lines in the American anthem:

Whose broad stripes and bright start through the perilous fight
O'er the ramparts we watched, were so gallantly streaming
And the rocket's red glare, the bombs bursting in air,

To readers of the *Times* piece, memories of the Battle of Okinawa, the most
savage of the Pacific campaign (Manchester, 1987), were likely still fresh as the
82-day struggle saw "over 200,000 lost American, Japanese and Okinawan lives"
(Manchester, 1987, p. 42). In the Battle, described by local witnesses as a *tetsu
no bofu* (storm of steel), US forces alone sustained over 75,000 casualties (Nash,
2015, p. 143), the shocking losses no doubt weighing especially heavy upon
American public consciousness. While the "perilous fight" for Okinawa was, for
the Americans, a key piece in the larger Pacific War puzzle, recent memories and
emotions of the "rocket's red glare" and "bombs bursting in air" over Okinawa
would certainly be activated by the positive postwar developments enumerated in
Barrett's "Rampart We Built".

Barrett's article seems to illustrate a sort of patriotic pride felt by a Western
reporter assigned to tour the East-Asian outpost and describe the vast "magical" reorientation of Oriental culture subsumed by Occidental development. His
survey of the island, which "quietly mushroomed into a first-class island bastion,
barbed with batteries of long-muzzled 120's", dispossessed of control over its land
and sea, remains a key study in the free flow of transnational capital to the island
fortification constructed by Western military forces. "The construction project",
Barrett notes, "which in effect is converting the lower third of Okinawa from
tropical barrenness into a series of self-contained communities, is roughly the
equivalent in manpower effort, . . . , to building a city the size of Indianapolis
from scratch" (1952).

In erasing the agency of the island's war-torn local survivors, the journalist can
effectively frame for his readers the myth of postwar Okinawa as an inert waste-
land devoid of life (Broudy & Simpson, 2013). The caricature can, then, serve to
justify the fundamental transformation of the island, which "in the savage transfer
of title . . . [became] a rivet-hammering, rock-blasting, $500,000,000 construc-
tion project" (1952). Thus, what was once a "memorial" to the war dead is now
a "construction project" presented to *New York Times'* readers as evidence of
capitalism's unassailable ability to unfold massive projects of development on foreign shores. In this postwar period, the military planners and engineers produce

in the island a concrete illustration of impressive developments made possible by their careful calculations and surveys.

Barrett admits to his readers that the precise size and scope of the post-war project are confidential. While "several communities with their schools and stores and club houses and block after block of residential homes account for only about 25 percent of the Okinawan project, all the rest", he notes, "is military" (1952). Visitors to Okinawa today might be staggered by the general imposing appearance of US bases throughout the island, but Barrett's article in the early 1950s serves, arguably, as the most graphic description of anti-democratic development during the occupation period.

> If all the asphaltic concrete used on Okinawa could be put into a single-lane road 11 feet wide, the highway would go from New York to Chicago; if the poured concrete could be formed into a sidewalk 4 feet wide, it would start in New York and end in San Francisco; and if the cement blocks could be laid end to end in the United States, they would make a wall 4 feet high complete across the country, with an extension of another 1000 miles into the sea.
>
> *(1952)*

Today, in the northern part of the main island, an audacious program of development has, in recent years, been resurrected from the 1966 occupation (Yoshikazu, 2006) in a major "rivet-hammering" and "rock-blasting" construction project entailing massive land reclamation opposed, in the latest island-wide referendum, by the majority of local people (Johnson, 2020). Before analysing contemporary local resistance to programs of military-industry development, we trace the history through which the promises of reversion from military occupation to Japanese governance produced the present status quo.

Development in the reversion era

Initially, Okinawa Governor Chobyo Yara's 1971 postreversion manifesto (*keng-isho*) proclaimed the aim of Okinawan people to remove all bases and to assert their collective desire for self-determination based upon the region's unique history, language, and culture distinct from Japan's (Shimabukuro, 2012, p. 47). Throughout the 1970s and 1980s, however, a more conservative and pragmatic bloc came to dominate local politics and charted a different tack away from Yara's progressive manifesto. This course fully embraced Japan's mainstream postwar regime of "dependent development". The regime was arguably ingeniously devised for Japan's neocolonial control of Okinawa. It locked Okinawa's economy into the post-war bifurcated military-industrial system organised under the Washington-Tokyo mutual security alliance.

Through the Okinawa Development Agency and later directly under the Prime Minister's Cabinet, the Government of Japan centrally planned a series of special "development budgets" for Okinawa, led bureaucratically by the highly acclaimed Japanese developmental state. The special development budgets for Okinawa have, since then, been justified by Tokyo's interest in ensuring the survival of its Mutual Security Treaty with Washington maintaining the majority of the politically unpopular anachronistic and colonial US military presence away from the Japanese mainland and largely concentrating it on the geographically remote Okinawa. Indeed, it has long been argued that the regime of "dependent development" has been the principal means by which Tokyo has camouflaged its dependence on Okinawa.

Since its 1972 reversion from American postwar military occupation and administration to Japanese governance, Okinawa has remained "suspended in time" (Teshiba, 2003) as a US military outpost serving as a key strategic base of operations in East Asia. The question of why Okinawa appears to be caught in suspended economic animation can be addressed, in part, by comparing key regions in the world where development and the needs for national security intersect with postwar history.

According to Escobar, for example, as military assistance agreements were made by the US and all Latin American nations in Rio de Janeiro in 1947, the connections between strategic military planning and the origins of development have been scarcely examined by scholars (2012, p. 34). In time, these pacts, Escobar notes, would morph into doctrines of national security, intimately linked to economic development strategies (2012, p. 34). When viewed in the same light, the present situation for Okinawa can be traced back over the past several decades when victory for western forces produced the post-WWII global hegemonic order through similar security pacts signed by the United States and Japan in 1951 in San Francisco. Former Okinawa Governor Masahide Ōta, notably, called attention to the many observers who have noticed over the decades the

> subsidies and other material incentives [used] as a blunt instrument for dealing with local protests over base issues [as] such subsidy politics exploits the economic weakness and dependence of Okinawa on the central government because . . . handouts have become such a necessary prop to the prefectural economy.
>
> *(Ōta, 2003, p. 25)*

Weaknesses in the "dependent development" system, however, began emerging when the global economy began shifting towards full-on neoliberal globalisation (Hook, 2003, p. 41).

Recent development projects in Okinawa serve as salient examples of the continuing tension between claimed imperatives of the dominant postwar "modern ontology" and local struggles that move towards a pluriverse (Escobar, 2011, p. 139). Prompted by the need to both maintain the long-standing security arrangement and close the old US Marine Corps Air Station in Futenma (in the island's southern region), Tokyo refined its *quid pro quo* politics in Okinawa by using special financial aid "sweeteners" and subsidies linked to local acceptance of the substitute US military facilities (Tanji & Broudy, 2017, p. 189). Since its announcement in 1996, the most controversial project to date remains the development of a sprawling US Marine Corps Air Station in Henoko in the northern region of the island, an economically and demographically depressed area, especially in need of investment. Seen increasingly as outmoded, such was the reclamation project that called for more of the same stereotypical industrialisation and environmentally destructive construction.

Significantly, the 2013 "All-Okinawa" coalition, which embodied bipartisan local opposition to the new US Marine Corps sea base in Henoko, has revealed a decline in Tokyo's ability to control Okinawa through its post-reversion system of "dependent development". The first-ever bipartisan, anti-base "All Okinawa" coalition was made possible by the deflection of traditionally prodevelopment, pro-US base conservative Okinawan business leaders, to join the anti-US base progressives against the new base construction. In the early 21st century, these conservatives expressed a higher awareness of autonomy as *Uchinanchu* (people of Okinawa)—a sense of need to re-assert local identity against Japan, triggered by the 2007–8 history textbook controversy. The turning point was the conservatives' financial and organisational support for the 2008 "All-Okinawa" people's protest against Japan's censorship of history textbooks to delete descriptions of the Japanese military's complicity in collective compulsory suicides in Okinawa (Matsumura & Wright, 2015) and of "all references . . . to the controversial term 'comfort women'" (Nozaki & Seldon, 2009).

These feelings of local pride and a desire to recover the past in a region whose culture, language, and history had been battered and subsumed by the plans of two major world powers began finding expression in scholarship; political activism; and the performing and fine arts. Though each area of resistance deserves its own book-length treatment, we focus our analysis on the voices of people who seek justice through the arts.

Concrete: a medium of construction and communication justice

When media theorist Marshall McLuhan observed that, "the medium is the message" (1964, p. 1), his insight might appear fully crystallised to observers of Minoru Kinjo's most notable works of art. The artist works as both creator and curator in his Yomitan gallery. On approaching the site, we saw his two-story house beside which stood a fenced-off area partially camouflaged by subtropical foliage. We entered the main open-air exhibit through a gap in the tall grass with palm trees enclosing the foyer. The warm breeze and surrounding landscape seemed to serve as integral natural elements of Kinjo's installation. A cinder block wall dividing the museum's "floor" space from a neighbouring property stands as an intriguing boundary between the so-called bulldozers and bayonets exhibit and present life beyond the enclosure. Here we felt, standing in the midst of his work, as though history were reconstituted in the sculptures of local figures standing against uniformed men with weapons drawn and another handling the levers of a bulldozer (see Figure 8.1).

Minoru Kinjo had worked for decades to recreate the dreadful scenes of his witness to US military base expansion operations when local people in Isahama, and in Ie-jima, were pushed off of their land and out of their homes to make way for the new colonial outposts. Each piece cast in cement and plaster paralleled, to Kinjo, the cold and emotionless faces of US forces competing for power and control over local land—American soldiers armed with the machinery of war (and post-war development) and the people with their ancestral ties to *terra firma*. The artist lectured us for hours on how that era saw American forces capture land and coastlines from local people and pour countless yards of concrete into forms for new homes, runways, and seaports. Even the rice paddies in Kamiyama and the potato fields in Awase, he noted, which had long produced daily staples, were not spared from the development of military garrisons.

FIGURE 8.1 The sculptures show a figure standing against uniformed men with weapons. Photograph by Jason Aaren Arbogast, 2020.

Kinjo's description of that time reminded us of Escobar's critique of the literal limitations of globalisation grounded in a pervasive and deceptive belief that the entire world is some kind of limitless "global space" that can and will invariably accommodate all the needs and demands of the captains of capitalist modernity. There is something fundamentally perverse about this fanciful construction of the world, imagined and literal, Escobar points out (2011, p. 139). "If we are to take the pluriverse seriously", he notes, "let alone if we are to confront the ever worsening ecological and social crises" (2011, p. 139), we must awaken to the ways in which globalisation—a universal, fully economised and delocalised system—is normalised through "the immense power of corporations and maintained within manageable levels of dis/order by military might" (2011, p. 139).

Escobar points out that "from its very global conditions are emerging, however, responses and forms of creativity and resistance that make increasingly visible the poverty, perniciousness, and destructiveness of this imaginary" (2011, p. 139). For Kinjo, the apt artful response in calling wider attention to these conditions is concrete—the natural medium of choice that made the witness of his own postwar memories of military development even more meaningful. In times of both war and peace, the bulldozer reappears to take its place in the perpetual march towards what elite movers and shakers of the global system claim to be progress and development. Kinjo saw the American post-war project to dispossess people of their land as part of the explicit effort to throw the people of Okinawa into a state of constant concern and dependency.

Imbued in arresting high relief concrete sculptures that capture scenes of battlefield horror during the 1945 Allied invasion of Okinawa is the distinct message that the medium communicates as much meaning as its various creative forms. Kinjo's work in concrete, among other media, reminds his audience that the physical and structural changes imposed upon our ways of living, introduced in subtle and insidious ways over long periods of time, must not fade from public consciousness.

During the Pentagon's official administration of Okinawa (1945–1972), when base expansion was at its peak and the increased necessity for more land at its most intense, US authorities poured countless yards of concrete for the emerging aircraft aprons and runways, support structures, and homes for the machines and members who would comprise the new governing presence. For local people, Kinjo observed that concrete came to typify foreign domination as it would come to dominate the bombed-out, flame-thrown landscape and cover, through a campaign of land annexation, the agricultural fields that people had used for centuries to practice self-sufficiency.

In surveying his artwork, one cannot help but see in Kinjo's sculptures how cement and plaster combine to carry memories from the past into the present, integrating conceptual images conjured up by historical narratives into truly concrete representations of what local people in the postwar era endured. Kinjo himself, a traumatised witness to the tragedies of that time, expanded in an interview with us on the experiences of his youth.

After graduation from high school in neighbouring Hamahiga Island, he set off for college in Tokyo, full of promise at 19, but was ultimately denied entry to the many schools he had applied to. Dejected and wandering for a time in Tokyo with no permanent place to rest, he awoke one morning from a shelter in Ueno Park to behold the splendour of an art exhibit featuring the work of Auguste Rodin. Kinjo admits to his shock and awe at the stark contrasts between what he saw in Tokyo and what he had known while growing up in Hamahiga. The visual beauty and cultural capital residing in the Rodin exhibit caused him to reflect on his own impoverished beginnings as he stood gazing at the works of the famous French sculptor. To Kinjo, the great gaps in social and economic wealth situated in Tokyo, as compared to Okinawa, were astonishing.

In returning to Okinawa, he and his mother felt embarrassed and were periodically mocked by members of the local community because he had not been able to secure a seat at a university in Tokyo. The intolerable treatment in his hometown forced him to relocate to Osaka to undertake studies in English education and to acquire a teaching license whereupon, after graduation, he began work as a high school teacher in the city. His memories of the Rodin exhibit and their larger meanings, nonetheless, continued to haunt him.

During his tenure, he became inspired by the resolve of common people to unite in a shared struggle against more powerful political and economic interests. As he read news of the unfolding movements for reversion in Okinawa and the civil uprisings in the early 1970s, he empathised with people who struggled everywhere as he also witnessed around him resistance movements in Osaka. There, at the time, he became aware of parallel movements in communities throughout the city. Korean students and other historically marginalised groups, such as citizens with various physical or mental impairments, struggled against racism and discrimination, and these citizen efforts to fight injustice emboldened him all the more to act beyond the commitments and responsibilities of his own teaching profession. This period marked the time he began contemplating alternative outlets of creative expression.

Having also witnessed his own sister sold into servitude to Itoman Village, along with countless other girls, and his female cousins coerced to live with American military men for support, Kinjo felt that he could never forgive himself for remaining powerless to alleviate the suffering around him. He said that he wanted to find an excellent medium to help express the profound anger and sadness he saw in the faces of Okinawan women.

Out of his observations, decades earlier have come countless works drawing upon themes of war, discrimination, and centrally planned forms of poverty. The sculptor focuses on these themes as a witness to the ongoing struggles of people everywhere. "Okinawa is so very interesting", Kinjo observes, "because there are so many problems, and so many people are resisting, and this is why we never grow old". He muses and shakes his head, "I don't become depressed; living here is much more interesting than sad" (2018).

His work is a careful study of the stark contrasts between serenity and stoicism. Each piece in this part of the exhibit representing American military might, and its excesses, is striking in the parallel relationship the sculptor draws between the medium itself and the expressionless faces of the men. The concrete cast of a military man seated at the controls of a bulldozer stares blankly at the sculpted forms of members of a local crowd standing in resistance to him and his fellow soldiers armed with rifles with fixed bayonets (see Figure 8.2).

One can begin to grasp the full effect of Kinjo's intent by beholding the stone visage of the men and their cold business-like manner as they move the machinery of military development forward. A mild trace of emotion can be found in the slight sneer of another American face contrasting sharply with the equanimity of an Okinawan man calmly seated before them in opposition.

FIGURE 8.2 The sculptures show a military man seated at the controls of a bulldozer. Photograph by Jason Aaren Arbogast, 2020.

First-hand textual accounts of this kind of opposition also appear in the historical record, in newsprint. In his 1953 article "Play Fair with Okinawans", Otis Bell described then what visitors to the museum today might imagine to be eerily similar to the scenes that unfolded during the 1950s when, "army troops had to be called out to suppress [what they called] 'a communist uprising'", which happened to be an "unarmed group of Okinawans . . . protesting use of their land without agreement and without payment" (Bell, 1954). Viewers will also note expressions of anger and resolve to resist the movement towards base expansion displayed in the concrete figures of farmers standing (and some sitting) amidst the commotion (see Figure 8.3).

As an extension of their hard feelings of resistance, the various historical characters cast in this particular medium might appear to onlookers to signify a solid resolve to remain strong. Upon closer observation, too, we might further notice that Okinawan concrete itself comprises the very life forms that help the island thrive, at least at the level of organic chemistry, as the calcified corpses of organic bodies, once alive, are now recast as core components of the medium. In keeping with the interaction of these ingredients—the aggregate of sand, ash, coral, and limestone—the people, when mixed in with the right conditions, represent an inflexible and unyielding desire to defend and stand firmly on their land.

It has long been suggested that the authentic symbols of Roman imperial power cast in concrete architectural designs occupying regions in far-flung

FIGURE 8.3   The sculptures show farmers amidst the commotion. Photograph by Jason Aaren Arbogast, 2020.

provinces of the Empire had served as daily reminders that Rome was, indeed, the global centre of military and economic power in the classical world. Visitors to the gallery in Yomitan might speculate whether Kinjo had in mind to use this medium as a way to regain some control over that world, past and present, and to reform it for some peaceful, environmental, and (re)creative purpose. While local movements against the Henoko development show that Kinjo had selected an apt medium, other Okinawan practitioners have taken the message of resistance outside the prefecture with much success.

1945 ± 66 years: reexamining pastness of Okinawa history in 2011

Kaoru Kinjo is a philosopher who puts his thinking into everyday practice. Born in Okinawa but transplanted to Osaka, he has been involved in Okinawan cultural activism since the 1970s through *Gajumaru no kai*, a local Okinawan youth group that supports Okinawans living in Osaka who are facing difficulties adjusting to the harsh environment in which Okinawans have often faced discrimination. As a cofounder of the group, Kinjo was deeply involved in an Okinawan diasporic awakening and cultural renaissance in Osaka.

In 1985, he bought a three-story house and established *Kansai Okinawan Bunko* (Bunko hereafter) on the second floor with his older brother selling Okinawan merchandise in a shared space. Bunko offers books, newspapers, photos, DVDs, films, artwork, objects, and materials related to Okinawa. In examining two of his flyers, we assess Kinjo's creative hand at work in the discursive symbols he chooses to address an international diplomatic controversy that still divides people.

2011 Flyer 1945 ± 1966 did the war end for Okinawa?

Each year, Bunko hosts events on Okinawa's historically important anniversaries such as 1879 (annexation of the Ryukyu Kingdom); 1903 (Pavilion of Anthropology); 1945 (the Battle of Okinawa); 6/23 (Memorial Day); 12/20/1970 (Koza Riots); and 5/15/1972 (Okinawa's Reversion to Japan). Bunko events are also connected to current events such as elections and rallies for peace that remain ongoing on the mainland. In 2011, America's lead diplomat in Okinawa Kevin Maher was fired from his post for calling Okinawans "lazy" and "masters of extortion" (Talmadge, 2011; Broudy & Simpson, 2013) monikers that recall the *quid pro quo* politics cited by Masahide Ōta but developed by Tokyo to keep Okinawa dependent on so-called handouts. Bunko routinely reexamines the status of the ongoing war in Okinawa revealing the long period of historical domination from 1879 to the present system: US militarism and Japanese economic hegemony.

As a creative performative medium, Kinjo's flyer embodies the content, context, and form, and it functions as conceptual art, an approach grounded in the avant-garde movement of 1960. Since conceptual art is driven more by concept than form, an art exhibition's catalogue itself may serve as a work of art. In the words of a conceptual art publisher, "Reproductions of traditional art in catalogues are inevitably (distorted) 'secondary' information. If the information is PRIMARY, the catalogue itself can be an exhibit" (Higgins, 2002). Often drowned in the provocative text, the critical and creative signs/logos (such as 66 on leaflets, posters, and flyers) that Kinjo creates can be read as conceptual, disseminating its message even after the event has ended.

In the following sections, we critically examine two flyers for three events: 15 May 2011 and 16 May 2004. The flyers refer to important dates in Okinawa's post-war history: 15 May signals the end of US military domination in Okinawa and its return to the Japanese nation-state.

May 2011 Flyer "1945 ± 1966: did the war end for Okinawa?"

During the 15 May event, Ko Nakazo, an Okinawan writer and cultural critic, spoke about the unfinished business of 1879 when the independence of the Ryukyu Kingdom was disposed of and, at once, the Ryukyuans became Okinawans and the Ryukyu Islands became Japan (see Figure 8.4). The title of the event itself was "To End the Ryukyu Disposal" which recounts the history of what had happened and the ongoing lack of resolution. Kinjo uses both the

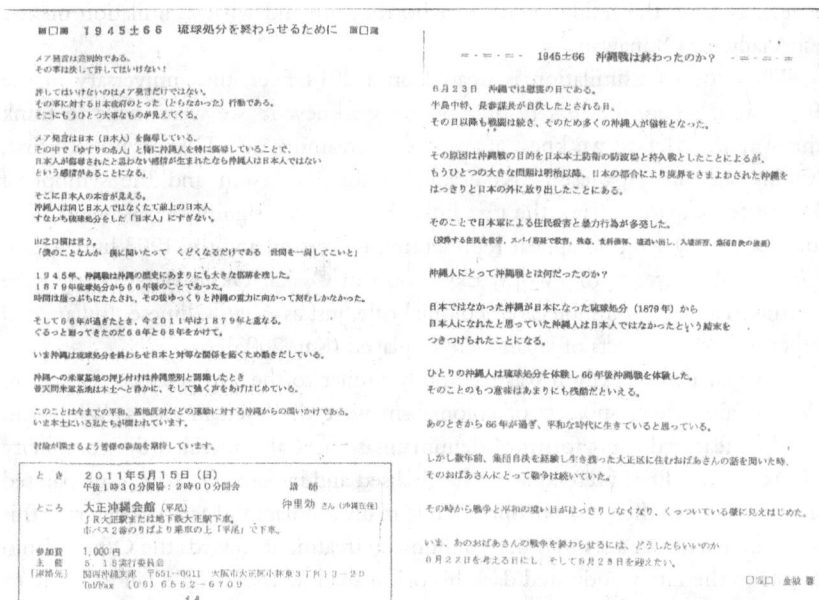

FIGURE 8.4   May 2011 Flyer, archival collection of Ariko Ikehara at the Koza X MiX-topia Research Center, Okinawa, Japan. Photograph by Ariko Ikehara.

rhetorical and the symbolic to decry the falsehood, "Maher's statement is discriminatory. We should never accept it!" alluding to Maher's criticism of Japanese, but especially of Okinawans. With his use of bold font and bold assertions, Kinjo points out that the Ryukyuans never "became" equal to the Japanese and urged an end to what occurred 66 years ago. He called for people to forge an equal relationship between Okinawa and Japan and referred to the heavy burden of military bases placed upon Okinawa and the solution of transferring the bases to Japan. This is the line that divides the people: Japanese supporters willing to take the burden and those who are not. On this side of the flyer, the text reads: "We expect to deepen the debate with your participation".

Diverging profiles of the reversion: Japanese and Okinawan

Another side of the sheet features the content of the actual event: "The profile of the reversion—Japanese Profile, Okinawan Profile", a pun on the expression, "Profile of War". Wordplay acts as a critique of the predominant one-sided view that helps maintain the status quo. The trope is deployed to critique the meaning of Reversion from the front and side views so as to dislodge the notion of only one legitimate face (or side) of war and one truth but to examine them from all profiles (or sides) of war, such as in the Battle of Okinawa. In the same spirit of critique, the event also examines the profiles of Okinawans and Japanese, especially from the hidden truth of who they are and what assimilation means, especially for Okinawans.

The issue of assimilation is treated on a 2014 flyer, the anniversary of the Reversion, where the text reads: "Before we knew it, we were made to think this way . . . Before we knew it, we were screaming . . . Then, who said first, 'Okinawans are Japanese'?" Referring to the Reversion and the symbol of Hinomaru (Japanese flag), the text links these various significant events of 1903 and 1972. Key symbols appear representing Reversion and the 1903 human zoo (*Jinrui-kan*). Here, at the World Exposition in Osaka, Okinawan women were portrayed as captured subjects of colonial rule, just as Ainu, Chinese, Indian, and other imperial subjects of Japan were displayed (Kai, 2005).

This particular pavilion was uncannily similar to the 19th-century European World Fairs where subjects of colonialism were displayed in cages. While this incident featured overt forms of dehumanisation, it also revealed the complicity of Okinawan elites, pretending to be civilised and irreproachable, who separated themselves from their own people. While many scholars and activists describe this incident as only an act of Japanese inhumane treatment towards the Other, Kinjo points to the rarely addressed dark historical shadow that people fail to come to terms with. While questions about the dispossession and marginalisation typified in the 1903 Osaka exhibit remain unanswered, there is another time in history that Okinawans desired to be Japanese, an attempt unfulfilled.

May 2004 "Dōka Shichatta Watashi Tachi What is Wrong with us?"

On the anniversary of the reversion (15 May 2004), Bunko produced a flyer that addressed the same question that Kinjo asks. For some Okinawans, reversion in 1972 signified a hopeful belief that Okinawans *would* become Japanese (see figure 8.5). The flyer also features a provocative question: "What Is Wrong With Us?" The question serves as a perlocutionary act: "convincing, persuading, deterring, surprising, or misleading" (Austin, 1962/1975). Kinjo's question refers to that time when people thought they would assume full citizenship with all Japanese rights and responsibilities and, thus, take on new names and new ways of living and looking at the world. In Japanese, the phrase is also a clever pun. *Dōka* means both "what happened" and "assimilation". The meanings strike the hearts of the guilty especially hard. The text also alludes both to the Japanese appropriation of Okinawan culture and land and to those who resist its theft. At the heart

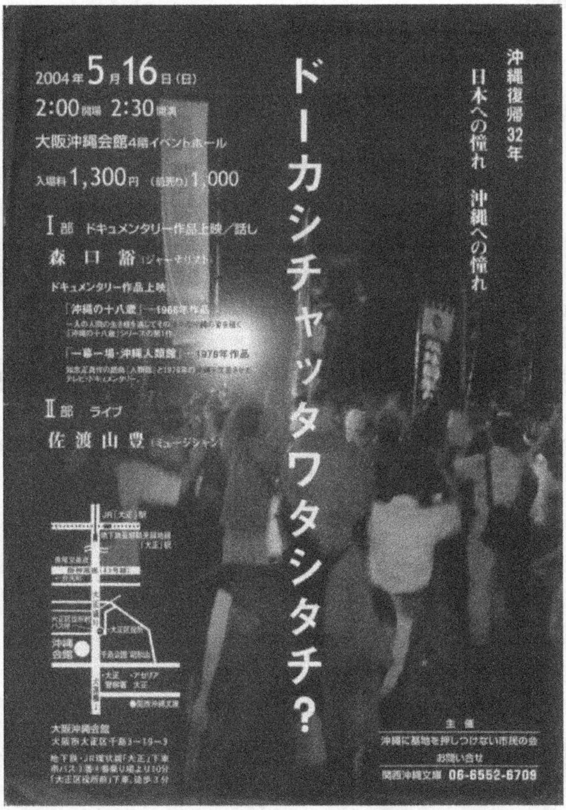

FIGURE 8.5   May 2004 Flyer, archival collection of Ariko Ikehara at the Koza X MiX-topia Research Center, Okinawa, Japan. Photograph by Ariko Ikehara.

of this event is a call for unity among Okinawans and Okinawan-Japanese to ponder their own complicity in the maintenance of the status quo.

The flyer serves a performative function when folded in half. In our interview, Kinjo reveals the relationship between this cycle of past-present-future events as each circle back to the original—that is, Ryukyu Disposal (1879) all of which cause us to repeat the question *ad infinitum*. The shape of the flyer, whether folded or straightened, is impacted by what he calls the gravity by which people are drawn to act and move together. The flyer, when flattened, symbolises "the gravity" (desire) pulled towards Japanese affecting the natural process of assimilation into Japanese. When two sides are folded back-to-back or face-to-face, the gravity is pulled towards Okinawan roots, returning, reclaiming, rebuilding, revitalising that which was lost. We can locate in Kinjo's work not only a rejection of the forces of modernity that have worked to create the modern Japanese status quo but also, just as importantly, an effort to respect "relational ontologies . . . that eschew divisions between . . . individual and community, and between us and them that are", as Escobar observes, "central to the modern ontology" (2011, p. 139).

Conclusion

Okinawa might be well understood as a space where competing views of what the island was, is, and should be are in constant flux. The hegemonic view promoted by the United States and Japan is based on Modern, capitalist, military, neoliberal, and neo-colonial development, which expresses itself globally and oppresses alternative, local possibilities. However, there is also a counterhegemonic pluriverse of different actors striving to retain and expand local culture, arts, language and agricultural practices, relational ontologies and epistemologies, and historical memory while counteracting cultural, economic, and military subjugation by both superpowers.

The sense of losing something invaluable and expending the energy to regain it pervades so much of the conceptual and geographical spaces occupied by people concerned for Okinawa's future. Minoru Kinjo, as we have shown, uses the three dimensions of space in sculpture to regain the past and retell stories obscured by myth and interest in maintaining the prevailing order. Kaoru Kinjo uses space for meetings, study groups, gatherings, and events to reassert Okinawan agency, to uplift Okinawan people living in Japan and the mainland.

The philosophical position of Kinjo's Bunko is "Looking at Okinawa from Taisho Ward! Okinawa space where Ryukyu people can interact" (Kinjo, 2009). He sees Bunko as a harbour, a place where people, ideas, events, and objects related to Okinawa can come and go like Foucault's concept of the boat,

> a floating piece of space, a place without a place, that exists by itself, closed in on itself and at the same time given to the infinity of the sea and that,

from port to port, from tack to tack, . . ., it goes back as far as the colonies in search of the treasures that they conceal in their gardens.

(Foucault & Miskowiec, 1984, p. 9)

Such are the associations that reveal Kinjo's philosophical and avant-garde disposition, his keen artistry in the flyers he makes, inviting critical reflection, critique, and participation. Throughout Okinawa, we also see many more spaces than these occupied by common people striving to make common cause against what they see as an ongoing occupation of the land, sea, and air.

Given the region's immeasurable importance to the security and economic might of two major world powers, we extend the insights offered by Robert Eldridge: Okinawan academics, journalists, and opinion leaders must fill the great void if they want the local perspective on their postwar and postreversion experience better understood by their fellow citizens and those of other countries, rather than issues of topical import (2004, p. 129). We feel that this sort of work has begun at the grassroots with the voices of many determined and talented local people reconstructing parts of Okinawa's cultural and linguistic story lost to the past but reemerging to challenge the old paradigms.

Acknowledgements

The authors express gracious thanks to Minoru Kinjo for his time in the interview and Hideki Yoshikawa for his insightful comments and suggestions on early drafts.

References

Austin, J. L. (1962 [1975]). *How to do things with words* (J. U. Sbisa & M. Sbisa, Eds.). Harvard University Press.

Barrett, G. (1952, September 21). Report on Okinawa: A rampart we built. *New York Times*.

Bell, O. (1954, January 20). Play fair with the Okinawans. *Christian Century*, 77.

Broudy, D., & Simpson, P. (2013). Naming and framing in (post)colonial Okinawa. In D. Broudy, P. Simpson, & M. Arakaki (Eds.), *Under occupation: Resistance and struggle in a militarised Asia-Pacific*. Cambridge Scholars.

de Fontenelle, B. B. (1728). *Oeuvres Diverses. Vol. 1: De L'Origine des Fables*. Chez Gosse & Neaulme.

Eldridge, R. D. (2004). *Post-reversion Okinawa and U.S.-Japan relations: A preliminary survey of local politics and the bases, 1972–2002*. U.S.-Japan Alliance Affairs Division, Center for International Security Studies and Policy, School of International Public Policy.

Eldridge, R. D. (2012, February 3). The Okinawa 'base problem' today. *Nippon.com*.

Escobar, A. (2011). Sustainability: Design for the pluriverse. *Development, 54*(2), 137–140.

Escobar, A. (2012). *Encountering development: The making and unmaking of the third world*. Princeton University Press.

Falk, R. (2016). *Why Okinawa should matter: Global justice in the 21st century*. Palgrave Macmillan.

FBIS. (1969, May 9). *Daily report, foreign radio broadcasts, 1969, no. 101–110.* Foreign Broadcast Information Service: Daily Report. Retrieved December 12, 2019, from https://babel.hathitrust.org/cgi/pt?id=osu.32435063627590&view=1up&seq=281&size=125

Feifer, G. (2001). *Battle of Okinawa: The blood and the bomb.* Lyons Press.

Foucault, M., & Miskowiec, J. (Trans.). (1984). *Of other spaces: Utopias and heterotopias.* Architecture/Mouvement/Continuite.

Fujiwara, S. (2020, April). Okinawa's plane spotters chase data on flights U.S. won't reveal. *The Asahi Shimbun, 24.*

Higgins, H. (2002). *Fluxes experience.* The Regents of the University of California.

Hook, G. D. (2003). Responding to globalization: Okinawa's free-trade zone in microregional context. In G. D. Hook & R. Siddle (Eds.), *Japan and Okinawa: Structure and subjectivity.* Routledge.

Johnson, E. (2020). More than 70% in Okinawa vote no to relocation of U.S. Futenma base to Henoko. *Japan Times.* www.japantimes.co.jp/news/2019/02/24/national/politics-diplomacy/okinawa-residents-head-polls-referendum-relocation-u-s-futenma-base-henoko/

Kai, E. J. (2005). *Jinruikan: Funin Sareta Tobira (Jinruikan: The sealed gate).* Atto Wakus.

Kinjo, K. (2009, November 9). *Kansai Okinawa Bunko.* Retrieved December 28, 2020, from http://okinawabunko.com/

Kinjo, M. (2018). Personal interview with the artist. Yomitan Village, Okinawa.

Komatsu, H. (2017). The negotiating process around the 'homeland level status' reversion between Japan and Okinawa. *International Relations of the Asia-Pacific, 18*(1), 71–98.

Lummis, C. D. (1996). *Radical democracy.* Cornell University Press.

Manchester, W. (1987, June 14). The bloodiest battle of all. *New York Times Magazine.* https://www.nytimes.com/1987/06/14/magazine/the-bloodiest-battle-of-all.html

Matsumura, J., & Wright, D. (2015). Japanese military suicides during the Asia-Pacific war: Studies of the unauthorized self-killings of soldiers. *The Asia-Pacific Journal: Japan Focus, 13*(25), 2.

McLuhan, M. (1964). The medium is the message. In *Understanding media: The extensions of man.* The MIT Press.

Mears, H. (1956). Okinawa: Orphan of conquest. *Nation, 183*, 368.

Minority Rights. (2018). *Ryukyuans (Okinawans).* www.minorityrights.org

Morningstar, C. (2020). *The great reset: The final assault on the living planet [it's not a social dilemma—it's he calculated destruction of the social, part III] Wrong kind of green.* www.wrongkindofgreen.org/?s=sdgs

Nash, D. E. (2015). *Battle of Okinawa: III Mef staff ride.* History Division US Marine Corps.

Nozaki, Y., & Seldon, M. (2009). Japanese textbook controversies, nationalism, and historical memory: Intra- and inter-national conflicts. *The Asia-Pacific Journal: Japan Focus, 7*(24), 5.

Ōta, M. (2003). Beyond Hondo: Devolution and Okinawa. In G. Hook & R. Siddle (Eds.), *Japan and Okinawa: Structure and subjectivity.* Routledge.

Phillips, P. (2018). *Giants: The global power elite.* Seven Stories Press.

Shimabukuro, J. (2012). Okinawa Kaihatsu Shinko Taisei e no Chosen (Challenging the Okinawan development regeneration system). *Sekai, 48*, 45–53.

Smits, G. (2010). Romanticizing the Ryukyuan past: Origins of the myth of Ryukyuan Pacifism. *International Journal of Okinawan Studies, 1*(1), 51–68.

Smits, G. (2019). *Maritime Ryukyu 1050–1650.* University of Hawaii Press.

Talmadge, E. (2001). Scientists shed light on why Okinawa is 'land of immortals'. *The Washington Post.*

Talmadge, E. (2011, March 9). U.S. diplomat replaced over Okinawa uproar. *Star Advertiser.*

Tanji, M. (2006). *Myth, protest and struggle in Okinawa.* Routledge.

Tanji, M., & Broudy, D. (2017). *Okinawa under occupation: McDonaldization and resistance to neoliberal propaganda.* Palgrave.

Tedeneke, A. (2019). *World economic forum and UN sign strategic partnership framework.* Press Release. World Economic Forum. www.weforum.org/press/2019/06/world-economic-forum-and-un-sign-strategic-partnership-framework/

Teshiba, R. (2003). Suspended in time: Okinawa's continuing struggle. *Alchemy: Swarthmore.* www.swarthmore.edu/writing/suspended-time-okinawas-continuing-struggle

Tokuyama, Y. (2013). Collective traumatic memory in a jointly-colonised Okinawa. In D. Broudy, P. Simpson, & M. Arakaki (Eds.), *Under occupation: Resistance and struggle in a militarised Asia-Pacific.* Cambridge Scholars.

Yoshida, R. (2008, March 25). Basics of the US military presence. *Japan Times.* Retrieved December 12, 2008.

Yoshikazu, M. (2006). U.S. dream come true? The new Henoko sea base and Okinawan resistance. *The Asia-Pacific Journal: Japan Focus, 4*(2).

9

ONTOLOGIES AND ECOLOGIES OF THE OTHERWISE

Notes on postdevelopment practices in Malawi

Carlos A. Segovia

While visiting Malawi in July 2019 to learn about the environmental-justice initiatives put forward in various villages by the Lilongwe-based NGO Youth for Sustainable Development (YSD) over the past eight years—practices that have effectively enabled such villages to recover their precolonial agricultural practices and thereby strengthened their economic self-sufficiency and their resilience vis-à-vis climate change—professor Boyson H. Z. Moyo, former Dean of the Faculty of Natural Resources at Lilongwe University of Agriculture and Natural Resources (LUANAR) with whom I had the pleasure of colecturing at Bunda College in Lilongwe on the deconstruction of progress and other modern myths in light of indigenous knowledges, informed me that in 2001 the United States Agency for International Development (USAID) had set forth in Mzokoto village, Rumphi (northern Malawi), a Water Project destined to supply its population with an *in-situ* water well so that the Mzokoto women need not daily walk several miles to a distant in-between-villages water spot where all local women use to fetch water. In short, the USAID consultants envisaged this as the "solution" to what they perceived as a "problem". Accordingly, they built their projected water well. Yet to their perplexity the women in Mzokoto continued travelling to the aforementioned spot to fetch water. What the Western consultants had perceived as a "problem" was no problem for them: their daily excursion allowed them to visit their fellow women and exchange with them, and hence to build and maintain social relations with their neighbours; and since they had no problem in doing this, they needed no "solution" for it. Consequently, the USAID-built water well in Mzokoto remains abandoned to this time.

As it is well known, the USAID was created from several predecessor foreign-assistance agencies in 1961 (under John F. Kennedy's administration) with the purpose of "lead[ing] international development and humanitarian efforts to save

DOI: 10.4324/9781003316220-10

lives, reduce poverty, strengthen democratic governance and help people pro-gress"[1] and—I propose to read the following clause less as providing additional information than as a conceptual clarifier of the political framework of its mis-sion—"[i]n support of [the United States of] America's foreign policy" so as to "promote American prosperity through investments that expand markets for U.S. exports [and] create a level playing field for U.S. businesses".[2] In fact, its ideo-logical discourse draws on the economic-growth doctrine of Walt W. Rostow (1916–2003), who, after contributing to the Marshall Plan (1948–1952) in his quality of assistant (since 1947) to the Executive Secretary of the Economic Com-mission for Europe, persuading—with fellow CIA-connected MIT economist Max F. Millikan—Dwight D. Eisenhower (in the 1950s) to implement US for-eign aid, and publishing (in 1960) *Stages of Economic Growth: An Anti-Communist Manifesto*, served first as Deputy Special Assistant for National Security Affairs under J. F. K.'s presidency (1961–1963) and then as National Security Adviser to Lyndon B. Johnson (1963–1969). Now, as the subtitle of his 1960 book makes plain, Rostow's agenda must be put into the perspective of the Cold War: it aimed at substantiating the thesis that economic investment could be a means for the USA to gain political influence abroad against the USSR; moreover, Rostow was not only one of the main theorists behind what is known today as post-1945 USA-backed-up development, but he was also one of the main ideologues behind the Vietnam war (Milne, 2008), for which he received the Presidential Medal of Freedom in 1969.

According to Rostow's discourse on economic growth, there are five stages of social development: (1) a sort of ground-zero, represented by what he labels "tra-ditional societies"; (2) the preconditions needed for these to economically "take-off" (which, in his view, transforms them into "transitional societies"); (3) their effective "take-off"; (4) their drive to "technological maturity"; and (5) "mass consumption", which Rostow equates with "economic modernisation". A two-fold reduction visibly operates here: of society to "economy"[3] (Esteva, 2010, p. 8) and of economy to "mass consumption", which is thereby understood by him to provide the *telos* to "human history". Back, then, to Adam Smith, for whom "the social body is a body composed of things, a web of commodities", and the abun-dance of these "the litmus test that distinguishes 'civilized and thriving nations' from 'savage' ones, 'so miserably poor' they are reduced to 'mere want'" (Ashcroft et al., 2007, p. 149),[4] save that now everyone is invited to join the economic-growth model.[5] Or forced to. In fact, the ambiguity of this logic—the fallacy of its alleged inclusiveness, that is—should be patent by now, as it has produced and cannot but produce many subaltern worlds[6] for the profit of a single, dominant and self-centred, world . . . and hence an asymmetric universe, as any universe is.[7]

Against such pretension, then, I find the aforementioned anecdote on the USAID-built water well in Mzokoto village particularly eloquent in terms of the cognitive justice required in the making of a pluriverse—which must not be confused with a more inclusive universe. For a pluriverse is, by definition,

Multiple, and this means, among other things, that "problems" and "solutions" cannot be the same everywhere. Put otherwise: in a pluriverse, each world has its own problems, and it is only the problems that are acknowledged as such in each world that demand solutions. The opposite—the claim that we all have common problems, the pretension that there is out there a single regime of truth: ours—reflects rather accurately the colonial, power-driven mindset on which all universes stand. And countering it requires, in turn, to speak of different ontologies instead of epistemologies or ecologies of knowledge,[8] as there is no one world diversely interpreted depending on each culture's epistemological specificity, that is, various situated knowledges of a presituated (a priori, objective) univocal reality, but as many situated realities as worlds in a pluriverse.[9] It is the idea of a one-world world, of a universe of which what Arturo Escobar calls "patriarchal western capitalist modernity" would hold the interpretative key—with its annexed notions of "progress", "development", and so on—that we must get rid of. As Escobar (2018, p. 118) himself observes, "[t]he project of 'reworlding' [the world otherwise] is . . . necessary ontological in that it involves eliminating or redesigning not just structures, technologies, and institutions but our very ways of thinking and being".[10] Plus in addition to cognitive justice, there can be no truly sociopolitical, communicative, and economic justice either beyond this premise—which is both the counter-premise of any form of racism[11] and a globalisation-disrupting axiom.[12]

But why use the term "ontology" to name other "ways of thinking and being"? Is philosophical terminology not too Western-centric and too abstract? Philosophy is indeed a Greek phenomenon. But Greek does not mean Western.[13] Furthermore, philosophy's constitutive openness to otherness and exteriority—put differently: its hypersensitivity and passionate stance towards the problematic qua problematic—makes it untimely against any form of identity—that is, against sameness. Philosophy is an activity—a "practice", as Althusser used to say—consisting—as Deleuze (1983) and Deleuze and Guattari (1994) in turn suggest—in a multi-faceted (i.e., complex or non-reductive) theoretical delimitation and life-oriented evaluation of notional problems and their corresponding "components" and "variations" via the creative production and communicative sharing of "concepts", in which it differs from both the scientific production of "prospects" through the selection of "variables" that enable to operate in the world under a specific (i.e., reduced) set of circumstances, and the artistic production of "percepts" and "affects" through which the sensible "varieties" of the real can be experimented and explored. Yet it is also, as Althusser likewise observed, a "battle field" for the "politics of theory"[14]—and thus anything but "abstract" in the ordinary sense of the word. Simply put, then, reclaiming other "ontologies" amounts to taking sides—as Althusser himself might have ventured—in the battle between "materialism" and "idealism" on the issue of whether it is each culture's (ideal) interpretation of a one-world world or universe, or else the irreducible (material) multiplicity of a non-metaphorical pluriverse, that must be advocated today. Needless to say, only the latter can be taken to be a rigorous materialist position.

Moreover, I would like to make the point that it is only by implementing cognitive justice in terms of acknowledging ontological difference that what I propose to call the de-colonial strategy pyramid can be fulfilled. I take such a pyramid to contain three levels: a lower one represented by economic self-sufficiency, a middle one amounting to political autonomy, and an upper one coincident with communicative (and conceptual) independence. Economic self-sufficiency is essential, but it is not enough. And the same applies to political autonomy. Without the latter, an economically self-sufficient community might be constrained to subscribe to external political decisions. And without communicative independence, neither political autonomy nor economic self-sufficiency can be fully achieved. The making of a pluriverse requires these interconnected, superimposing levels, which I have distributed vertically to emphasise the decreasing degree of awareness and the increasing degree of subtlety that one comes across with when moving upwards from the bottom level to the upper level of the pyramid.

An example of what may fall within the latter is offered by two Tumbuka words—Tumbuka being the Bantu *lingua franca* in northern Malawi—which stand in semantic opposition to one another, namely, the (plural) nouns *wanthu* (sing. *munthu*) and *wazungu* (sing. *muzungu*). As per their morphology and semantics, these nouns belong in the first and second noun stems (classes) existing in Tumbuka, which include "agent" nouns. This means that what we—but only we: non-Bantu, Western Indo-European speakers—would agree to call "people" nouns and at least certain "animal" nouns merge in these two lexical categories, the first of which is reserved to the singular form of such nouns (*munthu*, *muzungu*), whereas the second one is assigned to their plural form (*wanthu*, *wazungu*).[15] Let me add that non-Bantu, Western Indo-European speakers commonly take *wanthu* to be an ethnonym: the ethnonym for "Bantu" (*wanthu* = the Bantu). Conversely, they take *wazungu* to denote the "white people", and thus to be another kind of ethnonym, though a less-precise one (inasmuch as "white" is a more extensive category than Bantu). From this standpoint, therefore, *wanthu* and *wazungu* denote, if somewhat unevenly, two different "human types"; that is to say, they denote possible subdivisions of a common genus: "human". For it is in this (arborescent) way that we tend to view (and classify) things. Not only Aristotelian philosophy—whose categories have become, it would seem, our a priori forms of reasoning: modern biology with its likewise arboriform taxonomies, Christianity with its notion of a universal filiation for all men and women, and the modern State that makes us all surveilled, number, and taxed citizens of various nations, have all diversely contributed—as also has Marxist humanism, in its own way—to persuade us that, whatever their subdivisions, "humans" naturally form a single category. Yet as puzzling and unnatural as it may sound to us, there is no way to persuade Bantu speakers of this—unless they are forced to substitute their language for a different one, that is. English, for instance, is (present tense) the language of most Christian missionaries in Malawi, as well as the administrative—and, together with Chichewa, the educational—language of the Malawi State. *Wanthu* in Tumbuka (and something very similar may be said about the other Bantu languages spoken in Malawi) does not mean the "Bantu", nor does *wazungu* mean the "white people". *Wanthu* ("bantu") means, more simply, the "people". Like in most indigenous contexts, three categories must be carefully distinguished here. First, there is—to use here a pleonastic paraphrase—the "true (or real) people": those who speak like you and do things in the way you do them, that is, your own group (the "people").[16] Then there are those who "look like (true) people" without being "(true) people", that is, other groups that have a similar if not identical language to yours, etc.[17] And, finally, there are the "others": those who do not "look like (true) people" cannot be said to be "(true) people".[18] *Wazungu* is the Tumbuka term for such "others". Consequently, *wanthu* and *wazungu* are deictics that do not function as two logical subdivisions (or species) of the "same" genus. They stand, instead, in an inverse relationship. Put otherwise, they are the multiplicative inverse of one another, for which reason they cannot be subsumed into a single category;[19] in fact, the *wanthu* have more in common with their totems, in which they transform, than with the *wazungu*.[20]

The implications of this opposition are clear. If they denote two altogether different things rather than two subdivisions internal to a single genus, *wanthu* and *wazungu* cannot have the same needs. They must be forced into a single category in order to be allocated common needs and provided with, say, water wells, or any other thing that may help improve what the modern "imaginary representation of [any 'human'] conditions of existence"—if I may recall here Althusser's (2014, pp. 257–259) definition of "ideology"—calls the "material conditions" of human life. The idea of "progress" works as a regulative universal thereof, together with the recommendation to "accumulate" material goods and services. But we are here again before modern Western notions ("to be more", "to have more") that are hardly translatable into any Bantu language, in which normally—as it is the case, for example, with the Tumbuka affixes *-li* (to "be") and *-li na* (to "have")—"being" and "having" only make sense in the present tense, that is, now. But in this, the Bantu languages only prove incredibly logical. For if one had something in the past, it means one no longer has it, and if one has something in the future, it means one does not have it yet. Put otherwise: to "have" is an action exclusively linked to the present, that is, neither past nor future; and the same stands for "being", since one cannot say "I was something" or "I will be something" without implying that one is not that something now, that is, without paradoxically turning such expressions into statements about one's nonbeing. Interestingly, however, we tend to forget that an analogous linguistic violence was needed to transform the Latin term *progressus*, which originally meant "movement" (not necessarily forward, it should be remarked), into something like an "improvement" vector (Latouche, 2004, p. 129). One that if indistinctly applied in terms of market economy and technological development, as is often the rule, can only impoverish those human populations that, being affluent in terms of food supply, privilege immediate freedom over the technological control of everyday life and the communal unprogrammed enjoyment of their free time over the individualist and consumerist-planned offering of the tourist sector—for it perversely

presents such populations as being underdeveloped, thus justifying colonialism . . .
of which, as I have written elsewhere,[21] "humanism", redressed today as humani-
tarianism, is but the metaphor. More generally, the discourse on progress has been
repeatedly adduced to whiten colonial violence.[22] Therefore, a pluriverse will
have no chance to exist under its spell. Communicative independence oriented
towards communicative justice is, therefore, required to expand other forms of
pluriversal language.

Yet I should also like to stress that for a pluriverse to take shape anthropocentrism must be overcome, or more bluntly ruled out. In other words, humans[23]
cannot exert a dominant, supremacist position in what must be viewed—for a
pluriverse to be there, that is—as the intersection of multi-species worlds.[24] Furthermore, environmental justice will never be put into effect if this supplementary
premise is overlooked.[25] Now, moving beyond anthropocentrism demands two
things: it forces us to question—as Elizabeth A. Povinelli (2016) suggests—any
prevalent distributed boundaries between Life and Nonlife, and it obliges us to
simultaneously challenge any prevalent assumptions concerning any hierarchical
distributions within Life itself. For in a pluriverse everything is equally alive, which
means that all things refuse to fall under the tutelage of a single principle—or,
the pluriverse less as a system than a non-centred number of existential a-parallel
trajectories and disjunctive synthesis which cannot be totalised despite their many
intertwined lines of composition.[26]

Let us return briefly to the Bantu languages and what I am tempted to
call their "magic of the otherwise".[27] First, the polycentrism of their nominal
classification—which I have already alluded to—defies any clear-cut dividing line
between what we commonly identify as "humans", "animals", "plants", "rocks",
"natural phenomena", and "things", which frequently coexist within the same
noun stems, that is, inside macro semantic fields whose boundaries, moreover,
have to do with distinctions relative to qualities assignable to their members
through the combination of sensible intuition and mathematical thought. Thus,
for instance, there is a noun stem in all Bantu languages for all things that can be
qualified as extensive or extended, from bamboo trees to months (which are still
measured in Malawi by the phases of the moon), fields and villages (which can
always grow larger), or lips (insofar as these can engage in a prolonged conversation, one may deduce).[28] Second, ideophones (i.e., onomatopoeias), which play a
paramount role in the languages of Sub-Saharan Africa, should not just be viewed
as human "iconic depictions" (Dingemanse, 2012) of the environment, but as
receptors, reproducers, and eventually amplifiers of the voices of the "others"
inhabiting a shared ecosystem, for ideophones "do not just represent; they evoke,
they convey" (Nuckolls, 2011, p. 1). Lastly, nominal polycentrism (which opposes
the mainstream arborescent logic of the West) and "interspecies" polyphony (via
the pervasiveness of ideophones) inscribe in the Bantu pluriverse an intense sense
of relationality and animacy that are needed for communicative justice.[29]

I must add that many of the places I visited in Malawi in 2019 (in
Mchinji, Mzimba, Rumphi, and elsewhere) contain the physical remains of a

nowadays-partly-gone, as well as the promising rudiments of a yet-to-come, multispecies pluriverse.[30] For instance, local farmers are engaging there in multicrop cultivation, and if they initially adopted the latter to implement climate resilience, the fact is that in doing so they have favoured the emergence of multisided ecosystems of which they are part and parcel. For "you cannot dominate nature", as they told me using a word, "nature", that has no strict equivalent in Chichewa, Tumbuka, Tonga, Ngoni, or any of the other Bantu languages spoken in present-day Malawi (and beyond). Yet there is a profound "epistemological divide" (Moyo & Moyo, 2013, p. 400) between the prodevelopment ideology and the indigenous mentality. Thus, even if in contrast to the large-scale monocrop cultivation prevalent since colonial times—whose pernicious effects, including biodiversity loss, are easily appreciable at first sight—traditional indigenous agriculture, with its stress on small-scale cultivation and crop diversification, proves more adaptive than industrial agriculture to the increasing irregular seasonal cycles caused by climate change, as well as more effective by ensuring permaculture, and even if traditional crops prove more fertile and resistant than hybrid ones, so that over the past two decades more and more Malawian agriculturalists have decided to go back to traditional agricultural practices, and those receiving subsidies from the State have opted to prioritise such traditional practices above modern forms of cultivation,[31] supporters of economic modernisation continue to lament Malawi's "low ratio of development" and to attribute "food insecurity" to "erratic or poor rainfall" (Rasmussen, 2018, p. 8).[32]

But in addition to the transcendent "needs" dictated by the modern mindset, there is another ideological difficulty that Malawians must cope with today, especially in the urban areas, namely: the infiltration of Christian anthropocentric views and dogma in general, which is taught in secondary education as a plausible substitute for history. Christian anthropocentrism, with its stress on human interiority and sovereignty over "nature" and, thereby, its endorsement of "human exceptionalism" represents another obstacle for the worlding of a pluriverse—if it makes sense to speak in this way, for a pluriverse is what there is out there whether one sees it or not. Furthermore, Christianity was introduced in Africa as a regime of colonial submission capable of guaranteeing the subserviency of the local populations to the settlers. And therefore, it is an obstacle to both the recovery of traditional ways of living and the invention of new ones. For Christianisation entailed—and entails—the destruction of any ontologies and ecologies of the otherwise. This is evident, to mention but one example, in the way in which Christianity has in many places more-or-less-effectively replaced indigenous forms of relational "dividuality" (Strathern, 1988), both "social" and "natural" (i.e., towards other humans and other-than-humans), with the idea of an individual interiority indebted to a surveilling God[33] and, later, to the State. It should be highlighted, in this sense, that the indigenous peoples of Africa had no proper names before the arrival of Christianity: they were called by their (horizontal) relational names (mother/father of . . ., sister/brother of . . ., daughter/

son of . . ., wife/husband of . . .), their grandmother's or grandfather's (vertical) relational names, and their nicknames (i.e., their oblique relational markers).[34] So it was their "relations" as well as their "bodies"[34] that conferred them polyvalent identities open also to theriomorphic becomings and other forms of "interspecies" interactions.[35] Recovering these possibilities or rethinking them in new ways therefore requires to jump outside the Christian and modern mentalities that have recurrently undermined them. And to be sure this will be easier in those contexts in which the aboriginal cultural stock still subsists under the colonial dressing than in those contexts in which, conversely, the aboriginal terminology is either used to label colonial realities and/or transformed into folklore.

Yet these and other related obstacles are far from being exclusive to Malawi: one finds them here and there in different proportions. Besides, the fact that a number of nontranscendent, existential needs are gaining relevance today in the rural areas of Malawi as well as the open attitude that, driven by the acknowledgement of such needs, many Malawians show even in the urban areas towards pre-modern and no-longer-modern ideas alike, allows for optimism; and the same must be said about the survival, despite all, of what exceeds the sphere of human needs and consequently the production, acquisition, and reproduction of the means that satisfy them—what Bataille (1991) famously called the "accursed share". All this suggests that, however homogenous and self-referent, the modern one-world world attempts to become, new spaces of freedom outside it are possible and present and that Malawi is an especially interesting place for these to be further explored.[36]

Specific educational initiatives must be undertaken to support these, of course. Lecturing consecutively at LUANAR on modern myths and extramodern ontologies in the context of the activities programmed by YSD in Lilongwe in July 2019 helped me to tackle the complexities inherent in any communication process aiming at fostering dialogical exchange needed for communicative justice on these and other related issues.

To begin with, indigenous knowledges are still today deemed inferior to modern science, whose "objectivity" is often celebrated as though the roots of modern science were not constitutively religious and colonial—the two things. One just needs to look carefully into the engraved title page of the work which laid the foundations of the scientific method: Francis Bacon's *Novum Organum*. It has a galleon passing between the Pillars of Hercules, which mark on either side of the Strait of Gibraltar the exit from the Alboran Sea—the westernmost portion of the Mediterranean—into the Atlantic Ocean. For in his quality of Lord Chancellor of England, Bacon played a key role in establishing the British colonies of Newfoundland, Virginia, and the Carolinas. The interplay of religious yearnings, utopian politics, colonial expansion, and the rise of modern science in early-17th-century England should be moreover clear by now.[37] Thus, Bacon's *Confession of Faith*, a 1603 pamphlet posthumously published in 1641, provides the earliest shortest compendium of the protomodern ideological cocktail: Christian fanaticism, scientism, human exceptionalism, colonialism, domination of nature, and—of course—patriarchalism. As Caroline Merchant (2003, pp. 71–72) writes,

[t]he principal villain in Bacon's secular Recovery Narrative was nature, cast in the female gender. Although Eve's inquisitiveness may have caused "man's" Fall from "his" God-given domain, for Bacon, the relentless interrogation of nature (as fallen Eve) could regain it. Bacon used the inquisition and the courtroom as models for cross-examination of nature" to therefore help man reconquer his pre-fallen status. And while "science and technology made the material transformation of nature possible", she adds, "capitalism gave the emerging bourgeoisie the economic tools to change the earth" (74). In fact, the notion of private property elaborated by Hugo Grotius, Samuel Pufendorf, and John Locke pointed to what the colonists—unlike indigenous peoples, who do not relate to the world in such a way—could extract and appropriate from nature with their labour. And, of course, it was Grotius, Pufendorf, and Locke—plus Hobbes, *contra* Rousseau's "romantic" version of "savage" life—whom Adam Smith vindicated in his lectures at Glasgow University during the 1750s and 1760s. But all this would seem to be anecdotical, as modern science is often naively taken to have been born like Athena from Zeus's forehead. And it is impressive to see how widespread this view of modern science is, even in the institutions of higher education of former colonies like Malawi, where positivism reigns almost free and which thereby contributes to reproduce the very colonial ideology that Africans continue to suffer from. And yet there can be little doubt that, in the cities at least, it is mostly in the universities—their serviceability to colonial structures of power/knowledge notwithstanding—that one can question the modern myths by invoking what higher-education institutions should foster all the same: critical thinking. First paradox, then, in the form of an undecidable and double self-refuting mixture. A second paradox, or rather this time an irony, is that while the African people have been taught by Western missionaries, officials, doctors, teachers, and their own Westernised elites how to unbecome Africans, and they have done their best to learn the lesson, I, coming from what is called today the Global North, was instead willing myself to learn about their pre-Christian traditions and encouraging Malawian undergraduate, graduate, and PhD students to unlearn the Western ways they had been taught and go back to these. Not that I was alone in this, as my colleague and friend professor Moyo held a similar discourse and there were many students willing beforehand to recover indigenous knowledges, but it was anyway curious to notice this sort of positional chiasm. Lastly, the fact that many Malawians cling to Christianity out of respect for their ancestors represents a somewhat unfathomable paradox, since respect for the ancestors is a pre-Christian African motivation bafflingly directed, in this case, towards those ancestors who converted to Christianity and, by doing so, did not respect their own ancestors' beliefs and practices—we are here before a sort of conceptual oxymoron. These are a few examples of what I have labelled complexities in the communication process leading towards justice; complexities that render it eventually wavering but fascinating at the same time.

FIGURE 9.1 Climate-resilience assembly in Madzi village, Mchinji, Malawi, July 2019. Photograph by Carlos A. Segovia.

FIGURE 9.2 Traditional granary with traditional crops in Madzi village, Mchinji, Malawi, July 2019. Photograph by Carlos A. Segovia.

FIGURE 9.3 Theatre play on the benefits of indigenous agriculture, improvised by the inhabitants of Madzi village, Mchinji, Malawi, July 2019. Photograph by Carlos A. Segovia.

Notes

1. Retrieved 19 August 2019, from www.usaid.gov/who-we-are
2. Retrieved 19 August 2019, from www.usaid.gov/who-we-are/mission-vision-values
3. Exclusively thought of in terms of production and acquisition, as Bataille denounced in 1933 (Bataille, 1997).
4. Smith's quotations are from his 1776 *Inquiry into the Nature and Causes of the Wealth of Nations* (Smith, 1994).
5. The two most-recent instantiations of this invitation are Nordhaus and Shellenberger's (2009) "ecomodernist" manifesto and Steven Pinker's (2018) agitprop pamphlet *Enlightenment Now.*
6. Ecologically destroyed through ongoing extractivism, socially impoverished through massive proletarianization, and mentally eroded by systematic subjective standardization, to put it in terms of Guattari's 1989 "three ecologies" (Guattari, 2000).
7. It is possible to read the lemma behind such logic as a modern permutation of the Christian moto: *extra ecclesia nulla salus* ("there is no salvation outside the Church"). Cf. in this sense Margaret Thatcher's popular adagio (after Herbert Spencer): "there is no alternative", and the words of the 2016–2017 special adviser to the UN Secretary

on sustainable development, David Nabarro, concerning the UN Africa Renewal plan: "no one will be left behind" (Retrieved 22 August 2019, from www.un.org/africarenewal/magazine/april-2016/sdgs-no-one-will-be-left-behind).

8. I am drawing here on an idea which is gaining force in contemporary anthropology. See, e.g., Holbraad and Pedersen (2017).

9. Cf. Mario Blasser's (2016) use of the term "uncommons" in connection to today's cosmopolitics.

10. On the interconnectedness between epistemology and ontology, see Ndlovu-Gatsheni (2020, pp. 2–3, 101, 145, 149).

11. As Deleuze and Guattari (1987, p. 178) put it, "[r]acism never detects the particles of the other; it propagates waves of sameness until those who resist identification have been wiped out".

12. Cf. Ndlovu-Gatsheni's (2020, p. 38) distinction between the "postcolonial", which he sees as being "located within a Euro-North American-centric modernist discursive, historical, and structural terrain", and the "decolonial", born, he stresses, "at the borders of Euro-North American-centric modernity and fuelled by a decolonial spirit of epistemic disobedience and delinking"; thus, he concludes, "[w]hereas postcolonial theorists' horizon is universalism and cosmopolitanism, decolonial theory gestures towards pluriversality and a new humanism". Still, decolonial alternatives to development suffer at times from what could be labelled epistemological and ontological naivety; notice, for instance, the wording in the online presentation of Aram Ziai's ongoing research project at the University of Kassel (Retrieved 25 November 2021, from www.uni-kassel.de/forschung/icdd/research-1/research-since-2015/post-development-decolonial-alternatives-to-development), which aims at "[e]stablishing a network devoted to decolonizing development studies and investigating conceptual and practical alternatives to development": "The popularity of Buen Vivir/Sumak Kawsay/Suma Qamaña in Latin America, Swaraj in India and Ubuntu in South Africa clearly manifests", one reads therein, "a desire to transcend the cosmovision of homo oeconomicus, Cartesian rationality and a Baconian, anthropocentric view of nature, in favour of alternatives which see humans [sic.] as spiritual beings [sic.], as embedded in social relations [sic.], or as part of nature [sic.]"—"humans", "spiritual beings", "social relations", and "nature" being Western-centric ontological and epistemological categories.

13. No need to cite Heidegger here, however—though it would be possible to. See the brief comment on the opening lines of the *Iliad* and the issue of the "body" on n. 31.

14. See, e.g., Althusser (1990, pp. 205–211).

15. On nominal semantics and noun classification in the Bantu languages, see Katamba (2003), Dingemanse (2006), and Bostoen and Bastin (2016).

16. Which includes not only your extended family but also other families in the same clan and other clans in the same tribe.

17. In short, the members of other tribes, who are potentially affines or enemies.

18. These are always potential enemies . . . or affines—notice the ordinal role-shift with respect to the roles listed in previous category.

19. See further Viveiros de Castro (2012). Using a binary scalar logic, I apply here to the group's "others" what he writes therein about any binary group's two constitutive moieties, whose relation (which is always of the type $\sqrt{2}/2 = 1/\sqrt{2}$) cannot be rendered in the form of an addition (be it of the type $1/2 + 1/2 = 1$ or of the type $1 + 1 = 2$).

20. On indigenous "becomings"—which are always the quality "of an *act*, not of the *subject*," so that "[e]ven if the object of the becoming is imaginary, the becoming [itself] is real"—see Viveiros de Castro (1992, p. 271). They can be ritual or random, purported, or induced.

21. In a paper titled "On Humanism and the Spirituality of Ethnocide" (Segovia, 2018) in homage to Pierre Clastres's "De l'Ethnocide" (Clastres, 2010, pp. 101–113).

22. Contemporary indigenous-American claims to "good living" instead of "better living" are a powerful example of today's decolonial counter-discourse; see Escobar (2018, p. 148).
23. For a discussion on the questionable extensiveness of this noun, see Segovia (2019). I use it here for simplicity's sake.
24. Cf. Donna Haraway's (2016) notions of "living-with" and "making kin", as well as her subsequent emphasis on that of "sympoiesis", and Eduardo Mendieta's (2012) defence of an "interspecies cosmopolitanism."
25. The adjective "environmental" proves likewise problematic, as it remains human-centred; I endorse it here to keep within the word choice of the editors of this volume.
26. In ontological terms a pluriverse is always—as Guattari anticipated in 1989—"chaosmic", with chaos being, in the absence of any overall ruling principle, the "hyper-complex" domain of all "morphogenesis"; and "being", in turn, being a name for the mutational energy out of which multiple possible worlds take form (Guattari, 2013, pp. 103–108). On the "animist" character of any true pluriverse, see Segovia (2020).
27. *Magie pour magie* ("one type of magic for another one"), as Artaud (2004, p. 1543) once provokingly claimed (in 1947): *à la magie . . . d'un monde infâme doit répondre . . .* [une autre] *magie curative* [et] *réelle* ("to the magic of an infamous world a different type of magic, curative and real, must respond").
28. On indigenous logics and their "rationality", see Lévi-Strauss (1966).
29. Which contrasts with the Aristotelian distribution of "rational", "sensible", vegetal", and "mineral" beings, which made its way into modernity through medieval scholasticism.
30. Cf. Hilan Bensusan's (2017, p. 26) lucid use of the term "retrofuturism".
31. An excellent overview of the situation in northern Malawi will be found in Briggs and Moyo (2012). On the official concern to make agriculture more resilient against the backdrop of climate change, see the 2017 report by the Malawi Government (2017, pp. 56–60). On the international pro-growth assessment of the institutional attempts put forward in this respect in Malawi in the 2010s, see the World Bank Malawi Economy Monitor of 2017 and the UNDP, 2018 report.
32. Despite significant changes after 2004, which have had positive effects on its agriculture, the "national economy" of Malawi remains "structurally unbalanced", as Jonathan Kaunda wrote in 1995. "The agricultural sector", he explained, "is dualistic, with smallholder farmers growing subsistence [sic] crops, and the estates concentrating in producing tobacco, tea and sugar for export . . . The export economy has . . . little reflect on the smallholder subsector, and it does not significantly benefit rural masses who grow crop for domestic consumption" (Kaunda, 1995, pp. 307–308). And needless to say the economic liberalization of the past two decades—in consonance with the neoliberal directives of the International Monetary Fund and the World Bank—has not helped to solve this dualism (Booth et al., 2006, p. vii). One wonders, however, whether the issue is to find a balance between such polarized terms. In fact, the recovery of land expropriated for the production of sugar, tea, and tobacco is an interesting post-development phenomenon in present-day Malawi.
33. With the help of his representatives on earth: the missionaries.
34. Like in Ancient Greece: cf. *Iliad* 1.3–5, where the dead Achaeans are "themselves" (*autous*) eaten by the birds and the dogs, while their shadows (*psychai*) are sent forth to the Hades, and the Chichewa expression: *zidza pa thupi pache*: "they came for his body", meaning "they came for "him". In this sense, Ancient Greece and Africa—as also Greece and Amazonia, on which it is eloquent to compare the stories of Diomedes, Patroclus, and Apollo in *Iliad* 5.432–444; 16.702–711, 783–822 and the fate of the Arawete warriors as glossed by Viveiros de Castro (1992, pp. 238–251)—stand closer to one another than Ancient Greece does to the Christian and modern worlds (of which, rather pompously, the former is popularly said to be the "cradle").

35. For it is the "body" that can take such and such relations (of consanguinity, affinity, and totemic alliance). Thus, the absurdity of translating "soul" (*psyche*) as "life" (*moyo*) in the Chichewa versions of the New Testament, since indigenous "life" in inseparable from blood-, affine-, and totemic relations.
36. On the presentness and immanence of any "futurability", see Berardi (2017, pp. 31–33). Aside: by "spaces of freedom" I mean "spaces" *au sens fort*; cf. Amoo-Adare's (2013) suggestive rethinking of spatiality.
37. See, e.g., Voegelin's (1952), Webster (1975), and McKnight (1999).

References

Althusser, L. (1990). *Philosophy and the spontaneous philosophy of the scientists*. Verso.
Althusser, L. (2014). *On the reproduction of capitalism: Ideology and ideological state apparatuses*. Verso.
Amoo-Adare, E. A. (2013). *Spatial literacy: Contemporary Asante women's place-making*. Palgrave Macmillan.
Artaud, A. (2004). *Œuvres*. Gallimard.
Ashcroft, Bill, Griffiths, G., & Tiffin, H. (2007). *Post-colonial studies: The key concepts* (2nd ed.). Routledge.
Bataille, G. (1991). *The accursed share: An essay on general economy* (Vol. 3). Zone Books.
Bataille, G. (1997). The notion of expenditure. In F. Botting & S. Wilson (Eds.), *The Bataille Reader* (pp. 167–181). Blackwell.
Bensusan, H. (2017). *Linhas de animismo futuro*. Mil Folhas do IEB.
Berardi, F. (2017). Bifo. In *Futurability: The age of impotence and the future of possibility*. Verso.
Blaser, M. (2016). Is another cosmopolitics possible? *Cultural Anthropology, 31*(4), 545–570.
Booth, D., Cammack, D., Harrigan, J., Kanyongolo, E., Mataure, M., & Ngwira, N. (2006). *Drivers of change and development in Malawi*. Overseas Development Institute.
Bostoen, K., & Bastin, Y. (2016). *Bantu lexical reconstruction*. Oxford Handbooks Online. Retrieved August 20, 2019, from www.oxfordhandbooks.com/view/10.1093/oxfordhb/9780199935345.001.0001/oxfordhb-9780199935345-e-36
Briggs, J., & Moyo, B. H. Z. (2012). The resilience of indigenous knowledge in small-scale African agriculture: Key drivers. *Scottish Geographical Journal, 128*(1), 64–80. Retrieved July 8, 2019, from http://dx.doi.org/10.1080/14702541.2012.694703
Clastres, P. (2010). *Archeology of violence*. Semiotext(e).
Deleuze, G. (1983). *Nietzsche and philosophy*. The Athlone Press.
Deleuze, G., & Guattari, F. (1987). *A thousand plateaus: Capitalism and schizophrenia* (Vol. 2). University of Minnesota Press.
Deleuze, G., & Guattari, F. (1994). *What is philosophy?* Columbia University Press.
Dingemanse, M. (2006). *The semantics of Bantu noun classification: A review and comparison of three approaches* [MA Thesis, Leiden University].
Dingemanse, M. (2012). Advances in the cross-linguistic study of ideophones. *Language and Linguistics Compass, 6*(10), 654–672.
Escobar, A. (2018). *Designs for the pluriverse: Radical interdependence, autonomy, and the making of worlds*. Duke University Press.
Esteva, G. (2010). Development. In W. Sachs (Ed.), *Development dictionary: A guide to knowledge as power* (2nd ed., pp. 1–23). Zed Books.
Guattari, F. (2000). *The three ecologies*. The Athlone Press.
Guattari, F. (2013). *Schizoanalytic cartographies*. Bloomsbury.

Haraway, D. J. (2016). *Staying with the trouble: Making Kin in the Chthulucene*. Duke University Press.

Holbraad, M., & Pedersen, M. A. (2017). *The ontological turn: An anthropological exposition*. Cambridge University Press.

Katamba, F. (2003). Bantu nominal morphology. In D. Nurse & G. Philippson (Eds.), *The Bantu languages* (pp. 103–120). Routledge.

Kaunda, J. M. (1995). Malawi: The postcolonial state, development, and democracy. *Africa: Rivista trimestrale di studi e documentazione dell'Istituto italiano per l'Africa e l'Oriente, 50*(3), 305–324.

Latouche, S. (2004). *La Méga-machine. Raison technoscientifique, raison économique et mythe du progrès* (2nd ed.). La Découverte, M.A.U.S.S.

Lévi-Strauss, C. (1966). *The savage mind (La Pensée sauvage)*. Weidenfeld & Nicolson.

Malawi Government. (2017). *The Malawi growth and development strategy (MGDS) III: Building a productive, competitive and resilient nation*. Retrieved August 25, 2019, from https://cepa.rmportal.net/Library/government-publications/the-malawi-growth-and-development-strategy-mgds-iii

McKnight, S. A. (1999). Voegelin's challenge to modernity's claim to be scientific and secular: The ancient theology and the dream of innerworldly fulfillment. In G. Hughes (Ed.), *The politics of the soul: Eric Voegelin on religious experience* (pp. 185–205). Rowman & Littlefield.

Mendieta, E. (2012). Interspecies cosmopolitanism. In G. Delanty (Ed.), *The Routledge handbook of cosmopolitanism studies* (pp. 276–287). Routledge.

Merchant, C. (2003). *Reinventing Eden: The fate of nature in Western culture*. Routledge.

Milne, D. (2008). *America's Rasputin: Walt Rostow and the Vietnam war*. Hill & Wang.

Moyo, B. H. Z., & Moyo, D. Z. (2013). Indigenous knowledge perceptions and development practice in Northern Malawi. *The Geographical Journal, 120*(4), 392–401. Retrieved July 8, 2019, from https://doi.org/10.1111/geoj.12056. Reprinted in Ngulube, P. (Ed.). (2017). *Handbook of research on social, cultural, and educational considerations of indigenous knowledge in developing countries* (pp. 280–302). IGI-Global.

Ndlovu-Gatsheni, S. J. (2020). *Decolonization, development and knowledge in Africa: Turning over a new leaf*. Routledge.

Nordhaus, T., & Shellenberger, M. (2009). *Break through: Why we can't leave saving the planet to environmentalists*. Mariner Books.

Nuckolls, J. B. (2011, October 30–November 2). *Ideophones in bodily experiences in Pastaza Quichua (Ecuador)*. Paper presented to the 2011 Symposium for Teaching and Learning Indigenous Languages of Latin America (STLILLA). University of Notre Dame.

Pinker, S. (2018). *Enlightenment now: The case for reason, science, humanism, and progress*. Penguin.

Povinelli, E. A. (2016). *Geontologies: A requiem to late liberalism*. Duke University Press.

Rasmussen, P. E. (2018). *2018 African economic outlook: Malawi*. African Development Bank. Retrieved August 22, 2019, from www.afdb.org/fileadmin/uploads/afdb/Documents/Generic-Documents/country_notes/Malawi_country_note.pdf

Rostow, W. W. (1960). *Stages of economic growth: An anti-communist Manifesto*. Cambridge University Press.

Segovia, C. A. (2018, April 26–28). *On humanism and the spirituality of ethnocide*. Paper presented to the International Symposium L'Humanisme en questions, co-organized by the Université libre de Bruxelles (ULB), the Association des sociétés de philosophie de langue française (ASPLF), the Fonds de la Recherche Scientifique (FNRS), and the

Académie royale de Belgique (ARB). Université libre de Bruxelles (ULB), Brussels. www.academia.edu/35935353/On_Humanism_and_the_Spirituality_of_Ethnocide_ 2018_Conference_Paper

Segovia, C. A. (2019). Spinoza as savage thought. *Rhizomes: Cultural Studies in Emerging Knowledge, 35*, Forthcoming. www.rhizomes.net

Segovia, C. A. (2020). *El nuevo animismo: Experimental, isomérico, liminal y caósmico*. Themata, Revista de Filosofía, Forthcoming.

Smith, A. (1994). *An inquiry into the nature and causes of the wealth of nations*. Modern Library.

Strathern, M. (1988). *The gender of the gift: Problems with women and problems with society in Melanesia*. University of California Press.

UNDP. (2018). *Human development indices and indicators: 2018 statistical update—Malawi*. United Nations Development Programme. Retrieved August 19, 2019, from http:// hdr.undp.org/sites/all/themes/hdr_theme/country-notes/MWI.pdf

Viveiros de Castro, E. (1992). *From the enemy's point of view: humanity and divinity in an Amazonian society*. Chicago University Press.

Viveiros de Castro, E. (2012). *Radical dualism: A meta-fantasy on the square root of dual organizations, or a savage homage to Lévi-Strauss/Radikaler Dualismus. Eine Meta-Fantasie über die Quadratwurzel dualer Organisationen oder Eine wilde Hommage an Lévi-Strauss*. dOCUMENTA (13).

Voegelin, E. (1952). *The new science of politics: An introduction*. Chicago University Press.

Webster, Ch. (1975). *The great instauration: Science, medicine, and reform, 1626–1660*. Duckworth.

World Bank Malawi Economic Monitor. (2017). *Land for inclusive development*. The World Bank Office in Malawi. Retrieved August 21, 2019, from http://documents.worldbank. org/curated/en/422571510808901529/pdf/121419-REVISED-PUBLIC-Malawi-Economic-Monitor-6-Land-for-Inclusive-Development.pdf

10

FURTHER ROADS FOR COMMUNICATIVE JUSTICE IN PLURIVERSAL DIALOGUES

Eliana Herrera-Huérfano, Joan Pedro-Carañana, and Juana Ochoa Almanza

Based on the reflections, debates, findings, and conclusions developed in each of the experiences discussed in the book, this chapter explores a dialogue of knowledges based on the category of communicative justice. We understand this dimension of pluriversal justice as a working alternative to the monoculture of technocratic, corporatised, and oppressive communication that responds to the logic established by capitalist, racist, patriarchal modernity. The monoculture of communicative injustice establishes constrictions to communicative justice that ought to be identified and analysed to re-think how they can be overcome. Moreover, we observe how the experiences of communicative justice contribute to improving other dimensions of pluriversal justice. Thus, this dialogue of knowledges makes visible the learnings and contributions to the process of planetarisation of the pluriverse.

The dialogue we created amongst the different chapters of this volume is guided by some key questions: How do hegemonic communication systems and processes limit the possibilities of building a pluriverse? What do the experiences studied in this book tell us about the need for communicative justice? What are the characteristics of this dimension? How does it contribute to other dimensions of pluriversal justice? What are the main communication practices and technologies used?

We designed a model to identify the main characteristics of communicative justice to carry out the dialogue. This model is an approximation, a representation to provide a descriptive and analytical account of what we found. As a nomothetic model that includes only a few variables, there is a risk of simplifications because it does not allow us to see the interrelationships and nuances. Nonetheless, it allows us to identify key monocultural tendencies that we should deconstruct and dismantle as well as pluriversal tendencies that we should visualise, imagine, and create.

DOI: 10.4324/9781003316220-11

The model synthesises the key aspects that each chapter allows us to reflect on. Moreover, it allows us to contrast monocultural communicative injustice with pluriversal communicative justice in terms of its protagonists, communicative practices, key concepts, characteristics, and dimensions of justice/injustice.

Protagonists

The protagonists correspond to the key social actors of the communication processes. They are collective or individual subjects, such as institutions, organisations, companies, leaders, or ordinary people who mobilise and engage in different actions. The difference in the protagonists is based on and feeds back into the verticality of communication controlled by minority elites versus the horizontality of participatory communication.

In the monocultural trend of communicative injustice, social actors have a messianic character of saviours based, as argued in Chapter 2, on the understanding of "Man [humans, but particularly male] as the king of creation". This relationship implies an exercise of vertical domination. Man/power/violence is exercised by colonial powers (colonial Britain in Chapter 3), corporations and industrial conglomerates in geostrategic sectors (shrimp farms in Chapter 4), media and cultural industries (the *glocal* music industry lived in Madrid as discussed in Chapter 7, and corporate media according to several chapters), the military sector (armies in Japan in Chapter 8), governments (of both democratic and authoritarian regimes, as argued in Chapter 6), and international cooperation organisations prone to the unproblematised promotion to achieve development indicators (like those in Africa and Latin America discussed in Chapter 5 or USAID in the case of Malawi in Chapter 9).

In contrast, pluriversal communicative justice is mobilised and managed by "Los Nadie"[1] (Galeno, 1993, p. 52), who have a capacity for agency and fight for the various needs of justice. Communities and grassroots social collectives are at the forefront and in many cases are supported by NGOs and international cooperation organisations (not marked by a developmentalist vision). These are the cases of Indigenous women weavers in Bolivia (Chapter 2), the global human community, led by the poor and the youth (Chapter 3), communities of ancestral inhabitants in the Gulf of Guayaquil in Ecuador (Chapter 4), the cooperation programmes for social change between Latin American social organisations and African journalists and facilitators (Chapter 5), media activists and anti-colonial and anti-capitalist collectives (Chapter 6), female alternative and hybrid music bands in Spain (Chapter 7), local resistance movements in Okinawa (Chapter 8), and, actually, all species (Chapter 9).

Media and communication practices

Media and communication practices in the monoculture of communication resort to all forms of technology but have a special interest in monopolising mass and digital media (see the cases of India in Chapter 3 and the United Kingdom in

Chapter 6). Communication injustice uses these technologies for vertical communication practices of social control as presented in the cases of the big music industry discussed in Chapter 7 or the lack of access to technologies in remote communities exposed in Chapter 4. Meanwhile, communicative justice adopts a creative approach and uses all means possible, including textiles (Chapter 2), sculptures (Chapter 8), or music (Chapter 7) to share experiences democratically. The experiences refer to a wide range of technologically-mediated and non-mediated communication practices. They include rituals, music, ceremonies, dialogues, indirect or direct resistance actions such as demonstrations, pamphlets, theatre, carnivalesque symbolism, and humour, among others (Scott, 2000, p. 234). Such a creative approach can be seen in the cases of the media festival organised by the UK-based Media Reform Coalition (Chapter 6), the protest actions conducted by communities in Ecuador (Chapter 4), and the performances in Malawi (Chapter 9) or the different practices of nonviolent communication in India, including pilgrimages and fasting (Chapter 3). Pluriversal communicative practices also encompass educational activities like those discussed for capacity building between Latin America and Africa (Chapter 5), and all kinds of meaning production generated in daily life practices (see the case of Andean weaving as communication in Chapter 2 and women's cooperative spaces for music production in Chapter 7). The first communication technology is the body and its expressive capacity, whether human or non-human (Chapter 9).

It is important to note that, from a pluriversal perspective, what really matters are the practices of communicative justice and that technologies are mere instruments. The characteristics of the technology are subordinated to the structural power relations that affect them and the hegemonic-counterhegemonic practices which communicative justice aims to alter in favour of the pluriverse, as revealed in Chapters 5 and 9. Different chapters show that communicative practices of injustice reflect capitalist, neoliberal, and colonial logic, while uses of technology based on communicative justice aim at cooperative practices (Chapter 7) through nonviolence (Chapter 3). The concept of pluriversal communicative justice provides analytical tools to comprehend mainstream and alternative communication in different channels used in the present or that may be used in the future.

Key concepts

The key concepts to understand how each case presents communicative injustice and justice bring together various constitutive elements that sustain justice/injustice and allow them to exist and reproduce. These concepts highlight the core from which exclusionary differences are constructed and, in turn, provide clues to propose ways out of the injustices of the prevailing monocultures.

The key concepts of monocultural communicative injustice appear across the chapters in this volume. Ethnocentrism is discussed in Chapter 4 when referring to the appropriation and exploitation of the mangrove ecosystem despite the damage this does to humans and other species. Developmentalism is at the core of Chapters 8 and 9, while a patriarchal, racist, and classist order is analysed as a core problematic in Chapters 2 and 7. The experiences of Japan (Chapter 8) and India (Chapter 3) address a capitalist, colonialist, and warmongering system. Each concept contrasts with those of communicative justice. For example, Chapter 4 shows that *Buen Vivir* presents an alternative to the devastating practices of communicative injustice. The pluriversal possibilities of existence are supported by the voices, thoughts, and feelings of women and other invisibilised and negated populations (Chapters 2, 4, and 8), permanent dialogue based on biocentrism (Chapters 2 and 4), community and cooperative work (Chapter 8), nonviolent relationships (Chapter 3), different cosmologies (Chapters 5, 8, and 9), and reverse media policies (Chapter 6).

The main difference between the key concepts of monoculture and pluriverse that account for communicative justice is that the latter aims to eliminate any form of exclusion (race, class, gender, belief, species) from the daily conversation that marks the political, economic, cultural, and environmental life of any population, community, or group of beings. In opposition, communicative justice seeks horizontal, reflexive, respectful, and active listening relationships. As shown throughout the book, these are the pillars that structure the existence and vindication of the pluriverse.

Characteristics of the monoculture of communication and pluriversal communication

The characteristics presented in the following describe the features of communication in monoculture and pluriverse, the ways in which they function in everyday life, the discourses they promote, and the type of relationships they generate. As explained at the beginning of this chapter, each experience presents particularities anchored to specific contexts, cultures, histories, and territories. In the following, we summarise general tendencies from them.

Individualism and hierarchal relations are the bases of a monoculture of communicative injustice that seek to exploit nature, animals, and human and non-human beings (Chapters 4, 8, and 9) through social constructions relying on anthropocentrism (Chapter 2) as well as on class, race, gender, and speciesism hierarchies. Chapter 7 discusses this through the experiences of women musicians of different nationalities and Chapter 3 through xenophobia and hate speech. Under these divisions, violent practices are naturalised and justified by universal ideas that delegitimise any form of difference, opposition, or questioning, as shown in Chapters 5, 6, 8, and 9.

Other ways of being and living on the planet become the target of developmentalist and neocolonial processes that wipe out local practices of socialisation and production of communication and other goods, as the Ecuador case exposes in Chapter 4. The characteristics that emerge through critique and dissent in communicative justice account for the communal and local bonds of solidarity. They speak of and highlight mutual care between species, specifically human and non-human, as Espejo and Mora discuss in Chapter 2. They also expose the need to introduce and maintain local forms of communication that promote constant, respectful, and dignifying dialogues. These dialogues guarantee caring for language and paying attention to the use of words as the starting point of any relationship. Chapter 3 argues this through the soul-to-soul communication and emotional bridge-building, whereas Chapter 9 through inter-species communication and valuing the conceptual richness of local languages. Permanent dialogue implies the recognition of and respect for multiple forms of knowledge (Chapter 7), the dismantling of developmentalist and neo-colonialist processes (Chapter 5), advocating for media democracy, and the right to communication (Chapters 6 and 8).

The characteristics of monocultural and pluriversal communication are completely opposite. Communicative justice always seeks to build links and bridges to recognise, and dignify each other in our differences, whereas monocultures build barriers to communication.

Dimensions of justice/injustice

The hegemonic paradigm uses communication injustice to facilitate systemic oppressions in cognitive, political-economic, sociocultural, spiritual, environmental, and sociopolitical relations. Chapters 2 and 8 provide an overview of gender-based violence, oppression, and undervaluation of women's practical and everyday knowledge. Chapters 3, 5, and 6 discuss cognitive violence in academia, where science is the only valid way of knowing, and colonialism eliminates other knowledges and ways of being. Chapter 4 observes environmental injustice in the exploitation of natural resources in Ecuador. Finally, Chapters 6, 7, 8, and 9 examine experiences of sociopolitical and political economy violence.

Communicative justice opposes these asymmetrical power structures by making key contributions to all dimensions of pluriversal justice. Devaluation of the other, inequality, naturalisation of exclusionary differences, violence against the natural environment, and internal and intergroup conflict give way to recognition and amplification of the other (as a form of cognitive justice in Chapters 2, 5, 8, and 9), socioeconomic equality (Chapter 6), political autonomy (Chapter 8), interculturality in diversity (Chapter 7), harmony with nature (Chapters 2, 4, and 9), and dialogue and mutual support within and between groups (Chapter 3).

These key contributions relate to communicative justice in making visible the injustices of monocultures (*what is not named, does not exist*) to demand and propose transformations (*naming what does not exist yet may contribute to its coming into existence*). At the same time, pluriversal communication makes visible and facilitates alternative ways of organising life, living, and communicating not as unattainable utopias, but as existing realities.

The key concepts of each paradigm reflect their differences and how communicative justice and injustice interrelate in opposition. The former fosters the inclusion of different ways of communicating; the latter is only the dominant one. Verticality/horizontality marks the different approaches to communication. It also differentiates the way protagonists participate (from above or below). Social control of communicative injustice presents barriers to the just harnessing of the dialogical and emancipatory possibilities of media. Pluriversal Media and Communication Practices decentre technology and bring solidarity to the front. Since injustice is multidimensional and interdimensional, communicative justice is oriented to improving the degrees of justice in the different dimensions of the pluriverse, ideally through an intersectional approach. Thus, communicative justice is a synonym of pluriversal communication.

At the risk of oversimplifying and homogenising, communicative justice is a key dimension of pluriversal justice that aims at the decentring of and transitioning from exclusionary, vertical, oppressive monocultural communicative injustice to inclusive, horizontal, and democratic pluriversal communication. This occurs due to the protagonism of ordinary, exploited, and oppressed realities, especially, subaltern populations. These people's knowledges, worldviews, and cosmogonies characterise communicative justice. They practice the right to communication through communicative practices of cooperation among humans and with other beings, in harmony with nature. Communicative justice resorts to a variety of mediated and nonmediated communication practices of and for life, love, and struggle for its planetarisation and that of other dimensions of the pluriverse. It reduces all forms of injustice, be it political economy, cognitive, sociopolitical, sociocultural, spiritual, or environmental.

As developed in Chapter 1, the most valuable methodologies to study the pluriverse are those in which the researcher engages in communication and knowledge-generation processes with communities. The different chapters of this volume emphasise the importance of starting research with the recognition of local—situated—experiences that contribute to the planetarisation of the pluriverse. These experiences do not have a universal application but are of global relevance. They offer learnings to experiences and struggles elsewhere. The concept of *glocalisation* applies here, as local conditions of communicative production are affected by global conditions, and locally situated communication shows there are other ways of understanding and living. They reveal the many different and valuable perspectives on this planet—a pluriverse. Thus, local does not mean micro. In the context of the pluriverse, communicative justice operates on transscales, whereby the local contributes to global transformations.

Note

1. As Eduardo Galeano illustrates in his poem *Los Nadie*, we refer to the dispossessed, marginalised, and excluded by the dynamics of the world system.

References

Galeno, E. H. (1993). *El libro de los abrazos*. Siglo XXI.
Scott, J. (2000). *los dominados y el arte de la resistencia*. Editorial Era.

11

POSTSCRIPT

Justice, sustainability, and communications: a pluriversal approach

Ashish Kothari

In March 2022, I was sitting on the banks of the Indus River in Ladakh, India's trans-Himalayan region bordering Tibet. My colleague and I were holding a session on "rights of rivers" with students of the Government High School at Chumathang village. She asked the students to list what they thought was a river's rights. The "right to flow", the "right to be unpolluted", and the "right to not be stopped by dams" were some of the responses. And then one girl stunned us by proclaiming "it has the right to sing"!

Such a perspective can only come from a kid born next to a river, used to its gurgling and gushing and not yet "educated" into thinking only in a "rational", intellectual way. Or it can come from Indigenous peoples and other local communities whose cosmovisions encompass, seamlessly, the rational and nonrational, the intellectual and the emotional, and the materialist and the spiritual-romantic. For whom, as the Iwi Indigenous people in New Zealand say about the Whanganui, flowing through their territory, "the river is us, we are the river".

500 years of colonialism has dealt a death blow to many such cultures and worldviews, but several still survive, and some are making a comeback. Anticolonial, ecological, Indigenous rights and other related movements are challenging the homogenising project of western modernity and reasserting the value of diverse epistemologies and ontologies—ways of knowing, being, acting, and dreaming. With language diversity being as threatened as biological and ecological diversity, and languages being libraries of knowledge that could hold clues to many of our problems, such movements are vital for the future of humanity, and for all life.

The challenges such movements face are from not only the ongoing heritage of colonialism, very much alive in various neo-colonial ways, but also a multitude of inequalities stemming from both tradition and modernity. These

DOI: 10.4324/9781003316220-12

include discriminations and marginalisations of gender and sexuality, class, "race" and ethnicity, caste, ability and disability, and many others. Economic growth-based "development" approaches, led by nation-states or capitalist corporations (increasingly, both together), have added to these, especially by significantly enhancing economic and wealth inequities, destroying the ecological base of the livelihoods of hundreds of millions of people, and making the lives of much of humanity more vulnerable due to climate, biodiversity and pollution crises. Many of these inequities and vulnerabilities are intersectional, for instance, in gender, economic, and ecological injustice affecting women in low-income groups in mutually reinforcing ways.

At the heart of these crises lies the injustice of communication and learning, as this book vividly brings out. The lack of spaces for the voices of the marginalised (including the nonhuman) in various aspects of political and economic life, massive inequalities in the media power of the elite versus the "masses", the invisibilisation of so many forms of communication and media as "social"/digital media takes increasing control, the displacement of multiple forms of community and nature-based learning, and so on are aspects of this injustice. On top of this is the appropriation of many progressive movements and spaces and articulations by governments or big NGOs, such as, for instance, the hijacking of radical world-views like "buen vivir" and "ubuntu" and "swaraj" by so-called revolutionary (but ultimately still authoritarian and centralising) parties and governments in Latin America and Africa and South Asia, respectively.

But the situation is not all bleak—far from it. For across the world, there is local-to-global resistance against the forces of exploitation and unsustainability, as also myriad alternative initiatives at meeting human needs in ways that are ecologically responsible and socially equitable. In India, some of us refer to these movements as part of "eco-swaraj", or Radical Ecological Democracy, in which transformations are taking place or envisaged in five spheres of life: political, economic, social, cultural, and ecological. We depict this as a flower of transformation (see Figure 11.1).

As the Vikalp Sangam framework notes, transformations in these spheres include:

a. **Ecological integrity and resilience**, including the conservation of nature and natural diversity, maintenance of ecological functions, respect for ecological limits (local to global), and ecological ethics in all human actions.

b. **Social well-being and justice**, including fulfilling lives (physically, socially, culturally, and spiritually), equity between communities and individuals, communal and ethnic harmony; and erasure of hierarchies and divisions based on faith, gender, caste, class, ethnicity, ability, and other such attributes.

c. **Direct and delegated democracy**, with decision-making starting in spaces enabling every person to participate meaningfully, and building from this to larger levels of governance by downwardly accountable

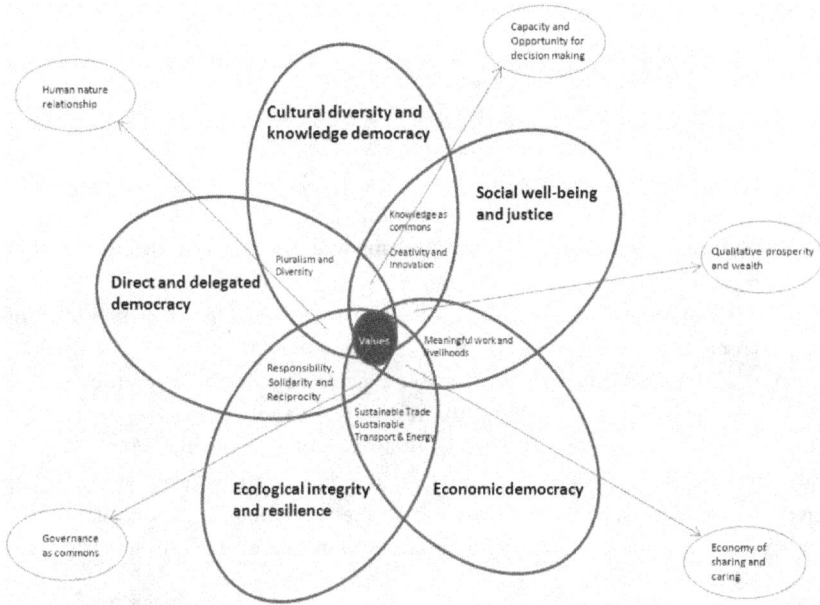

FIGURE 11.1 Flower of transformation. Credit: "In Search of Radical Alternatives" the framework developed by the Indian network Vikalp Sangam.[1]

institutions, and all this respectful of the needs and rights of those currently marginalised.

d. **Economic democracy**, in which local communities and individuals have control over the means of production, distribution, exchange, and markets, based on the principle of localisation for basic needs and trade built on this; central to this would be the replacement of private property by the commons.

e. **Cultural diversity and knowledge democracy**, with multiple coexisting knowledge systems in the commons, respect for a diversity of ways of living, ideas and ideologies, and encouragement for creativity and innovation.

The most crucial part of this framework of transformation is a set of ethical values or principles that emerge implicitly or explicitly in grounded alternative initiatives. These include solidarity and love, diversity and pluralism, autonomy and self-determination, relationality and interdependence, human rights and the rights of nature, dignity and justice, equality and equity, peace and nonviolence, harmony, commons and collective interest, and others (all of these diametrically opposite to the values—of lack of them!—of the currently dominant system).

Transformations along these lines are of course still marginal and exceptional, compared to the dominant juggernaut of the current nation-state-capitalist-military-industrial system, built on patriarchy, racism, and human centredness.

But across the world, they show the enormous potential of what we are capable of, if could get our act together in collectives that reclaim power but exercise it with responsibility towards other people and species.[2]

Importantly, and linked to one of the central themes of this book, there is no single alternative approach, no "model" that should be exported around the globe. Rather, there is a "pluriverse" of them,[3] an enormous diversity of approaches, each relevant in its own context and not immediately replicable (and definitely not to be "upscaled"!) but perhaps with several common ethics (such as the ones listed earlier).

One of the most crucial elements of such transformation is the agency of the dispossessed and marginalised, for they are not inherently powerless. They have a voice, and movements of justice enable that voice to come out strongly. This includes listening to and enabling the rest of nature to speak also—not only, as the book says, "communication with other beings that inhabit Mother Earth" but also communication *by* these other beings and elements of nature including rivers, mountains, and deserts. Do we have the wisdom—can we relearn it from Indigenous peoples and from children—to listen to these voices, to practice communicative justice in the interests of the pluriverse?

22 April 2022

Notes

1. www.vikalpsangam.org; see Sangam, V. *In search of radical alternatives.* https://vikalpsangam.org/about/the-search-for-alternatives-key-aspects-and-principles/
2. https://vikalpsangam.org/article/these-alternative-economies-are-inspirations-for-a-sustainable-world/
3. Kothari, A., Salleh, A., Escobar, A., Demaria, F., & Acosta, A. (Eds.). (2019). *Pluriverse: A post-development dictionary.* Tulika and Authors Upfront. https://radicalecologicaldemocracy.org/pluriverse

INDEX

Note: Page numbers in **bold** indicate a table on the corresponding page.

For Product Safety Concerns and Information please contact our EU
representative GPSR@taylorandfrancis.com
Taylor & Francis Verlag GmbH, Kaufingerstraße 24, 80331 München, Germany

9 7 8 1 0 3 2 3 2 6 1 8 4